THE SPACE OF BOREDOM

THE SPACE OF BOREDOM

HOMELESSNESS IN
THE SLOWING GLOBAL ORDER

Bruce O'Neill

. . .

Duke University Press · Durham and London · 2017

© 2017 Duke University Press
All rights reserved
Printed in the United States of America on acid-free paper ∞
Typeset in Minion Pro by Graphic Composition, Inc., Bogart, Georgia

Library of Congress Cataloging-in-Publication Data
Names: O'Neill, Bruce, [date] author.
Title: The space of boredom : homelessness in the slowing global order / Bruce O'Neill.
Description: Durham : Duke University Press, 2017. | Includes bibliographical
references and index.
Identifiers: LCCN 2016040911 (print)
LCCN 2016041958 (ebook)
ISBN 9780822363149 (hardcover : alk. paper)
ISBN 9780822363286 (pbk. : alk. paper)
ISBN 9780822373278 (ebook)
Subjects: LCSH: Boredom—Social aspects. | Globalization—Social aspects—
Romania. | Homelessness—Political aspects—Romania. | Romania—Social
conditions—1989– | Romania—Economic conditions—1989–
Classification: LCC HN643.5 .O54 2017 (print) | LCC HN643.5 (ebook) |
DDC 306.4—dc23
LC record available at https://lccn.loc.gov/2016040911

Cover art: Photo by Bruce O'Neill.

To Helen

CONTENTS

PREFACE

"Whatever you do when you're homeless, you feel bored (*plictisit*)," Florin, an unemployed low-skilled laborer (*muncitor necalificat*) in his early thirties, explained to me on an autumn morning.[1] Florin lived in a squatter camp with his wife near Stefan's Place, a popular nongovernmental organization in Bucharest, Romania, where homeless men and women went to meet with one another, as well as to access a social worker or doctor, or to take a shower. "Especially whenever you think about tomorrow," Florin continued, "what to do, what to eat, where to go, and where to work. Winter is around the corner, and I think, 'Where will I live?' I'm outdoors, the wind blows hard, and the snow is coming. And this is the life that you have to think about, because no one is going to come look after you and make sure you're all right." Florin paused for a moment to gather his thoughts. His broad shoulders rolled forward, and his face drooped. "And then I get this feeling of boredom from having to tighten my belt as far as I can manage, until the knife scrapes against the bone. You can't do anything worthwhile if you don't have a job and if you don't have money." Florin spent the remainder of his morning pacing up and down the main road in an effort to busy himself.

. . .

THIS IS AN ETHNOGRAPHY about being cast aside to the margins of Europe amid a prolonged global economic crisis. Set in postcommunist Bucharest, Romania, this book explores the internally felt space where the promises and possibilities of European-style consumer capitalism cut against the limitations of economic turbulence and scaled-back government protections. The nearly three years of ethnographic research discussed in this book began during the optimism over Romania's accession to the European Union and followed the aftermath of the global financial crisis. The ethnography weaves between homeless shelters and day centers, squatter camps and black labor markets, in order to detail how people internalize and make sense of deepening poverty over and against the anticipation of rising, consumer-driven prosperity. Organizing the book's narrative is a widely shared sense of boredom among Romania's new homeless population. How and to what effect, this book asks, does deepening immiseration come to be understood and embodied through boredom? And how does this ordinary affect provide a window into the cultural politics of displacement in a global economy in crisis?

The voices animating this ethnography are predominantly male, because homelessness is an overwhelmingly male phenomenon.[2] While the Romanian government did not define homelessness until 2011, much less keep demographic information about the homeless population, ethnographic observation suggested that three out of four homeless persons in Bucharest were male.[3] This makes sense given that women displaced out onto the street proved time and again to be more capable of mobilizing relations with family and friends to stay indoors. When these strategies fell short, women also enjoyed better social protections. Bed space in Bucharest's handful of night shelters, for example, was largely reserved for women and children, despite the disproportionate presence of single men living on the streets.

To be sure, those women unable to avoid homelessness also wrestled with boredom. Inside family shelters, I leaned against kitchen walls and took note of how to prepare Romanian dishes, I spent afternoons sitting in a women's dormitory watching Spanish soap operas, and I sat in a shelter courtyard and helped keep watch over playing children. In these moments the gendered dimensions of boredom became clear. Homeless women, both young and old, felt bored with the kind of life homelessness afforded. Homeless shelters placed on women much of the same domestic drudgery that their privately housed counterparts dealt with. The proper functioning of shelters depended on women's unpaid domestic labor without providing any of the creative craft or pleasure of homemaking. Boredom reverberated throughout women's daily repetition of thankless laundering, scrubbing, and child rearing.

Sitting alongside these women in the shelter, but also populating the vast majority of day centers, squatter camps, and black labor markets, were men who also spoke of being intensely bored with life (*plictisit de viață*). In contrast to the boredom of the repetitive and thankless labor experienced by women, the boredom of unemployed men had an inert character. Unable to serve as breadwinners, men were bored not because their labor was repetitive and underpaid but rather because they could no longer find consistent work. Employers no longer found these men to be worth exploiting. Men awoke each morning to the realization that they had little meaningful activity around which to structure their days: no job, no family, and too little money to buy a hot meal, much less a movie ticket. Rather than doing or making something recognizably meaningful, homeless men instead spent their days sitting and reading the classifieds, smoking, drinking coffee, standing and chatting, pacing and thinking. Days dragged into nights only to give rise to more empty days.

These homeless men and women, furthermore, did not identify as Roma, or so-called gypsies as many Romanians initially assumed. This is because being homeless and being Roma are not the same thing. Although imagined across Europe as an uprooted and transient population, only a small portion of the Roma can correctly be described as such.[4] Those Roma who do regularly move from opportunity to opportunity, furthermore, do not necessarily identify as homeless, a social and bureaucratic category that pathologizes the absence of a stable residential address. To be sure, some of the men accessing services in night shelters and day centers, and hanging out in public parks, were ethnically Roma. These men also insisted that being without formal work and housing was both unusual and distressing for them. Without prompting, ethnically Roma men would detail their employment histories and list their previous home addresses. "I might be Roma, but I'm not a gypsy," an ethnic slur loaded with connotations of deviance, was a common refrain. The importance that homeless Romanians placed on differentiating themselves from "the gypsies" no doubt contributed to the boredom of their everyday life, as acts of self-policing to maintain some semblance of a working-class respectability curtailed much of the rule breaking and excitement so often associated with life at the margins of the city.[5]

Although particular to Bucharest, this study of boredom and homelessness resonates in many direct and indirect ways far beyond Romania's borders. At the time of this research, a debt crisis was reverberating across the

European Union. The unemployment rate for the euro area hit 10 percent, indicating that some twenty-three million men and women across Europe were unemployed.[6] The crisis in the Eurozone destabilized the economies of the very places homeless Romanians imagined moving to in order to establish a better life, with unemployment rates as high as 19.1 percent in Spain, 10 percent in France, and nearly 8 percent in the United Kingdom.[7] At the same time, persistently high unemployment in the United States following the collapse of its housing market resulted in equally troubling (and persistent) unemployment levels of 10 percent, prompting the economist Paul Krugman to lament that "for the first time since the Great Depression many American workers are facing the prospect of very-long-term—maybe permanent—unemployment."[8] Scholars studying cities across the global south also raised concerns about the development of populations of unemployed men with little to no prospects of being folded into the formal labor market.[9] Simply put, these men had been expelled from the local, national, and global economies.[10]

At the onset of the twenty-first century, in both the global south and the global north, people wearing both blue and white collars found their lives held in limbo by unemployment, their spending curtailed by strained savings accounts and mounting credit card debt, with no hope for a quick solution. Faced with scaled-back government protections and the predominance of flexible, lean-and-mean production styles, millions of men and women around the world lived through an economic stagnation not unlike that experienced by the people described throughout this book: they were unemployed, broke, and skeptical about the future and felt as though there was nothing to do in the present. Left to wrestle with long moments of quiet reflection, they undoubtedly experienced worry, anxiety, and self-doubt, but there was also the ambient and difficult-to-shake sense of boredom.

The Fieldwork

This ethnographic study was based on the classic anthropological methods of participant observation, recorded interviews, and documentary photography detailing the daily lives of homeless men and women in Bucharest, Romania. These efforts captured not only the grinding routines, strained relationships, and thoughtful insights of Bucharest's homeless but also the collectively shared feelings and emotions that showed what it meant to inhabit a changing city, particularly in its most marginal dimensions. This work began at a pair of institutions catering to homeless men and women. One was a government-administered night shelter located outside the city limits of Bucharest that I call the Backwoods Shelter. The Backwoods Shelter offered its homeless beneficiaries little else beyond basic accommodation and two meals a day. The facility had no educational, employment, or entertainment programming of any kind. The toilets clogged regularly, the halogen lights flickered, and cockroaches (*gândaci*) crawled across walls and bedspreads and down shirts and pant legs. A single bus line stopped immediately outside the front gate. Otherwise, a cemetery, a gas station, and a kennel housing stray dogs surrounded the shelter. The austere utility and isolation of the shelter called to mind a warehouse.

The other institution was a day center, which I call Stefan's Place, administered by a nongovernmental organization. Located fifteen minutes by bus from the city center, this organization offered access to doctors and social workers, the opportunity to shower and to change one's clothes, and a place to spend the day in relative peace. In the summer men and women followed the shade as it shifted across the center's parking lot. In the winter, in lieu of an indoor waiting room, Stefan's Place made available an unheated toolshed where homeless men and women huddled together. The hours of operation were nine o'clock to five o'clock, though people could be found waiting to enter as early as six thirty in the morning.

In both places, the topic of boredom was unavoidable. "*Plictisit*" (bored) was how almost every person at the Backwoods Shelter and Stefan's Place day center responded to my initial salutation: "Hey—how are you doing?" As I came to understand boredom as a window into the cultural politics of exclusion in a moment of troubled global consumerism, I detailed when, where, and with whom people spoke of being bored. I also became attentive to absences, inquiring as to who or what was missing from people's lives in moments of boredom as well as where people would rather be and what they would rather be doing. Boredom, though, is a slippery fish for an ethnographer to catch. As an American whose research took him throughout the city, whose presence brought questions to be answered, conjectures to be corrected, and (more importantly) a comparatively full wallet that could (within reason) be lightened, I proved endlessly entertaining. It was not uncommon, in fact, for even my most distant acquaintances to greet me on the street with exclamations like, "Thank God you're here—I was so bored! Let's go get a coffee!" In a testament to the reflexive nature of ethnographic research, my presence proved to be one powerful antidote to the boredom that otherwise shaped life on the streets. I became mindful that small gestures, like providing a shot of Nescafé or photographing someone's portrait, were great distractions. These gifts beat back people's boredom, and, in exchange, I received gratitude and patience. These gifts also led to invitations to hang out beyond the social worker's gaze. As the study evolved, I spent my afternoons eating lunch in squatter camps, my nights drinking beer in transit stations and public parks, and my mornings waiting for work on black labor markets before dawn. The research also took me to unexpected parts of the city, such as high-end shopping malls and IKEA furniture stores, where homeless persons attempted to not look homeless in order to gain access to cheap food, washrooms, and climate-controlled spaces.

My capacity to distract left me with the methodological balancing act of knowing when to create diversions, in the form of buying snacks or staging interviews, and when to hold back and allow "nothing" to happen. I came to view the moments of diversion as a kind of photographic negative, capturing through their inverse the boring times and places that my informants spent so much time and effort trying to escape. I balanced this perspective with attempts to confront their existential state of boredom head-on. In these moments I tried to fade into the background and to allow empty time, silent spaces, and idle fidgeting to press in on us. I then observed the practices, moods, and ideas that unemployment and poverty brought about, and I shared, as best I could, in the social condition that the homeless described as boredom. As it became apparent that my informants genuinely suffered from this state of boredom, this balancing act became shadowed by my own ethical questions and concerns.

Contributions

Most concretely, this book is an ethnographic account of the production and management of homelessness in Bucharest, Romania, the capital of one of the European Union's newest (and poorest) member states. It details who is homeless, and why, as well as how they get by in a perilous economic climate. It also explores the various ways that the homeless are (and are not) governed and raises important implications for urban planners and policy analysts alike. But the study also makes an additional set of interventions, the first of which is contributing to the theorization of downward mobility. While a thick literature theorizes the historical and material forces reproducing entrenched poverty, less well understood are the effects of falling into it.[11] This study, conducted in the wake of the global financial crisis of 2008 and within a broader history of postcommunist transition, traces the effects of becoming poor. It provides ethnographic insight into how men and women with stable work histories and high expectations for their quality of life come to terms with the lost ability to earn a paycheck and to spend it, as well as how a contracting capacity to participate in the economy reorients relationships not only with family and friends but also with the city, with Europe, and with globalism more generally.

The book also contributes to the politics of displacement by foregrounding its entanglement with heightened consumerism. Social theorists have long understood how social distinctions are made hierarchically and horizontally through consumption within a capitalist society.[12] With the fall of communism in Eastern Europe, and with the introduction of consumer capitalism to the region, anthropologists have taken considerable interest in how consumption practices emerged as a critical site for making claims to belonging to the nation, to a struggling middle class, and to Europe.[13] Less well understood is the inverse: how the inability to fulfill attachments to a new and growing array of consumerist fantasies shapes the lived experience of those displaced from work and home and into poverty. This study, set in the immediate aftermath of the global financial crisis of 2008, details how the politics of social exclusion, and ultimately of social death, gets interpreted and embodied as a lack of consumer stimulation.[14]

At its most abstract, the book contributes to a rethinking of the global, a scale of social and material relations most frequently defined by market-driven production and consumption. During communism, Western academics and politicians alike pointed to market competition as the necessary engine to reanimate Eastern Europe's stagnant economy. The market was seen as the solution to the failures of communism, from the prevalence of breadlines to the problem of stalled factory floors: communism wasn't productive of anything.[15] Yet two decades after the fall of communism and the introduction of political and economic reforms, there appears to be an escalation of inactivity. Anthropologists studying cities in Eastern Europe, but also in the global south, have observed growing populations of men displaced from a globally competitive marketplace and struggling with near-permanent unemployment.[16] The global financial crisis of 2008 only compounded the growing problem of inactivity. Without a steady paycheck, these men struggled to fulfill familial obligations, maintain a household, or develop professional expertise. Rather than accelerating the rhythm of everyday life, the pressure of competitive markets wore on the senses of millions of displaced people in unexpected ways. Disrupted daily routines and stalled life narratives left people with a sense of boredom that was difficult to shake. *The Space of Boredom* enters into this boredom, which is so central to the way tens of millions of people worldwide experience globalization, in order to understand the quiet ways in which the global impresses itself on individual subjects.[17] Ultimately, this book explores the affective ruins of the global economy to advocate for a different orientation of the everyday, one that seeks to incorporate people into, rather than discard them from, urban life.

ACKNOWLEDGMENTS

This book would have been unthinkable without the incredible kindness, patience, and openness of the homeless men and women I came to know over the course of nearly three years of ethnographic fieldwork in Bucharest, Romania. I also owe an incredible debt of gratitude to the administrators and social workers of the shelters and day centers where this study took place. I am deeply grateful for the trust and transparency they showed me. I have never taken this for granted. I would also like to thank Ian Tilling for helping me to make connections at the start of the project and for being a source of constant support and friendship throughout my time in Bucharest.

This research would not have been possible without the generous financial support of a Fulbright Hays Doctoral Dissertation Research Abroad Grant, a National Science Foundation Doctoral Dissertation Research Improvement Grant, a Student Fulbright Fellowship, the Institute for Romanian Culture's Seton-Watson Grant for Foreign Researchers, and the American Council of Learned Societies. I am thankful for the financial support of Stanford University's Department of Anthropology; Center for Russian, East European and Eurasian Studies; and School of Humanities and Sciences. Finally, I am grateful for the research support of the Department of Sociology and Anthropology and the Center for Intercultural Studies at Saint Louis University.

This research trajectory took shape while I was completing a master's in city, space, and society at the London School of Economics and Political

Science and then a doctorate in anthropology at Stanford University. At the London School of Economics, I am thankful to Sharad Chari, David Frisby, and Edward Soja for cultivating my interest in the historical and spatial dimensions of urban life. At Stanford, I was lucky to join a truly impressive collection of scholars who were a source of companionship and constant inspiration. Thank you to Lalaie Ameeriar, Nikhil Anand, Hannah Appel, Elif Babul, Stefanie Bautista, Hillary Chart, Mun Young Cho, Jesse Davie-Kessler, Damien Droney, Maria Escallon, Maura Finkelstein, Patrick Gallagher, Mark Gardiner, Aysha Ghani, Helen Human, Sarah Ives, Alexandra Kelly, Dolly Kikon, Tomas Matza, Curtis Murungi, Kevin Lewis O'Neill, Guido Pezzarossi, Lisa Poggiali, Eleanor Power, Jenna Rice, Trinidad Rico, Robert Samet, Rania Sweis, Anna West, and Austin Zeiderman.

I would also like to thank those who engaged with this project over the course of conversations, both long and short, at various conferences and workshops, or while in the field. Thank you to Elijah Anderson, Peter Benson, Philippe Bourgois, John Bowen, Harold Braswell, Victor Buchli, Elizabeth Chiarello, Amy Cooper, Talia Dan-Cohen, Dennis Deletant, Ilinca Diaconu, Donald L. Donham, Ger Duijzings, Elizabeth Dunn, Monica Eppinger, Alex Fattal, Krisztina Fehérváry, Martin Demant Frederiksen, Jack Friedman, Angela Garcia, Bruce Grant, Zeynep D. Gursel, Thomas Blom Hansen, Scott Harris, Michael Herzfeld, Amy B. Huber, David Kideckel, Stuart Kirsch, Jong Bum Kwon, June Hee Kwon, Alaina Lemon, Daniel Mains, Saikat Majumdar, Dan Monti, Yasmine Musharbash, Claire Nicholas, Christopher Prenner, Laurence Ralph, Michael Ralph, Tracey Alexandra Rosen, Nancy Scheper-Hughes, Jeffrey Schonberg, AbdouMaliq Simone, David Slater, Priscilla Song, Archana Sridhar, Rebecca Stein, Jon Stillo, Kedron Thomas, Marguerite van den Berg, Loïc Wacquant, Richard Walker, and Rihan Yeh. I would like to give a special thanks to Liviu Chelcea for commenting on several early drafts of chapters and for opening the University of Bucharest's doors to me. The Faculty of Sociology and Social Work provided me with timely direction and incredibly well-trained research assistants. I would also like to thank Crăița Curteanu, Ioana Iancu, and Svetlana Iuschievici for carefully transcribing hours of taped interviews. They helped me process a large archive of material in a timely manner. Thank you.

I am incredibly grateful for the support and insight of my new colleagues in the Department of Sociology and Anthropology and in the Center for

Intercultural Studies at Saint Louis University during the critical stages of completing this book. The interdisciplinary environment of both the department and the center provided constant inspiration to think beyond disciplinary boundaries in order to reach deeper insights. My thanks go to my department chair, Richard Colignon; to the director of anthropology, Katie MacKinnon; and to the director of the Center for Intercultural Studies, Michal Rozbicki, for their unwavering support and encouragement. I am also thankful to my colleagues in the Department of Anthropology at Washington University in St. Louis, and to John Bowen in particular, for the open invitations to participate in their workshops, and for their enthusiasm and insight.

There is no way to fully thank my committee members for their intellectual generosity, thoughtful guidance, and kindness over the years. It has been a true honor to study under Jim Ferguson. I am inspired by Jim's great intellectual curiosity and insight as well as his keen ethical vision. Jim has fundamentally shaped in the best of ways my understanding of what it means to be a scholar. I would also like to thank Melissa Caldwell for providing me with invaluable area studies support and professional advice. My understanding of Eastern Europe and postsocialism would not be what it is without her generous guidance. Thanks also to Liisa Malkki, who has been a constant source of support. Especially at the proposal writing stage, Liisa's vision helped me make connections across broad literatures and interests. Beyond my committee, I would like to thank Lynn Meskel, who helped me develop my interest in the materiality of cities, and Dennis Rodgers, whom I first met while studying at the London School of Economics and with whom I have had the pleasure of collaborating as my studies advanced. Dennis has been not only a tremendous conversation partner but also a constant source of advice. Thank you all.

Parts of this book began as shorter essays. The material has since been pulled apart, rethought, and fleshed out to support the larger argument of this book. A very early version of chapter 2 appeared in *Environment and Planning D* 28, no. 2 (2010), as "Down and Then Out in Bucharest." Parts of chapters 4 and 6 appeared in *Cultural Anthropology* 29, no. 1 (2014), as "Cast Aside," and a shorter version of chapter 5 appeared in *Public Culture* 27, no. 2, as "Bored Stiff." The work of revising and developing the argument of this book benefited from the thoughtful engagement of numerous audiences, including during invited talks at the Russian and East European

Institute at Indiana University, the Department of Anthropology at the University of Michigan, the Department of Sociology and Anthropology as well as the School of Law at Saint Louis University, the Department of Political Science at Villanova University, and Yale University's Workshop on Urban Ethnography. At Stanford University, I am grateful to audiences from the Humanities Center's Cities Unbound Workshop; the Center for Russian, East European and Eurasian Studies; and the Department of Anthropology. I also presented portions of this book at the annual meetings of the American Anthropological Association, the Association of American Geographers, the Romanian Association of American Studies, and the Romanian Society for Cultural Anthropology; the biennial meetings of the European Association of Social Anthropologists and the Society for Cultural Anthropology; and graduate student conferences at Columbia University, University College London, the University of California at Berkeley, and Stanford University.

I owe a very large debt of gratitude to everyone at Duke University Press, and particularly to Ken Wissoker and Elizabeth Ault, for their unwavering editorial support and their selection of such capable and thoughtful reviewers. It was a true pleasure to revise the book with reviewers who so clearly engaged with this manuscript not only openly but also critically. The editorial process pressed me to think bigger and more clearly, and the resulting manuscript is undoubtedly better because of it. Thank you.

I would like to thank my in-laws, Dan and Kate Human, for their encouragement. I am grateful for Dan's background in anthropology, which has been a welcome source of enthusiasm for my career. I would like to give a special thanks to my parents, Bruce and Mary O'Neill, for their support throughout my studies as well as for their genuine curiosity about my work. They have kindly read my articles and listened to me practice job talks, and they have always asked thoughtful questions. They have also helped me celebrate the small successes along the way.

I would like to express heartfelt thanks to my brother, Kevin, who is also an anthropologist. I have learned immensely from watching his own career unfold. Kevin has been a constant conversational partner and source of inspiration, as well as the best of friends. Thank you.

My final and greatest thanks goes to my wife and fellow anthropologist, Helen Human O'Neill. Helen has read, edited, and debated with me the content of every single page of this book, and her insight and clarity have made it infinitely better. Helen also joined me in Bucharest for much of my fieldwork, providing me with a sense of home that would otherwise have been unthinkable. More than anyone else, Helen has seen me through every stage of the research and writing of this book with her love and support, and so it is with deep gratitude and affection that I dedicate it to her.

INTRODUCTION

"I feel bored (*plictisit*) quite a bit," Tomas confided. We were sitting in a patch of shade in the parking lot of Stefan's Place. The July heat radiated from above and off of the asphalt, making the humid air especially sticky. Tomas, a stout man in his fifties, had been living on the streets since his wife divorced him four years earlier. Since then, he slept in public parks, the stairwells of apartment buildings, and the waiting room of the Gara de Nord train station, among other places. When he could find construction work, Tomas earned up to sixty lei (about $18) per day off the books.[1] This was not one of those days. Instead, Tomas sat with me for lack of anything better to do. Gazing at the floor just ahead of his feet, Tomas continued, "I feel bored when I think about the kind of life that I have to live here in Romania. I mean, it's an ugly life on the streets. You have neither perspective nor peace of mind. You look at your watch and see that night is coming, and you wonder, 'Where should I go?' 'What should I eat?' 'Who can I sit and talk to?'" Tomas looked up from his feet and around the parking lot. About a dozen men in the twilight of their work trajectory were scattered about. Some slept along the fence line. Others sat on the curb of the driveway reading the tabloids. A handful spoke quietly on the stairs that led to the clinic inside. All looked firmly anchored in place. "I mean, at times I just feel useless," Tomas added with a heavy sigh as he returned his attention to the space just beyond his feet. "I think to myself, 'Why should I go on living?' There is nothing for me to do here that makes me happy. I don't have money in my pocket to buy something to eat or anything else that I might

want . . . and in these moments I feel an overwhelming dissatisfaction with life. It's like my organs don't sense the world around me." Tomas lightly rubbed his hands against the rough concrete of the retaining wall beneath him before returning them to his lap. "Don't get me wrong—I'm a religious man, and I believe it is a sin to kill yourself; but sometimes I just feel like I want to die, or perhaps that it would be better to be dead. These feelings of boredom are pretty terrible for me." Tomas sat quietly for a moment. He used his sleeve to wipe away the sweat that had accumulated on his brow, and he arched his back until his spine cracked and popped loud enough for me to hear. The sound of a car engine zipped past along the side road. "Hey, do you want to get out of here and maybe drink a coffee?" Tomas asked with a forced upbeat tone, as though trying to change the conversation.

Two decades after the fall of communism in Romania, and in the aftermath of the global financial crisis of 2008, a profound boredom drew back and forth across the streets of Bucharest. Political and economic reforms intended to transition Romania out of state socialism and into global circuits of production and consumption resulted in a chronically unstable economy. While an elite class of professionals emerged with the means to rejuvenate Bucharest's historic downtown and to sustain the newly developed shopping malls, prosperity eluded most Romanians. Instead, life became ever more insecure: steady work grew scarce, personal savings drained, and support networks stretched as the young and capable moved abroad in search of better opportunities. Once unthinkable in the time of communism, when state guarantees ensured a baseline subsistence for all, thousands of low-skilled workers, such as Tomas, found themselves unemployed and pushed onto the streets. Cast aside by heightened market competition, a shrinking state, and struggling families, homeless men and women lacked the means to participate in a world increasingly organized around practices of consumption. Empty hours gave way to endlessly dull days. Boredom abounded.

In the pages that follow, this book details the life stories of those left in the wake of efforts to integrate Romania into a global network understood to be ever accelerating, one where labor flows across borders, where slick production chains radically expand what is buyable, where digitization renders trade instantaneous and simultaneous, and where those caught up by it all guzzle caffeinated energy drinks, pop Adderall, and snort amphetamines in an effort to keep up.[2] While the global conjures a politics of speed, promising the "annihilation of space through time," the global wears differently upon the senses of many Romanians.[3] Market pressures intended to heighten production and consumption instead had the opposite effect. The Romanian economy buckled as formerly nationalized industry proved unsustainable in a brutally competitive global economy. Heightened market competition rendered millions of Romanians un- and underemployed and without the savings to support themselves. The introduction of the global did not incorporate these men and women into a frenzy of market-driven activity, as they had expected, but instead displaced them from it. Once they were displaced, life slowed down, and it slowed down quite a bit. A growing number of Romanians, in fact, describe endless days without work and speak of feeling stuck in place. Rather than speed and excitement, boredom defines downwardly mobile men's and women's engagement with the global economy. It is an affective relationship that is most clearly visible among

Romania's most vulnerable population (the homeless), but that resonates more broadly. A feeling that time has slowed down and that one is stuck in place is the result of a brutal politics of displacement within the global order.

This book's guiding assumption, then, is that boredom correlates in ever-cruel ways with downward mobility. This makes sense, given that the two arose simultaneously. Homelessness, as an official social and bureaucratic category, did not exist during communism. There was also very little concern with boredom. Universal housing, employment, and food rations took care of basic needs, while widespread austerity tamped down expectations for leisurely consumption. However, with the fall of communism, the Romanian government scaled back its guarantees, a competitive labor market was introduced, and the cost of living rose. Whereas, under communism, the state had taken care of all, Romanians now had to care for themselves within a new and highly competitive marketplace. Those unable to compete successfully in the new environment found themselves moved out of work and onto the streets, but also into a marginal space marked by profound and persistent boredom.

Importantly, Tomas and other homeless persons in Bucharest were not by and large depressed (*deprimat*); they were observably and self-consciously bored (*plictisit*). This is an ethnographic fact that is easily misconstrued, given that Bucharest's homeless narrated their boredom with such dramatic language. Tomas's desire for death, for example, cut against the triteness of popular depictions of the bourgeois ennui affecting the well-to-do in between parlor games and parties.[4] Tomas's account was not unprecedented, however. It resonates with an alternative tradition for thinking about boredom, one that ties boredom to poverty, solitude, and despair.[5] Time and time again, even in the darkest of moments, Bucharest's homeless described themselves as bored. Rather than pathologize themselves as depressed, homeless persons attributed their existential crisis to a series of social and structural conditions. These conditions brought about a perfect storm of decreased opportunities to earn a wage or receive a state guarantee at the very moment consumer capitalism took hold in postcommunist Romania. New needs arose just as individual capacities to consume dipped. Those filtered out by liberal reforms became constantly aware of the new consumer possibilities and pleasures that existed, both for Romania's small but growing cadre of professionals and also in other cities across the European Union (EU). The homeless, however, had no means of accessing them. This resulted in a gnawing sense of isolation from work but also from social worlds that were made up of family and friends but were mediated by consumer practices, and boredom took hold. While at times homeless men and women might have felt depressed—a clinical diagnosis linked to its own ontology—depression is distinct from the difficult-to-escape boredom with which these men and women identified and which they described from their place at the margins of the global economy.

The global, this book argues, is more than a geographic scale or material set of flows. It is a feeling that shapes ordinary life.[6] And for millions of people in Romania, and for tens of millions more in similarly positioned societies across the globe, this feeling is about slowing down rather than speeding up. Boredom captures the way a brutally competitive global economy affects those it discards in pursuit of ever-greater profitability and efficiency. The aftermath of the global financial crisis brought this changing global affect into clear relief. As corporations streamlined payrolls, the national and municipal governments slashed budgets, and families struggled with doing less with less, a growing number of people found themselves dumped out of the global economy. Still surrounded by its trappings, these now-superfluous subjects were no longer shaped through their participation in global production and consumption but by their irrelevance to it.[7] Tossed to the margins of the city, the displaced spent their days in a state of "letting die." As Michel Foucault notes, letting die is not as simple as "murder as such" but is instead a form of "indirect murder: the fact of exposing someone to death, increasing the risk of death for some people, or quite simply, political death, expulsion, rejection, and so on."[8] Letting die is a slow process that opens up spaces in which people live every day, just not in a recognizably meaningful way.[9] The deathly dull boredom reverberating across the senses captured this cruel impasse between the fantastic promises of global capitalism and the brute materiality of displacement from it.

This book, in the end, does not trivialize boredom—the painfully mundane form that abandonment takes in Bucharest—but rather confronts it in order to raise a simple question: What does it mean that life now stands in such a way that a profound boredom draws back and forth over us?[10]

An Economy in Crisis

Economic struggle has defined Romania's economy since the full onset of industrial capitalism in the mid-nineteenth century. In that period, city administrators made investments in rail lines, paved roads, and piped water to support the growth of industry.[11] Land reform measures ended serfdom in the countryside, turning peasants into petty landowners.[12] While urban centers developed, the standard of living steadily deteriorated for Romania's overwhelmingly rural population as small peasant landholdings fragmented amid population growth.[13] Inequality grew between peasants and wealthy landowners until tensions erupted with the peasant rebellion of 1907, which was not quelled until some ten thousand peasants had been shot.[14] A period of neo-serfdom followed, in which large landowners exploited the economic vulnerabilities of peasant farmers.[15] Lacking the means to achieve self-sufficiency, peasants borrowed grain and seed from wealthier landowners at usurious rates. The arrangement generated increased revenues for already wealthy landowners while leaving peasants bogged down by unmanageable debts that could never be fully worked off.[16] By the interwar period, the appropriation of peasant labor had contributed to an uneven distribution of wealth, one that allowed the center of the capital city, Bucharest, to garner a reputation for being the "Paris of the Balkans," at least up until the onset of communism in 1947.

With the onset of communism, economic struggle shifted from the fields to the factory. The Romanian Communist Party, in its effort to build an industrial proletariat, oversaw a program of village consolidation, reducing them from thirteen thousand to six thousand, which encouraged the transfer of rural peasants from the countryside to cities.[17] A process of rapid urban expansion swept across Romania's major cities, where newly relocated rural migrants took up residence in newly constructed housing blocks, to be sent to work in newly constructed factories. These efforts at urbanization and industrialization generally improved the quality of everyday life for former peasants, until communism took an unusually austere turn following a major earthquake in 1977. It was then that making do without became a fact of everyday life in Romanian cities as the then-dictator, Nicolae Ceaușescu, undertook two costly initiatives simultaneously. The first was an attempt, in the name of advancing state socialism in Romania, to pay back all of Romania's outstanding foreign debt ($11 billion) within a decade.[18] Ceaușescu believed this aggressive fiscal policy was necessary to prevent debt relations with foreign creditors from interfering in the development of socialism in Romania. To generate the necessary currency reserve, the Romanian Communist Party heightened its exportation of food and durable goods while severely limiting imports. Store shelves quickly went bare. The state also reduced its social spending, making it all the more difficult for the population to cope with shortages.

Ceaușescu's second initiative was the redevelopment of central Bucharest around a new civic center. The construction project was a monumental undertaking in both cost and scale. The entire development took up a quarter of Bucharest's historic downtown and included the construction of what would become the second-largest building in the world: a parliamentary palace known as "the House of the People" (Casa Poporului). Crafted out of only fine materials such as marble, gold, and crystal, the civic center project carried an estimated price tag of $1.5 billion. This was a remarkable sum for a country whose gross domestic product (GDP) at the time was about $17 billion.[19] As money, labor, food, and industry flowed out of the country to pay down debts and to fund the making of a new capital city, the Romanian people were left with little on which to live. Rather than struggling to work themselves out of unmanageable debts to wealthy landowners, as had an earlier generation, Romanians under communism wrestled with chronic shortages as the food and other durable goods that Romanian factories produced headed to markets abroad. Rationing and poverty ensued, leaving Romanians with one of the lowest standards of living in Europe.

After a decade of deepening austerity, the Romanian people's frustration boiled over. In December 1989, an anti-Ceaușescu uprising culminated in the execution of the dictator and his wife on Christmas Day, bringing an end to communism in Romania. The country then turned away from central planning and toward incorporation into the global economy. Western reformers and foreign investors stoked imaginations about the materially richer quality of life that could be achieved through opened borders and global trade.[20] The turn toward capitalism, Romanians hoped, would bring about a new era of prosperity through market-driven production and consumption. To harness the power of market forces, the Romanian government privatized state-held businesses, factories, and utilities. While these efforts were aimed at streamlining operations and achieving market efficiency, they had the effect of laying off thousands of state workers and reducing industry's overall output. Just four years into Romania's transition to capitalism, industrial output had declined by over half, and agriculture's share of GDP increased from 14 percent to 24 percent; around one million workers—a quarter of the industrial workforce—exited the factory floor, and 350,000 workers joined agriculture.[21] Rather than seeing the value of their labor sold off abroad, many Romanian workers found that their labor was losing its value within a globally competitive marketplace.

With this economic downturn, Romania fell into the very kind of foreign debt that the communist government had acted so draconically to avoid. By 1993, debts resulting from unpaid and unserviced loans from public agencies, unpaid taxes, and social security contributions peaked at approximately $2.5 billion, a number that exceeded Romania's annual budget.[22] These macrostructural pressures weighed down on the population. Inflation ran as high as 150 percent in 1997; unemployment reached 12 percent in 1999, and by 2003 average real wages had fallen to 60 percent of their value in 1989.[23] While expectations that liberalization would bring about a better life abounded, these broad economic forces rendered the basic costs of everyday life increasingly difficult to afford. In 2003, for example, a one-bedroom apartment rented for €175 per month while the average wage was only €130 per month. Multiple incomes became necessary to make the rent, leaving the average household only €85 to cover the rest of their monthly food, clothes, utilities, medicine, and transportation costs.[24]

After a turbulent decade of postcommunist transition that left ordinary Romanians downwardly (rather than upwardly) mobile, Romania's economy began to improve in the early 2000s. Western Europe and the United States, impressed by Romania's commitment to economic austerity, allowed Romania to join NATO (the North Atlantic Treaty Organization) in 2004 and the EU in 2007. Also, in 2005 the Romanian people voted into power a pro-European democracy for the first time, leading some prominent Romanian intellectuals to announce the end of postcommunism.[25] The economy also expanded: between 2000 and 2007, Romania's economy managed to grow 6.5 percent annually, providing the country with the kind of sustained development that was necessary to pull 30 percent of its population out of absolute poverty.[26] Consumption drove much of this economic growth, with foreign banks providing Romanian households with cheap credit serviced in euros. Romanian households voraciously consumed imported goods such as cars, televisions, and computers, financed by foreign money.[27] Western-style shopping malls opened in Bucharest and beyond. New construction exploded, and businesses began to hire. While Romania remained at this time a very poor country, with an average per capita income that was only 41 percent of the EU average, Romania's acceptance into the EU—and the flow of trade, aid, and infrastructure that came with it—gave people tangible cause to believe that better days were coming.[28] After decades of hardship, Romanians had every reason to believe that they were finally on the cusp of achieving a so-called fully European standard of living.

This period of growth proved unsustainable.[29] The brief moment of prosperity that had lifted millions of Romanians out of absolute poverty unraveled in 2008. It was then that widespread financial troubles in the United States' banking industry, over subprime mortgage loans, reverberated around the world. The ripple effects rapidly instigated a global financial crisis that left few countries unaffected. By 2009, the Romanian stock market had lost 65 percent of its value, while the Romanian new lei depreciated by 15 percent against the euro, increasing households' foreign debt burden almost instantly.[30] Romania's already low wages prevented the unemployment rate from spiking.[31]

With the country's financial outlook worsening, the Romanian government quickly found itself facing a budgetary deficit. In need of a bailout, the Romanian government turned in the summer of 2010 to the International Monetary Fund (IMF). The loans came with strings attached. The IMF imposed a radical series of austerity measures to restructure government spending and taxation. At its ugliest, the IMF austerity program cut public wages by 25 percent, increased the value added tax (VAT) to 24 percent, and cut spending to social assistance programs. Additionally, the government laid off eighty thousand public sector employees, the retirement age increased, and eligibility for retirement and disability-related pensions tightened.[32] These measures compressed the already austere funding for social assistance in Romania. The Romanian government coupled these measures with a public apology, fully aware of the added difficulties they posed to the Romanian people. The BBC quoted Romania's finance minister, Sebastian Vlădescu, as saying, "I cannot hide that I am deeply disappointed that today we are raising VAT," adding that the measures were necessary to ensure Romania's financial stability and to meet the terms for a $20 billion IMF loan.[33] According to the World Bank, Romania's expenditures on social assistance were the lowest in the EU, and spending on poverty-targeted programs was low in proportion to expressed needs and the country's GDP.[34]

The global financial crisis rapidly undid for many Romanians the improvements in quality of life they had gained once admitted into the EU. Instead of entering into a fully European standard of living—one that would approximate the material well-being found in other EU capital cities—as they had hoped after the fall of communism, Romanians never found sustained prosperity. Instead, they experienced a prolonged state of economic instability that left a growing number of people unemployed and out of money, with fewer and fewer government protections on which to rely. Instead of experiencing upward mobility, thousands of Romanians found themselves unemployed, unable to afford their homes, and pushed out onto the streets.

Creating Homelessness in Bucharest

Under communism, homelessness was unthinkable in Romania. The Romanian Communist Party (PCR) staked its legitimacy on universal guarantees to housing, prompting an impressive boom in construction. From 1950 to 1985, the Romanian state built well over 4.4 million apartments and houses, with the lion's share of this development taking place in cities.[35] By 1985, the PCR had built nineteen urban residences for every one rural dwelling, and the PCR built forty-five residences for every privately financed one.[36] By 1990, the year after the PCR's removal from power, the deposed government's massive investment of money and labor had produced 73 percent of Romania's national housing stock.[37] These efforts accommodated almost everyone. The Romanian language at this point even lacked a word to denote "homelessness." It was only after the fall of communism, amid the process of accession into the EU, that Romanian bureaucrats adapted the English word *homeless* into the Romanian *homleși*.

To be sure, some people during the communist period did fall through the gaps of state guarantees. They stayed with sympathetic family members in overcrowded apartments, or, when left with no other option, they slept in underutilized basements, attics, or abandoned buildings. However, those without regular housing in communist Romania were not identified as "homeless" as they might have been in the United States or the United Kingdom.[38] Instead of using terms tied to liberal notions of social welfare, the communist state made sense of those without homes through the language and infrastructure of pathology. This system of categorization does not match the Western category of homeless in any cultural, political, or economic sense. The state, for example, interpreted some of the unhoused as orphans and located them in orphanages; the government labeled the healthy but unhoused as "sick" and placed them in sanatoriums and asylums; and the unproductive became understood as criminals to be stored in prisons.[39] In this context, homelessness proper did not represent an experience or object of knowledge. This communist categorization effectively addressed the need of unhoused people for food, shelter, and care, while also allowing the PCR to avoid larger questions about the failures of its social, political, and economic systems.[40]

The fall of communism disrupted this management strategy. Transitional economies provided the perfect conditions for producing the unhoused—what Western aid agencies and the EU would quickly dub *homelessness*. All at once, housing expansion slowed, the labor market contracted, and average wages dipped just as the cost of housing spiked.[41] Once rare, unhoused people became an increasingly common feature in Bucharest. This growing pool of unhoused persons, however, became identifiable as homeless only as Western aid workers entered Romania and as liberal reformers readied the country for EU accession. Aid workers and journalists walking through central Bucharest, for example, witnessed people living and sleeping on the streets, which led them to report having seen "homelessness" in central Bucharest. Through these speech acts, foreign journalists and aid workers created in Romania the cultural category of homelessness even as they reported it. The most widely circulated example is the American filmmaker Edet Belzberg's documentary *Children Underground*.[42] The documentary follows the lives of five children living in a Bucharest Metro station during the late 1990s. The camera lens captures images of children collecting leftover cardboard boxes from nearby kiosk vendors, arranging the boxes on the floor of the station, and then huddling together for the night. The documentary also depicts these children begging for money and scavenging through the trash for food and empty soda bottles. These images led the American filmmaker to declare, in a seemingly unproblematic way, that these Romanian children are experiencing homelessness, a cultural frame of reference not used by any Romanian featured in the documentary.

While Romania's faltering economy would suggest a growth in this new "homeless" population, no one was really certain about the population's dynamics. The Romanian government, simply put, maintained no official records on homelessness.[43] While the Romanian government first dedicated funds to address homelessness in the mid-1990s, the Romanian state adopted an official definition of homelessness only in 2011.[44] Drawing on EU-wide standards developed by the European Federation of National Organizations Working with the Homeless (FEANTSA), the Romanian parliament defines homelessness as a state in which an individual or family lives "on the streets or with friends or acquaintances and is unable to sustain a rented house or is threatened with eviction, or lives in institutions or prisons and is due to be released within two months and lacks a domicile or residence."[45] Universal in its tone and intent, this adopted definition of homelessness is at odds with the way ordinary Romanians think about those living on the streets. With furrowed brows, Romanians of a certain generation generally seek clarification, wondering if by *homeless* one might really mean *țigani*, a derogatory denotation for the Roma; *vagabond*, meaning "vagrant"; or *aurolaci*, a term denoting street children who huff paint.

As also became clear over the course of extensive ethnographic research, those seeking the assistance of homeless shelters and day centers did not always understand themselves as homeless, even if their living conditions were unheated, overcrowded, precarious, or informal. They also did not understand themselves as necessarily sharing a social or material condition with others sleeping in shelters, in transit stations, and on park benches. In contrast to the undifferentiated mass of homeless referenced by advocates, administrators, and politicians alike, those living on the streets insisted that there were at least four distinct populations making use of homeless services. As quickly became clear, the distinction between population segments was social and material but also moral, and it hinged on the ability to approximate a working-class demeanor.

The most obvious distinction was between those living in shelters and those living on the streets. Shelter spaces, as one might imagine, were coveted places. Shelters in Bucharest tended to be mid- to long-term-stay facilities, meaning that beneficiaries could stay at a shelter anywhere from three months at a time to indefinitely. Shelter spaces, however, were few and far between, with less than a thousand beds for Bucharest's often-quoted and highly conservative estimate of five thousand homeless persons. While shelters were widely understood as a form of communal living fraught with neighborly tensions and marked by an absence of personal privacy, homeless persons nevertheless sought them out because they provided all of the accoutrements usually associated with "home." This included access to showers and washing machines, beds and kitchens, television, and even the Internet. Equally important, shelters enabled beneficiaries to mask their lack of formal housing when walking the streets, talking with casual acquaintances, or applying for a job. With freshly shampooed hair, clean and pressed clothes, and a working knowledge of television plotlines, shelter beneficiaries could walk down the street, apply for a job, and carry on conversations at the grocery store without appearing homeless. Shelters enabled homeless persons to give the impression of maintaining a more integrated social position. It was a kind of performance that began to break down when homelessness placed one on the streets.

The street homeless population further divided into three subgroups. This was explained to me by Ion, who, in his fifties, regularly visited Stefan's Place and lived in a nearby squatter camp. Seated on a pile of cardboard used as a bed, Ion explained to me that he was an *om fără casă* (literally, "a man without a house"). Although living day in and day out on the streets, Ion explained, an om fără casă maintained his appearance: he bathed regularly, his face was shaved, his hair was combed, and he behaved politely in public. To illustrate his point, Ion invited me to observe that the white shirt he wore was indeed white (rather than yellow), his face was smooth (rather than stubbly), and his hair was combed (rather than unkempt). With a hint of pride, Ion explained that he did not draw undue notice when riding the bus because his appearance was neat and he did not have a pronounced body odor. Although lacking the infrastructure found in shelters, Ion maintained himself in such a way as to pass as an integrated member of the working class. His ability to do so, I would later learn, was aided by weekly invitations to use the showers and borrow the clothes of housed family and friends. It was not uncommon for homeless men in this category to sleep outdoors three to five nights a week while staying with friends or family indoors for the other nights. These stays indoors offered an om fără casă the much-needed opportunity to get uninterrupted sleep, to shower and to wash their clothes, enabling the better socially networked to maintain a neater appearance and, in turn, to gain better access to semipublic resources found in shopping malls, supermarkets, and fast-food restaurants.

Not everyone living on the street could maintain such a "polite" (*politicos*) aesthetic. Those unable to keep up appearances, Ion continued, were labeled *un boschetar* (literally, "a bushman"). The designation implied that the person looks as though he slept in the bushes. As the stereotype goes, the boschetar is a sort of bum: he wears dusty clothes and has ruffled hair, his body smells, and he is often publicly drunk. His demeanor offends a working-class sensibility, a fact illustrated by the disgusted looks and harsh comments that a boschetar receives in grocery stores and on public buses. Testifying to the enduring observations of Mary Douglas, the perceived dirtiness of the boschetar evidences his moral and social inferiority vis-à-vis an om fără casă.[46] Dirt not only signifies moral impurity but also suggests that one is less deserving of social assistance. Throughout my time in the field, people identifying as an om fără casă regularly warned me not to speak with or buy food for a boschetar. With earnest faces, they explained to me that the boschetar was as much a threat to my wallet as to my physical safety. These exchanges made it clear that the inability to keep oneself fresh carried biopolitical implications, ones that hastened the process of letting die.

Yet the figure of the boschetar did not occupy the bottom stratum of homeless society in Bucharest. Despite the stigma, someone labeled "boschetar" was not a pariah; he nevertheless received a certain degree of attention from social workers and administrators. The face of the undeserving poor, the people situated beyond the goodwill of service providers as well as the homeless population at large, was that of the aurolaci or *drogați* (drug addicts). Drug use remained highly taboo in Romania for the homeless and housed alike. For the most part, this population segment abused inhalant-based glues or paints. Injection-based drugs began to circulate among the teenage members of Bucharest's homeless community only around 2005, while homeless adults gravitated strictly toward alcohol. Those self-identifying as om fără casă and boschetar actively avoided homeless drug users, whom they perceived as unpredictable, untrustworthy, and potentially violent. Social service providers also avoided working with active drug users because they saw them as self-destructive and as a poor use of limited resources. Time and again, social workers, administrators, and cleaner-cut homeless persons warned me not to work with people who appeared too disheveled or intoxicated. Despite numerous warnings and concerns, however, I did not have a single serious incident with violence or theft while spending time with homeless persons of any kind.[47]

Whether sheltered or on the streets, smartly dressed or in need of a shave, intoxicated or sober, those pushed out of the working class and reconstituted as homeless experienced a shared sense of boredom. Everyday life no longer met the basic expectations of guaranteed work and a home established during socialism, much less corresponded to the accelerating quality of life that the global market was supposed to deliver. Importantly, Bucharest's homeless men and women attributed their boredom to being stuck "here." Whether they were referring to the shelter or the squatter camp, the city of Bucharest, or even Romania as a whole, the overwhelming consensus was that a life that was not boring, but instead meaningfully stimulating, existed "over there": in a home, in another city, or in another country. By and large, homeless persons wanted to move away from the boredom of their marginalized lives and toward a wider array of possibilities located on the horizon.

The Space of Boredom

I met Teo in the parking lot of Stefan's Place. He did not move from his perch on a retaining wall along the center's driveway, even when the morning shade shifted, fully exposing him to the afternoon sun. Much of his cemented demeanor had to do with his right foot. Although it was heavily bandaged, sores nevertheless bled through the gauze. When Teo reset his bandages about midmorning, other beneficiaries whispered to me with grimaced teeth and scrunched noses, "Holy shit—look at those feet!" The skin had peeled, and blood and pus oozed out of raw wounds. I walked over to introduce myself to Teo and to ask how he was doing. "I'm bored," Teo said softly in response. Unable to walk without wincing, it had been weeks since Teo had worked and days since he had eaten. His acrid breath was partially masked by the scent of burnt newspaper, which homeless men regularly used to roll the unspent tobacco scavenged from the discarded cigarette butts littered in public squares. "There's nothing for me here anymore." Teo sighed with exhaustion. He then asked if I could buy him a loaf of bread.

The boredom that Teo, Tomas, and thousands of others living on the streets of Bucharest described is a particular kind of boredom. While this boredom resonates with a commonsense notion of having "nothing to do," its entanglement with such physical and inwardly felt suffering no doubt gives pause, given boredom's association as an experience that is without qualities.[48] This is because boredom is almost always theorized from the perspective of privilege. From Charles Dickens to David Foster Wallace, and from Friedrich Nietzsche to Martin Heidegger, both literature and philosophy speak of boredom as a sense of slowed time endured by the well-to-do when not sufficiently engaged.[49] The writings of Anton Chekhov even suggest a bourgeois indecency to boredom, linking it to the moral emptiness and stunted intellect of the affluent.[50] Boredom in this popular literary and philosophical sense is acknowledged as a troubling but also trite burden of privilege. It is something the better-off should learn to conquer, or at least to ignore, until something more interesting comes along to take hold of one's attention.

When theorized from the perspective of poverty, however, boredom takes on an entirely different politics. Boredom becomes something chronic (rather than passing) and cruel (rather than petty). In the parks and public squares of Bucharest, boredom registered on the senses of downwardly mobile Romanians as the yawning gap between the rising standard of living promised by global consumerism and the deteriorating material conditions in which they were now living. Drawn into the global economy by the fantasy of regularized consumption in corner stores and megamalls, of remodeled homes and world travel, heightened market competition ultimately devastated, rather than renovated, the infrastructure of everyday life.[51] As the promise of heightened consumerism slipped further away from the actual conditions of ordinary life, becoming ever more fantastic, ever more desirable, downwardly mobile men and women found themselves moved not just into homeless shelters and squatter camps but also into a space of profound boredom.

This book traces the production of boredom in three types of spaces. At its most concrete, the book treats boredom as a material space, a claim that is grounded in the common lament among the homeless that shelters and squatter camps are boring places to be. The shelters themselves, the homeless insist, are boring. These kinds of places bring about boredom in the people who occupy them. While the homeless assert this with a kind of ontological certainty that calls to mind Martin Heidegger's analysis of train stations, this book takes a historical and ethnographic tack in thinking about boredom's material dimensions.[52] This book treats shelter boredom as a shared social orientation rather than a property of the shelters themselves.[53] Shelters and squatter camps are, after all, socially devalued places. As conversations and observations with Teo, Tomas, and others made plain, these places are marginal because they lack worthwhile things to do. They rest in opposition to the excitement and bustle of the main square, the construction site, or the terrace bar, for example. They are the discarded fragments of the city abandoned by those with the means to avoid them. These spaces offer no compelling reason for people to choose to visit them unless otherwise compelled by need. As places in the city removed from, and devoid of, meaningful activity, shelters and squatter camps become places where boredom is found, and so they effect boredom in those who occupy them. Boring space, in the form of shelters and squatter camps, constitutes an empirically observable field.[54]

In addition to being a kind of material space, boredom is also inwardly derived. Boredom is an individually held and collectively shared evaluation that the temporal rhythms and spatial practices that make up shelters and squatter camps are lacking in meaning and significance.[55] It is also an affect that is deeply felt within the space of the inner self, where thoughts, emotions, and abstract ideas animate and define individual personhood.[56] In the pages that follow, this book traces boredom's historical formation at the intersection of the material world and the abstract space of the inner self through an analysis of everyday social practices.[57] Through everyday movements like pacing, smoking, and conversing, individuals bring the exterior space of the material world into contact with the interior space of the self. The attention to space brings the specificity of the boredom at the margins of the city into view. It is an ethnographically distinct kind of boredom that works unrelentingly to devalue the personhood of those subjected to it. Ultimately, the boredom captured within these pages registers within the modality of time the homeless's displacement from meaningful places and marks their resignation toward occupying the discarded spaces of the city.

Stuck in the space of boredom, the newly minted homeless took stock of lives disorganized by capitalism. They could not help but wonder whether they were living a life at all.[58] No matter how long these men and women would sit, an antidote to their boredom would not arrive. Instead of waiting for relief, homeless men and women actively moved about in search of opportunity. Sometimes these movements were to different physical places: public parks, boulevards, and train stations, while at other times the homeless traveled to different "mental spaces," as in cases of addiction, fantasy, and eroticism. Although analytically distinguishable, these efforts at moving out of the space of boredom were ethnographically intertwined. This intersection gave insight into the homeless's embodiments, emplacements, and practices while revealing a surprisingly violent and distinctly postsocialist set of relationships among the self, the city, and the global economy.

By entering into the space of boredom, this book ultimately examines the subtle ways in which global circuits of production and consumption slow the rhythm of everyday life. It details the subjective and affective fallout of consumerist fantasies that will not be fulfilled now, nor later. The kind of boredom that follows is no trivial matter. Rather, as will become clear in the pages that follow, this boredom is a critical site of attachments, internalizations, and bodily practices that go to the heart of the politics of displacement in a brutally competitive global economy.

1

SPACE-TIME EXPANSION

. . .

"Back under communism, you had a stable routine—you knew what to do with your day: school or work, then the line, then back home," Alex recalled to me as we sat in his squatter camp. Overturned cartons served as chairs, while an exposed heating pipe warmed the late-autumn air. "There were lines day and night," added Ionel, who shared the camp with Alex. "Let's say you needed milk. You had a bottle, and you waited in the evening in front of the creamery, and you stayed there until morning when the delivery came. You'd stay up all night to get three to four kilograms of milk to give to your children. All night you would wait there." Another neighbor, Ion, had worked in transportation and cargo during the Ceaușescu era and offered a more systematic reflection: "The timing of lines depended on when goods arrived. Often shipments arrived in the afternoon, so let's say three o'clock. You'd need to stand in line from dawn until four, five, or six o'clock. By eight o'clock the stores closed, so that was it. But you scheduled for this: you'd go to work while your wife stood in line. Then when your kids came home from school, they would stand in line for your wife. And then when you came home from work, you would stand in line for your kids." The family routine, these men insisted, was entirely organized around standing in line. Idleness and waiting made up the majority of the day. But as Alex noted, "Standing in line took a long time, it's true, but it wasn't stressful at all. We would sit with people from the neighborhood and read, play checkers, play cards, chess, or backgammon. And we would drink hard!" Ion and Ionel both irrupted in laughter and nodded knowingly. "There was almost

FIGURE 1.1. Camp. Photo by Bruce O'Neill.

always beer, wine, and *țuică* [plum brandy] around," Alex continued, "and there wasn't much else to do otherwise. It wasn't like today. There weren't so many televisions, and even then there were only two hours of TV programming each day! Sure, rather than stand in line I would have liked to have gone to the movies, kicked around a soccer ball, or maybe gone fishing, but life was generally alright."

"Were you ever bored?" I asked each of them and others. "No," they answered—sometimes with a shrug, sometimes with a curiously furrowed brow. "Why would I have been?" asked another.

. . .

IN OCTOBER 2010, homeless men gathered well before dawn at a black market for day labor in the hopes of finding some construction work off the books. About fifty men waited in the dark on this otherwise unused stretch of pavement for the opportunity to make less than fifteen dollars for a day of hard labor. Divided in small groups among themselves, they passed around old water bottles filled with țuică. "It gives you strength," Aurel, a homeless man, explained with a bounce in his voice as he passed me the bottle. The țuică registered an instant buzz in Aurel's empty stomach. He puffed up his chest and made as though he was lifting a heavy wheelbarrow: "It lets you forget that you haven't eaten or slept so that you can work through the afternoon." I tried not to wince as the predawn mouthful of brandy burned down my throat. I handed the bottle along to the next man while the group swapped information about various construction projects across the city. These moments before sunrise brimmed with optimism.

A contractor appeared soon thereafter, prompting those at the square to jockey for his attention. The waiting men gathered around the contractor. They all shouted their credentials and showed off the calluses on their hands, each trying to demonstrate that he was *un om serios* ("a serious man" or "hard worker"). The contractor, however, needed only three people; he selected a familiar face from the group and told him to quickly choose two more men. The newly minted captain of the work crew nodded in the direction of his two friends, and then the chosen three headed to the contractor's van while the rest of us continued to wait. As midmorning gave way to early afternoon and the bottles of țuică ran dry, it became clear to those left behind that no more work would be found that day. The brandy-boosted optimism of the early hours bottomed out entirely.

The remaining men gathered their things and drifted toward the city's parks, transit stations, homeless shelters, and squatter camps. By the time Aurel was ready to go, he had been stripped of all traces of his earlier bravado. Rather than puffing up his chest, he let his shoulders roll forward, and his eyes glazed over. On his way out, Aurel lamented to me, "*Ce plictiseală!*" (What boredom!). When I asked Aurel why he felt bored, he explained, "I was raised to work. I want to work. I don't want to stand around all day with nothing to do (*stau degeaba*). Tell me, what are you supposed to do all day with yourself when you can't find work, you smell bad, and you don't have any money in your pocket?" My own brows arched and my face drooped as I drew a breath to speak but found myself without a suggestion. A long pause was all I had to offer him. "Exactly," said Aurel, before walking off in the direction of a park.

. . .

THE ABOVE ACCOUNTS PROVIDE a window into two different moments of deprivation in Romanian history. In the first, homeless Romanians recall their days of communist-era austerity, when food shortages forced ordinary citizens to spend long amounts of time waiting in breadlines. These moments are remembered as idleness. In the second account, workers displaced by a globally competitive marketplace wait for day labor off the books. When the opportunity to earn some money, and eventually to spend it, does not come, these men consider themselves bored.

Roughly twenty years separate the idleness of breadlines and the boredom of homelessness. Within that period Romania underwent a dramatic set of political and economic reforms that injected a heightened sense of efficiency through market competition into Romania's once centrally planned economy. To be sure, the privatization of Romanian industry did away with breadlines. The shortages in everyday goods that had caused store shelves to run bare under communism gave way to hypermarkets such as Carrefour, which offered a taste of European-style consumerism in all of its abundance. These reforms, however, did not end deprivation for all Romanians. Instead, the introduction of market competition determined anew who experienced deprivation, what its cultural significance was, and how deprivation was internalized and embodied. While communist-era austerity was a collective condition tying a deprived people to a paternalistic state, market reforms refocused deprivation on particular population segments, such as the low-skilled, the elderly, and the homeless. As competitive market logics became more prevalent, these deprived populations were not affixed into slow-moving lines to eventually receive bread, as they had been under communism, but instead were labeled superfluous and cast aside to the margins of the city. There they waited for not much of anything. Amid the changing cultural politics of poverty and belonging—from incorporation into breadlines to displacement to the urban margins, from social reproduction to social exclusion—deprivation took on new characteristics. Time slowed, space expanded, and social relationships wore thin. Rather than being idle, those pushed to the margins of a global economy in crisis became bored.

The Breadline

In June 1948, less than a year after the Romanian Communist Party founded the Romanian People's Republic, the legislative branch of the newly formed communist state adopted Law 119.[1] This law legalized the Romanian Communist Party's mass appropriation of all companies, banks, and mines and the transportation, telecommunication, and utility industries as well as approximately 400,000 privately owned homes.[2] The implementation of Law 119 gave the Communist Party remarkable control over the means of production as well as the distribution of jobs, housing, and everyday consumables in Romania. Both industry and political power became highly centralized in comparison not only to Western democracies but also to other communist countries in Eastern Europe, particularly East Germany, Poland, and Hungary.[3] The Romanian Communist Party believed a highly centralized economy would allow for a coordinated and controlled push toward rapid development and, ultimately, the realization of socialism. To that end, government planners created a series of five-year plans intended to industrialize Romania's largely agricultural economy and to transform Romania's rural peasants into an urban proletariat prepared to build socialism.[4] Loans from Western banks provided the capital to develop new factories in cities across Romania. This boom in industry was coupled with a burst of urban construction to house a growing wave of rural-to-urban migration. State-owned factories provided Romania's urbanizing population with stable jobs, guaranteed housing, and steady wages. These state guarantees assured a baseline of material subsistence, but they also rendered Romanians dependent on the state for their general well-being.[5] Initial economic growth lent a certain degree of popular support to this arrangement.

In the 1960s Romania's economic successes enabled it to achieve membership in the World Bank and the International Monetary Fund (IMF), most-favored-nation trade status with the United States, and preferential trading status with Western European countries. Between 1971 and 1975, Romania's industrial output increased faster than that of any other Warsaw Pact country, and its GNP growth was the highest in Europe.[6] Romanian families achieved in this moment the kind of affluence that permitted regular weekend trips to the Carpathian Mountains and to the Black Sea, which were made possible by the development of new roads and hotels.[7] In this moment of prosperity, Romanian citizens had little cause to object to the centralization of political power, industry, and household resources around the Romanian Communist Party; its president, Nicolae Ceaușescu; and his vision of socialist modernity.[8]

The aggressive economic growth and impressive gains in quality of life, however, did not last. By the early 1980s, the Communist Party's efforts at central planning had produced what liberal economists call a "shortage economy."[9] Rather than allowing market pressures to allocate economic resources and determine the development of infrastructure, government planners made decisions based on projections and policy priorities. Despite the efforts of central planners, systemic miscalculations and misallocations of resources ensued throughout the Romanian economy. For example, while some factories received insufficient materials to meet their manufacturing quotas, others received an excess of materials and labor. Such imbalances led to stoppages on underresourced production lines, while other workers reported to overstaffed factory floors only to learn that they had nothing to do. Instead of working, they spent their day standing around.[10] This apparent misallocation of labor caused workers and machines alike to stand idle in ways that would not have occurred in a competitive, liberal market. Even when Romanian industry churned out an abundance of needed consumables, central planners did not store the excess for distribution to the Romanian people.[11] Instead, Ceauşescu's regime exported excess goods in order to build up a cash reserve to aggressively pay down its foreign debts and to fund elaborate construction projects in the capital city. These policies and inefficiencies directing the system of production contributed, in turn, to a lack of goods on store shelves. As store shelves ran bare, Romanians had to spend increasing amounts of time waiting in line for replenishments to arrive. The austerity that ensued from the government's (mis)handling of production and trade took its toll at home and abroad. As the 1970s came to a close, Romanians experienced a diminishing standard of living and a declining life expectancy.[12] Worsening conditions prompted Western journalists and politicians to recast Ceauşescu as a brutal dictator hostile to market-oriented reforms.[13]

By the 1980s, long and slow-moving lines defined much of the Romanian economy, as shortages of food, gasoline, and household goods compelled people to spend increasing portions of their day queuing. Several decades after the end of communism, Romanians collectively remembered these lines as a trying social experience that organized much of everyday life across the country. Dragoş Voicu, whose well-received novel *Coada* (The queue) was released at the time of this research, for example, represented life in Romania under communism as a giant and seemingly unending line for chicken scraps.[14] The novel depicts a people who had no choice but to marry and die, celebrate and mourn, within the framework of the breadline. Similarly, Romania's twenty-four-hour news station, Realitatea TV, broadcast viewer recollections of breadlines in a series of short films entitled *Comunism pe Burta Goală* (Communism on an empty stomach).[15] The series broadcast the testimonies of everyday workers who completed twelve-hour shifts only to spend the remainder of the day standing in long lines for bread, milk, and meat. Black-and-white photos depicted long lines that wound out of and around grocery stores bearing empty shelves. The time demands posed by queuing required the young and old alike to coordinate waiting, so that households would not lose their place when parents needed to work or sleep. The proliferation of lines left Romanians with little time to do much else but stand in anticipation.[16] Such lived experiences and recirculated accounts contributed to a general feeling of underdevelopment and resignation. As the Romanian journalist and critic Paul Cernat bleakly summarized with regard to the 1980s, "there existed a permanent uncertainty about the future: you could not know what idea might come to 'the chief above.' In general, you waited for things to get worse and worse. You did not know when or if the delivery truck would come. You just waited indefinitely."[17]

Deprivation, in a moment of communist-era austerity, defined much of everyday life. Shortages organized where people went and what they did, as well as how they felt. Of critical importance, however, is that this deprivation did not stigmatize individuals as it would in Romania's now-competitive marketplace. The experience of deprivation did not differentiate between the young and the old or between manual laborers and well-educated bureaucrats. Instead, deprivation in those moments was collectively shared. All but the very elite struggled to get the things they needed. In a time of communist austerity, deprivation lent itself to a politics of social attachment as almost everyone found themselves incorporated into the breadline. Despite its many abuses, breadlines were concrete sites that connected a people (reduced to dependency) to a paternalistic state that distributed (a minimum of) rations. In addition to food, the state also guaranteed each individual a job; to ensure that workers were well rested for the day ahead, the party also guaranteed each family a home.

In this moment, deprivation never implied that one was socially or economically *superfluous*, a term used by Karl Marx to reference capital's tendency to produce an overabundance, whether of human labor or of consumer pleasures.[18] To the contrary, during the depths of austerity, the Romanian communist government widely celebrated the productive value of each person, even as shortages forced people to miss meals or go without electricity in the evening. To that end, the state developed an elaborate "cult of labor" that heralded the contributions of ordinary workers to the production of Romanian socialism. Socialist art and literature depicted the herculean efforts of Romanian workers, just as government officials staged labor-related parades to celebrate the worker as the heroic source of all cultural and scientific achievement.[19] From the pages of newspapers to museum walls and down into central squares, the state's consciously crafted cult-of-labor policy imbued workers with symbolic capital, highlighting the contribution to the collective made by those idling between work, home, and slow-moving lines.

Behind the public celebration of the workers' productive capacity, the communist government also quietly monitored the speech and actions of nearly every Romanian. Through one of the largest and most elaborate secret police forces in Eastern Europe, the Securitate, the communist government collected information about the most banal elements of ordinary Romanians' daily routines. The secret police listened and observed while workers waited in lines, moved about the factory, and talked in their homes.[20] Workers reported on colleagues, friends on their neighbors, and children on their parents. While this extensive policing evidenced the paranoia of the Romanian communist government, it also demonstrated communist officials' profound interest in the most intimate thoughts and actions of the people, regardless of their social standing.[21] While in the 1980s the communist government fell far short of providing Romanians with a European quality of life, the communist party's efforts nevertheless positioned the state as a paternalistic entity that, at times all too literally, looked after the population.

Only those whose living conditions have worsened since the fall of communism recall the breadline fondly. Ion began to explain as we sat on his scavenged bed in his squatter camp. He had draped a plastic sheet over the hot pipe above to keep the rain off of his mattress and also to provide us with warmth. The heat building up in the makeshift room caused me to sweat through my shirt. "Sometimes," he said, "when stores ran out of supplies, there would be an uproar: pushing and screaming in these cramped lines: 'you broke my bag'; 'you tore my jacket, my blouse'; 'you pulled my hair.'" Ion knit his brows, scrunched his nose, and swung his elbows from side to side to illustrate the ugliness as well as the physicality of the scrum. "People hit you, pushed you, everyone grabbed what they could. I mean, if you stood in line that morning, worked throughout the day, returned to the

FIGURE 1.2. Bed. Photo by Bruce O'Neill.

line at night only to leave with an empty bag, then you got pissed." Ion sat pensively for a moment before adding in a voice of sincerity, "But in general it was better than it is now. Life was hard with those interminable lines, but it was good because you had a steady job, you had money to pay a stable rent. That's just not the case anymore." Ion's friend Radu concurred. "We ran like hell to queue without even knowing what kinds of supplies were being brought. We figured whatever it was, it was something. The lines were endless, but at the end of the line, you at least got to bring something to eat home to your apartment, to your family."

The social and material circumstances of homelessness led these men to recall breadlines with a certain degree of nostalgia, rather than focusing on the abuses of communist-era austerity. Reflecting on the breadline provided a foil for identifying a lost sense of security and belonging that was once tied up with the experience of shortages. To be sure, there was a brutalizing politics to deprivation under communism, but it was a type of politics that bred social attachments. The communist government's (mis)management of the planned economy nevertheless produced times and places where the state provided for people in need. The form of the breadline connected people to the state, just as the slow temporality of these lines connected family, friends, and colleagues in collective strategies of negotiating scarcity. The lines were slow and long, but the passage of time nevertheless brought people closer to something they either needed or wanted. For homeless men in Bucharest, a sense of meaning and belonging could be found in a communist-era routine of negotiating with family and friends during the constant moving back and forth between work, home, and the interminable line. Now that these men were awash in free time but with virtually no purchasing power, memories of a not-so-distant past when their time was entirely occupied with waiting for *something* to be provided by an overbearing state seemed almost too good to be true.

The idleness of the breadline disappeared with the end of communism in 1989. A series of political and economic reforms followed soon after, which intended to shift Romanians out of the idleness of its once centrally planned economy into a state of market-driven production and consumption. As Romanians moved instead from communist-era austerity to a global economic crisis, the social and political coordinates of deprivation changed dramatically, reshaping the way Romanians understood and embodied deprivation.

The Breadline Dissolved

With the fall of communism, Eastern European politicians turned to Western academics and institutions to guide their transition from a nationally planned economy to a liberal one integrated into the so-called global market. Jeffrey Sachs, the principal architect of the economies of former communist countries, asked rhetorically in 1991, "How can Eastern Europe succeed? The industry is so old-fashioned; the workers don't have the right skills; the enterprises are so dilapidated; the environment is despoiled."[22] This is a general comment on the region, but Sachs might as well have been talking about Romania specifically. Ceaușescu, with his commitment to Stalinist principles, had achieved a level of economic centralization that made Romania's national economy function almost completely contrary to the logic of a competitive liberal market. By the end of communism, Romania had one of the most centralized economies in the region, with what one area specialist described as "a highly distorted economic structure, which included obsolete fixed assets, low managerial skills, and declining economic competitiveness."[23] Despite such apparent troubles, Sachs remained undaunted: "Many other countries that were once cut off from the rest of the world by inward looking, authoritarian regimes have successfully opened up and become integrated into the global mainstream economy. By doing so, they have tended to enjoy enormous increases in real income. In effect, by rejoining the rest of the global economy, they are able to import some of the prosperity from the rest of the world."[24]

To "import some of the prosperity from the rest of the world," economic consultants, with the support of the IMF, the World Bank, and various Western democracies, advised postsocialist countries to harness the productive efficiency of competitive markets. From Poland to Romania, Western economists advised these newly minted democracies to rapidly privatize their industries and housing, as well as to quickly remove government intervention in market activities. In that spirit, the post-Ceauşescu Romanian government sold state-owned housing units en masse to their existing owners. Between 1990 and 1995, the state sold over four million units to private individuals.[25] The state also sold majority shareholder status in all of its nonessential industries, creating by 1994 no fewer than forty thousand joint ventures with foreign partners, totaling about $964 million in gross domestic product.[26] The state completely liberalized peasant markets to increase the supply of food, replaced the State Planning Committee with the Ministry of the National Economy, and redistributed land from agricultural cooperatives to peasants for "long-term use."[27] In the years immediately following the end of communism, the paternalistic relationship between the Romanian government and its people came to an end. No longer would Romanians turn to the state for their jobs, their homes, or their food, thus paving the way for a new set of social relations structured around a competitive global market.

To be sure, Romanians caught glimpses of what these new and expanding possibilities looked like. The privatization of companies and the rise of competitive markets brought an end to the shortages that defined life under communism. Factories and offices alike streamlined their production and removed unskilled and unnecessary employees, narrowing the communist-era gap between "having a job" and "having work to do."[28]

FIGURE 1.3. Unirii Square. Photo by Bruce O'Neill.

Restrictions on imports were eased as Romania recast itself as an emerging market open for business. As Romanian goods and services responded to a competitive marketplace, and stores started to maintain inventories, Romanian consumers enjoyed a growing level of choice. From sugary snacks and cigarettes to athletic sneakers and blue jeans, increased imports and improved domestic goods provided Romanians, for the first time in forty years, with more and better options—even if persistent poverty compelled shoppers to "choose" the cheapest among them.

While the Romanian economy struggled to gain traction in the 1990s, foreign companies and brands invested media advertising into this "emerging" economy. Billboards for major global brands such as Heineken, Nike, and Samsung illuminated the evening sky, altering the character and experience of central squares such as Unirii Square, Romană Square, and

Victoriei Square. Advertising extended from city streets into now-private homes through the proliferation of new commercial media and television programming. With the end of tight state controls, twelve hundred new newspapers and magazines went into circulation within the first year of postcommunism.[29] Cable television, once limited to two hours of political rhetoric each day under Ceaușescu, now offered hundreds of twenty-four-hour news and entertainment channels.[30] Foreign development firms also created new spaces for Romanians to pursue their consumerist desires. Abandoned communist-era developments, such as the food market, sarcastically referred to as a "hunger circus" (*circul foamei*), near Vitan Square, became an "American-style" shopping mall designed to meet "international standards for retail and leisure."[31] The introduction of American-style malls exposed Romanians not just to a variety of foreign retailers but also to a distinctly Western shopping experience—one that tethered the acquisition of new shoes and kitchenware to the ingestion of pop music, fast food, and carefully stylized spaces. As consumer culture gained traction in Romania, well-trained Romanian engineers and low-skilled manual laborers alike took advantage of the country's newly opened borders. They went on temporary work visas to places like France and Italy, but also to Israel and Abu Dhabi, for the chance to earn in a comparatively stronger currency.[32] Not only did these work trips allow many well-educated Romanian men to send remittances home to their families, but the time abroad also recalibrated these workers' sense of what a normal quality of life entailed.[33] Confronted with the excesses of global consumerism, life under communism appeared ever more austere. Capitalism aroused within the starved communist-era worker a desire to consume, and it seemed to be stimulated everywhere.[34]

Still miles away from the capitalist "dream worlds" of nineteenth-century Paris or twentieth-century New York, expanded access to cable television and magazines, malls and billboards, foreign films, travel, and the arrival of the Internet all converged to raise hopes that life in Romania would one day soon reach an imagined European standard of living.[35] The movement of goods and labor helped to structure Romanians' expectations about the accoutrements, aesthetics, and practices that would one day compose their future lives. As residents of Krakow, Moscow, and East Berlin transitioned into full-fledged consumer citizens, the average resident of Bucharest could not help but think that his or her moment would soon come too.[36] Romanians waited with eager anticipation for their chance to be caught up in this new wave of consumer capitalism.

FIGURE 1.4. Food market (*circul foamei*). Photo by Bruce O'Neill.

And wait for a European standard of living to take hold they did. It is well documented by now that while a small cadre of Romanian elites enjoyed an improvement in the quality of their everyday life, the economic and human impact of Romania's move toward privatization was generally disastrous. Transition merely teased Romanians with the prospect of a European quality of life rather than delivering one to them. As one commentator noted in the mid-1990s, "of the former Warsaw pact countries in Eastern Europe, Romania has numerous distinctions. It had the last transition. It had the most violent regime termination. . . . It is the country where the successor regime committed the most egregious violations of human rights. It is the only country where the democratic opposition has yet to win a national election. It is the only country where a former high communist official was not only elected to the presidency in the first free election, but re-elected."[37]

As Romania struggled politically to become a liberal democracy, its economy continued to falter rather than stabilize and strengthen. In 2000, when Romania made a major push toward European Union (EU) accession, EU analysts noted with distress that 40 percent of Romanians lived on less than one dollar a day and that Romania had the lowest gross domestic product of all candidate states, the highest inflation, the least foreign investment, and arguably the most corruption.[38] Immediately before its accession to the EU, analysts pointed out that the country's significant economic reforms still left Romanians with an average monthly wage of under $350.[39] At the same time, countries such as Germany and England, anxious over the apparent growing wave of Romanians trying to escape the troubled economy at home, tightened their visa restrictions for Romanian workers.[40] High rates of Romanian immigration to Italy, Spain, and France also led to overt hostility and, ultimately, to deportations.[41] Increasingly unwelcome abroad and compelled to return home, these workers joined the swelling ranks of Bucharest's unemployed, hustling for day labor on various black markets across the city. Rather than being caught up in the midst of a capitalist dream world marked by opened job prospects, discretionary spending, and foreign travel, Romanians entered the twenty-first century in a state of continued deprivation.

Deprivation, in this context of political and economic reform, took on a different social significance and set of material characteristics than it had had under communism. Poverty, in this moment of global consumerism, ceased to be a generalizable condition. Instead, it spoke to individual inadequacies as determined by competitive market outcomes. The young, entrepreneurial, and well-trained received validation in the form of rising salaries and the cultivation of richer tastes, while poverty now pressed in only on those unable to succeed in a brutally competitive labor market, such as the elderly, the low-skilled, and those otherwise deemed inefficient. The social significance of impoverishment shifted as it became entangled with near-permanent "unemployability." Under communism, the impoverished were workers central to the Romanian social and political imagination, but now impoverished Romanians came to be thought of as "redundant" and "expendable," as "human debris . . . eliminated permanently from producing society."[42] Simply put, poverty now implied an irrelevance not just to the city but also to the national and the global economies. Poverty for the first time carried an individualizing stigma. In this context, those experiencing poverty no longer received the attention of a paternalistic state as they had under communism. Now that the poor had been rendered super-fluous, neither the state nor private employers were invested in whether the poor ate or where they slept, much less what they thought.

Those who, for the briefest of moments, had enjoyed a foothold in the new economy were especially affected by the changing coordinates of poverty and belonging after they were eventually displaced by the global financial crisis of 2008. Five years of relatively strong economic growth had allowed many young Romanians to begin to enjoy the sugary rush of consumerism that was being advertised all around them. Salaries may have been small compared to those in other cities in Europe, but economic growth in the early 2000s nevertheless allowed even low-skilled workers to enjoy a regular stream of Coca-Cola at the Internet café or beers at the bar while watching the Steaua soccer team play. Rising wages engendered a new capacity for stimulation that could not be adequately fulfilled when currency exchange rates fluctuated or when market competition failed to streamline a business's operations, instead closing its doors altogether.

The lost capacity to buy into new consumer pleasures helped to cultivate a widely felt sense of boredom (*plictiseală*) among Romanian (under) consumers. Evidence of this was everywhere. The alleviation of boredom became the organizing theme of advertising campaigns, first for the Romanian television station Antena 1's "Anti-boredom Campaign" (Campanie Antiplictiseală), followed by the Nescafé brand's call to "Defeat Boredom!" (Învinge Plictiseala!).[43] Boredom served as a prominent theme of Romania's critically acclaimed new wave of cinema, including titles such as *Police, Adjective* (2009), *California Dreamin'* (2007), and *The Death of Mr. Lazarescu* (2005).[44] And streaming through the headphones of Romanian university students and disaffected teens was the prominent Romanian hip-hop star, Guess Who, who rapped about boredom as a way of capturing the darkness and monotony of life as a young Romanian in the late 2000s.[45] As rising consumer expectations cut against declining economic stability in Romania, boredom abounded. This boredom hit none harder than Bucharest's most vulnerable, the homeless, who found themselves suddenly pushed out of work and home with little savings to draw on. Within squatter camps and state-run shelters, those displaced by a global economy in crisis repeated in dull, anguished voices, day in and day out, "Mă simt plictisit"—"I feel bored." As became clear through a set of extended interviews with Mircea, a resident of the Backwoods Shelter located just outside of Bucharest, this deeply felt sense of displacement registered through such fundamental categories as the self, space, and time. As Romania's troubled incorporation into the global economy foreclosed on idle industries and turned underutilized employees into unemployable workers without the money to engage a growing constellation of commodities, space expanded, time dragged, and a profoundly bored subject emerged. Mircea's account below is illuminating not as an ideal type of this boredom but as a singularity that offers a clear vantage point for understanding how Romania's downshifting economy became internalized and embodied by its most vulnerable victims.[46]

Space-Time Expansion

> Something that's dull or opaque fails to provide enough stimulation
> to distract people from some other, deeper type of pain that is always
> there, if only in an ambient low-level way, and which most of us
> spend nearly all our time and energy trying to distract ourselves
> from feeling. . . . This terror of silence with nothing diverting to do.
> —DAVID FOSTER WALLACE, *The Pale King*

Shortly after the onset of the global financial crisis in 2008, Mircea, an ethnically Roma construction worker in his late twenties, found himself out of a job. Despite being a trained mason and a hard worker, Mircea was let go when his construction team needed to downsize. In the midst of an economic depression, there was not much demand to build in Bucharest. Mircea soon ran out of savings and was no longer able to make rent. He moved into the Backwoods Shelter with his fiancée and son. He spent most days alone in the shelter courtyard smoking cigarettes and sipping coffee. It was there that I found Mircea one afternoon sitting with his legs crossed, the left bouncing anxiously over the right, staring at the lawn before him while he smoked a cigarette. I walked over to say hello and to see what he was up to. Mircea gave his cigarette a final drag before looking up and explaining, "Today I'm just sitting at home and being bored. Yesterday I didn't stay here at the shelter. I left and I walked here and then I walked there." Mircea gestured with his cigarette toward the right and slowly dragged it across his body to the left, watching the thin trail of smoke slowly rise and dissipate into the air. Putting the cigarette back in his mouth, he continued, "Then I read a newspaper. But afterward I thought to myself, 'What was the point of all that walking?' and 'What was the point of that newspaper?' I was just running around to avoid doing nothing." With a shake of his head,

Mircea added, "It was all just a waste of time. So today I am going to sit at home and be bored."

In the absence of buildings to construct and homes to make, a global economy in crisis left Mircea feeling as though there was nothing to do.[47] Of course, no formal rules prevented Mircea from leaving Backwoods Shelter on any given day; he was free to spend his afternoons walking the streets or sitting in a park reading *Click*, a free daily tabloid. These freely available activities struck Mircea as empty, however. Their completion did not build toward any recognizable vision of a meaningful life: not a career, a family, or a home, or even a sense of momentary distraction. Their enactment left Mircea questioning whether he was not better off simply staying within Backwoods's fence line and "doing nothing" at all.

In this moment Mircea revealed a palpable tension between what he believed he ought to be able to do each day and the array of activities and practices that were immediately available to him. This tension was not so intensely felt before the global financial crisis. Mircea explained, "Before I came to Backwoods, we had work. We had it all the time. Where I stayed, around Militari, I could go back and forth [between construction sites], and everyone found work." His speech picked up tempo, and his eyes widened as he recalled this fleeting moment of prosperity. "We stayed in a small room, but life was easy then—everything in the day happened immediately (*imediat*): I'd get up, I'd go to work, and I'd be moving through the work fast (*repede*), and I made fast money (*bani repede*). I had a motor scooter, I had money, I had an apartment—I had everything!" Mircea went quiet for a moment as the excitement vanished from his face. "Then the crisis (*criza*) hit, and it all ended. Everything no longer worked. Now there is nothing here for me anymore." Mircea took another long drag from his cigarette.

Before the crisis, Mircea knew what to do. Each morning, he boarded his scooter, and he moved quickly between construction sites. Bucharest's boom in building in the run-up to Romania's EU accession created a wealth of opportunity that enabled Mircea to earn "fast money." This fast money, in turn, endowed him with the disposable income to rent his own apartment and to start a family to come home to at the end of each day. As one might expect, incorporation into the global economy quickened the pace of Mircea's day as he zipped between work and home. The accumulation of fast money left Mircea with enough time at the end of the day to head in the evening to the store, the restaurant, or even the movies.

In the wake of the financial crisis, as the global economy sought new stability by attaining ever-higher levels of efficiency through heightened competition, the everyday infrastructure for producing Mircea's life dissolved at a frightening clip. Rather than becoming further incorporated into global circuits of production and consumption, Mircea was displaced from them. Simply put, as competition for work ratcheted up, Mircea no longer made the cut. Mircea's fast money dissolved, and the global began to wear differently on his senses. Mircea recounted, "Now, because of the crisis, my life went '*caput*' [sic], you know? It sucks now. I lost the apartment, and I sold my scooter, I sold my computer, the television . . ." Mircea rattled off a detailed list of electronics and appliances with which he had parted ways. "I had to sell it all. We sold everything, and then everything slowed down. Now I'm here at this shelter feeling bored." I pressed Mircea to explain what he meant by everything "slowing down." "Take getting around," Mircea started without hesitation. "When I need to get around, I now rely on the bus, and it's slow. I have friends who stay at the St. Ignatius Loyola Shelter (a religiously affiliated homeless shelter on the outskirts of town).[48] It took five minutes on the scooter for me to get there. I timed it on my watch. But with the bus, it takes between an hour and two hours depending on the traffic and how you time the bus transfers. I timed that on my watch too. The bus takes a long time (*durează mult*). And it's like that for every other part of the day."

As the global recession turned Romania's lukewarm economy cold, work sites suspended construction midproject, leaving Mircea without a job to ride to in the mornings. He also no longer received a paycheck to bring home in the evenings. Rent quickly slipped out of reach, and so Mircea and his family had to leave their small apartment. Everyday needs like food, much less gasoline for the scooter, grew problematic. To generate cash, Mircea liquidated his possessions. The home gave way to a shelter, private transit to public, home computing to newspaper reading. A life once experienced not so long ago through metaphors of acceleration now downshifted quickly and seemingly came to a screeching halt. Mircea now struggled to adjust to much more cumbersome ways of moving, learning, and socializing. It left him feeling as though his life no longer had traction. Instead, life seemed to be in limbo. Mircea continued, "My nature is to go out and make money, you know? I want to do something, to produce something—for my wife and for my child. But now there is no [steady] work for me. . . . I now make around 700 lei ($235 per month) on the black market. At 700 lei, you cannot afford food, let alone to pay the rent to keep staying at Backwoods, the cost of a television, much less [monthly] cable or even cigarettes."[49] Shaking his head with frustration, Mircea added gloomily, "A man can no longer live here in Romania. All that is left for me to do is just to sit at this shelter feeling bored."

Mircea's understanding of what it means to have a life—a general vision including a developing career, a private home, and a certain capacity for leisure—came undone. In order to get by, Mircea improvised. He spent the mornings waiting at day labor markets in the hope of finding a day's worth of manual labor off the books. As a result of the crisis, though, black labor markets became flooded with other displaced workers like Mircea. It was now a buyers' market, and contractors knew it. Contractors offered decreased wages for a lengthened workday. Much like his slowed ride to the black market on a public bus, Mircea now had to work longer while earning less. The fast money that was once readily available gave way to a grinding competition for slow money. With frustration building in his voice, Mircea attested, "It's not like I don't want to work, but when I go out and work construction, I want more than sixty lei ($18 per day), but I don't see that shit anymore! And bosses want me to work for ten hours? Not eight hours like before the crisis but ten hours? At this rate, we're really just working for food!"

To be sure, newspapers advertised jobs offering more reasonable wages. When I pointed this out to Mircea, however, he rolled his eyes and wagged his finger in my direction. The job advertisements in the classifieds, he explained, were too good to be true: "Believe me, I'm afraid to go to work for one of those newspaper ads. I've gotten burned! Last year, I found in the newspaper a site advertising 2,000 lei ($600 per month) for a bricklayer." This kind of salary would have allowed Mircea to comfortably support his family in a rented studio apartment in a quiet neighborhood in the city. "I went to work there, but, man, I got played! I worked for a *whole month*, and at the end of it, they didn't give me any money. Nothing. Instead, they ran me off the site! Now I look at the newspaper with suspicion—I worry that they're all scams. I'll go to work for a month and then get nothing in return. It's bullshit," he concluded grimly.

Mircea's Roma ethnicity further complicated his efforts to make do on the black market, much less his aspirations of landing a formal work contract. Widely stigmatized throughout Europe, the Roma (so-called gypsies) are stereotypically seen in Romania as untrustworthy and lazy. Mircea's dark brown complexion made employers preemptively suspicious of him. With the glut of available labor on the black market, contractors could act on ethnic biases in a way they were not as prone to do when construction was thriving and skilled masons like Mircea were in demand. As Mircea explained while recounting the difficulties of his job search, "I went to one firm the other week because they told me over the phone that they were hiring. So I got on the bus and made the long hike over there to give them my résumé. But when they saw that I was black, that I was *ţigan*," Mircea paused, letting the word *ţigan*, the harshest slur referring to the Roma, hang in the air before continuing, "they said, 'No, we don't need anyone anymore. We have no use for you.' They turned me down because I'm dark. But this is the life for us in Romania: 'the discarded gypsies.' If employers see that I'm *ţigan*, they will have nothing to do with me."

Like many Roma struggling to make a life in Romania's working class, Mircea, defensively and without prompting, insisted on differentiating himself from the figure of the gypsy. With arched brows and widened eyes, Mircea exclaimed, "And it's infuriating because I have no criminal record—my record is clean. I have never stolen anything or been to jail. I don't even drink!," heightening the distance between himself and the main characteristics of the gypsy stereotype. "You can't say the same for the majority of [the predominantly white] men at the black market or even here at Backwoods. They all drink, and some of them have been to jail. But not me—not once! But I'm the one getting lumped in the same lot as the *ţigani*." With a heavy sigh, Mircea concluded with frustration, "The truth is that I've been working since I was fourteen. I'm good at what I do. But because I'm a *ţigani*, bosses see me at a construction site and say, 'We don't need this trouble.' I can't make money if I can't work."

Displacement from the global economy radically recalibrated Mircea's relationship to time and space. As his capacity to earn, and in turn to spend, contracted, he began to feel stuck in place. In a literal sense, Mircea had become less mobile. Whereas once he shuttled himself from place to place on a scooter, he now had to walk or take the bus. Trips that once took minutes suddenly took hours. In addition to his scooter, Mircea also sold off his television and his computer. He had less cash on hand to buy minutes on his cell phone or to visit Internet cafés, for example. Whereas he had once watched Premiere League soccer matches in his own living room, he now had to read about them the next day in a free tabloid; rather than keeping up with friends via instant messaging and texting, he found that friendships now drifted apart and grew fragile. Personally significant places felt further away, and the sensation of "immediate" mobility made possible by fast money gave way to prolonged exercises in waiting for slow money to trickle into his pockets. Roads looked longer, friends and familiar places felt further away, and time passed ever more slowly.

At the same time, Mircea also felt stuck in an existential sense. Most profoundly, his life narrative seemed to stall out entirely. No longer financially solvent, Mircea could not secure the everyday infrastructure necessary to develop his vision of a family life. His fiancée put their engagement on hold, even after the birth of their son. "I want to get married to my fiancée, to move forward with life, to buy a house, to get out of the shelter. But I can't do any of that without a stable job." I pressed Mircea, pointing out that the shelter where he was already living with his son and fiancée provided a sense of stability: a room with a bed and a guaranteed hot meal. I asked why he did not just move on with his life by getting formally married, if that was what he wanted. Mircea shrugged off the question: "The shelter gives me and my family food, a place to sleep, hot water for showers, and all of that, but . . . I want to make something better for my family. But instead of building our own life, I have to cling on to this. I have to hang onto this by a wire."

Romania's rationalizing economy produced the very opposite effects for manual laborers that postcommunist economic reforms had purported to offer. Rather than continually accelerating the pace of everyday life by further integrating Mircea into a global marketplace—a process that would compress his experience of both time and space by folding him into new circuits of private transit, communication, and media—a state of heightened global competition had in fact displaced him from the world around him.[50] All at once, global competition unleashed a wave of detachments that made space appear to expand, time to slow, social networks to strain, and digital stimulation to drop off. Few state guarantees were available to shield Mircea from the global's slowing down of his world, and it was not clear to Mircea what kind of opportunities could be found nearby. The material circumstances of Mircea's present drifted cruelly further and further away from his fantasy of a good life; and the future did not look any more promising. Romanian newspapers closely covered Romania's growing indebtedness to the IMF, which, while keeping the government afloat, did so by introducing a fresh set of austerity measures restricting government services. The media coverage left Mircea, and others, with the realization that there was no relief from mounting economic pressure in sight. "I think about the future a lot now," Mircea explained. "What future can I find here in Romania? I can't make anything, not a future for myself or one for my child. Romania is getting worse, and it will not get better. There was a crisis in America, it passed, and now it's done. But the crisis doesn't end here in Romania. Romania borrowed a large sum of money [from the IMF], and now we have to pay it back. It's just going to keep carrying on like this."

Stuck in place and cut off from any meaningful vision of the present and future, Mircea's hope for a better life became pegged to egress rather than progress. Mircea imagined fulfilling his fantasy of a good life not by waiting for better times to come to Bucharest but rather by moving toward opportunities located elsewhere in Europe. Testimonials from friends working abroad fueled Mircea's desire to emigrate. "Many of my friends left here, and they promised that they would call for me," Mircea began, "but they haven't. Now I'm waiting for some money to go to England. I know well from my friends that there aren't gypsies in England, and so it's great! There isn't the bias toward gypsies like in Germany or Spain. Plus the money is very good there. The minimum wage in England is 1,200 euros a month. That's a *minimum* of 1,200!" The minimum wage in Romania at the time hovered around 150 euros. The sum felt all the more paltry when viewed in a comparative framework.

From the young, educated, and upwardly mobile who frequented the chic cafés located in Bucharest's historic district to the unskilled workers in homeless shelters, Romanians across the class spectrum spoke discouragingly about the value of their wages compared to what could be found in other EU capital cities. Regular stories in the Romanian media kept these negative sentiments about depressed wages not only alive but informed.[51] While conceding that salaries are indeed higher in London, I pointed out to Mircea that the cost of living is also a lot higher in England. He waved away my objection. "I don't eat very much," Mircea countered, "maybe one full meal a day. And I'll be earning so much more a month that I'll definitely come out ahead—so yeah, I'm interested in working abroad. I just want to come into a bit of money so that I can make the trip—so that I can get a newspaper, call an employer in England, and ask for a job." In an effort to demonstrate his preparedness for life in England, Mircea simulated a phone conversation in English with a potential employer. Speaking each word slowly and deliberately, he continued, "And I know how to speak a bit of English—I could call an employer on the phone and ask, '*Sir—you—*

need—worker?' and I can respond, *'Sir—I know—to do—that—work,'* or something like that. But that's Romania. Everyone wants to go. Everyone wants to get away from here—to escape."

Mircea was not exaggerating. While Romania's population is approximately twenty-two million people, Romania's Ministry of Foreign Affairs estimates that between six and eight million Romanians work abroad.[52] Time and again, Romanians attempting to negotiate Romania's troubled economy do so by moving elsewhere. Yet Mircea's own great escape from the shelter on the outskirts of Bucharest to the "better life" he imagined in England or Spain now seemed financially impossible. He could not afford to move himself, much less his family. Importantly, Mircea had not always found the idea of immigrating unbelievable. He maintained an attachment to the fantasy of moving toward a better life abroad that made its unattainability painful in a way that his inability to afford a luxury car or win the lotto, for example, was not. Only a few years earlier, during the briefest moments of economic prosperity, he imagined himself as being only a day's road trip away from exploring such work opportunities. He even had friends who had made the trip to England or Spain and whose empty offers of assistance added fuel to his fantasies. It was only in the aftermath of the global financial crisis that the possibility of migration drifted out of his grasp. The changing economy recast the better life abroad—once just a day's ride away on a topped-up motorbike—to being impossibly out of reach, adding nuance to Homi Bhabha's observation that "the globe shrinks for those who own it; for the displaced or the dispossessed, the migrant or refugee, no distance is more awesome than the few feet across borders or frontiers."[53] For those displaced in a moment of heightened global competition, not only does opportunity feel further away, but it takes longer and becomes more arduous to move toward it. Rather than waiting on the cusp of movement toward betterment, Mircea found himself stuck within a complex cultural politics framed by expectations of upward mobility and the experience of downward mobility, the cultivation of a European-wide framework for evaluating one's quality of life and the withering away of the public and private infrastructure necessary for producing it. While the possibility of attaining a European standard of living became ever less plausible following the global financial crisis, Mircea still held tight to the fantasy of it. So he sat in the courtyard of Backwoods practicing his lines for imaginary phone calls with future employers and strategizing through his hypothetical weekly grocery bills to maximize his imagined future savings.

Amid the impasse of affective attachments to upward mobility and the immediate experience of displacement, Mircea clung optimistically to a working-class sensibility even as he was rendered downwardly mobile. He did not escape from his daily boredom by engaging in petty hustles in parks and transit stations or by entering into a world of alcoholism as is so often associated with life at the margins. His optimistic attachment to upward mobility left him anxious about acknowledging his actual downward mobility by enacting the lowly behaviors commonly associated with the figure of the "homeless bum" (*boschetar*), the addict (*aurolac*), or the "gypsy" (*ţigan*). Instead Mircea sat in a homeless shelter developed outside of the city limits, quietly sipping coffee and smoking cigarettes with his legs crossed, as though on a work break that refused to end. The quiet moment so coveted when on the clock now encompassed every waking moment, and reverberating within it was an unshakable sense of unfulfilled aspirations. With no clear sense of how to get life back on course, time slowed, space stretched, relationships strained, and stimulation dissipated. The cultural politics of attachment to global consumerism amid detachment from global production left Mircea feeling bored day in and day out.

2

BLEAK HOUSE

. . .

"When I first came here, I thought I was going to go crazy from boredom," began Aurelia, a resident of the Backwoods homeless shelter in her early sixties. We stood in the entryway of the shelter sipping Nescafé with Marian. Although of working age, Marian collected a disability pension that covered the cost of his room and board. Dependent on crutches, Marian was physically incapable of joining the other men who looked for work on the black market. Instead, he spent his days hanging around the shelter with the women and children. Aurelia continued, "When I first saw this place, I thought I'd been sent to a camp. I thought I was put in jail, or locked in a sanatorium. There's nothing to do here!" she exclaimed while throwing her free arm in the air in disgust.

Marian nodded knowingly as Aurelia took a long sip from her mug. "Life in Backwoods is hell," Marian confirmed. "We're bored all of the time because we don't have money to get out of the shelter and go into the city. It's this feeling of wanting to go into the city to do something but not having the money to do anything. It's a hard feeling to get rid of." Leaning back against the doorway, Marian added, "We're stuck here."

This widely shared sense of boredom among Bucharest's homeless population was not just psychosocial. It was also infrastructural. Their boredom was entangled with the planning and development of new urban spaces to manage Bucharest's growing homeless population. Some of these spaces were formal institutions, such as the Backwoods homeless shelter and the Stefan's Place day center. Although located in the most peripheral

FIGURE 2.1. Backwoods Shelter. Photo by Bruce O'Neill.

areas of the city, these formal institutions nevertheless addressed the homeless's most basic material needs for food and protection from the elements. For this reason alone, demand for shelter space far outpaced shelter capacity, prompting the vast majority of homeless persons to produce their own informal dwellings in the discarded spaces of the city: the unnoticed and underused spaces located within the landscaping of public parks, the stairwells of apartment blocks, and squatter camps set up on empty plots of land. Whether the homeless were situated in a formal institution or moving between such informal spaces, the development of this infrastructure to accommodate those displaced from work and home had the effect of moving homeless persons in need of services toward the physical and social margins of the city. Once there, the homeless found themselves far removed from the city's most socially valued places. Whether at the shelter, the day center, or the squatter camp, homeless persons felt stuck in nonplaces, and they were too broke and too far removed to participate in an urban life increasingly organized around practices of consumption.[1] The workings of this infrastructure contributed to an unbearably slow pace of everyday life for those cast aside in a moment of heightened global competition.

Developing Shelters: Placing the Homeless

As the 1990s drew to a close, after a decade of troubled efforts at development, Bucharest garnered a reputation in the international media for being overrun with poverty. A *BusinessWeek* column voicing an international businessman's apprehension of traveling to Bucharest provides a typical case in point. As the columnist describes:

> Western visitors familiar with Bucharest took a deep breath before taking on the Romanian capital's urban chaos. As you left the airport arrivals lounge, hordes of unshaven, unlicensed taxi drivers besieged you with offers to take their rundown jalopies through potholed boulevards to the city center. Once there, bypassing touts offering girls or wanting to change [your] money, you had to be wary of bites from Bucharest's 150,000 stray dogs. The mutts sent 30,000 people a year to the city's rundown hospitals, from where they often emerged sicker than when they went in.[2]

Contrasting the 1990s with Bucharest's pre–World War II glories, the same article continues:

> In the 1930s, this city's graceful streets, chic coffee houses and sophisticated shops earned it the sobriquet "Paris of the Balkans." In the 1990s, after 40-some years of communist neglect and the megalomaniacal projects of dictator Nicolae Ceaușescu, "Calcutta of the Balkans" seemed a fairer description. Half-starved orphans ran around neglected, garbage lay uncollected for weeks at a time, and the Dâmbovița River often stank.[3]

Municipal officials reacted to this Western gaze by working to manage poverty's presence across the capital city. Street orphans, sex workers, and stray dogs, to say nothing of the unshaven, had become a form of urban blight that, administrators feared, carried potentially costly consequences. Beyond aesthetic concerns that these living elements contributed to the

FIGURE 2.2. Old Town in 2010. Photo by Bruce O'Neill.

supposed degradation of the city, there was also the worry that they turned off Westerners whose investment was believed to be critical to Bucharest's future development. For the sake of attracting investment, poverty and all of its embarrassing traces needed to be cleared from view, particularly in the city center.[4] This movement culminated with the election of Traian Băsescu as the city's mayor in 2000. Băsescu instituted an aggressive campaign to "clean up" the streets of Bucharest, focusing at first on unlicensed street kiosks, sex workers, child orphans, and feral dogs.[5] While foreign animal-rights activists, led by the French actress Brigitte Bardot, winced, the majority of Bucharest's residents looked on approvingly. In a similar vein, the municipal government quietly began to address homelessness on the streets of Bucharest. A range of government bureaucrats, nongovernmental organizations, planners, and business professionals in Bucharest converged in the late 1990s to move homelessness off the streets and away from the city center.

This process began in 1998 when the municipal government approached Andrew, a British-born aid worker, to oversee the development of Bucharest's first night shelter, Second Chances. A retired police officer and former church deacon, Andrew came to Romania in the 1990s after viewing a series of television exposés on the child neglect and generally inhumane conditions inside Romanian orphanages. The local authorities became familiar with Andrew through his volunteerism and approached him about opening and managing a night shelter in Bucharest. After much negotiation, Andrew agreed to partner with the municipality, which ultimately allotted Andrew two buildings, one in northwestern Bucharest and the other in southern Bucharest. While Andrew was disappointed that the two allotted buildings were located outside of the city center, he was excited to learn of the buildings' dimensions. Both buildings were roughly the size of a grocery store. As Andrew recounted, "I wondered why the local authority would give a [nongovernmental organization] these buildings. They are both very, very valuable because their rent is quite small and their size quite large. . . . [W]e were absolutely astounded that we got them *fără șpagă* [without bribing]."[6] Andrew indicated that the local authority's transfer of two sizable buildings to Second Chances, without a customary bribe, signaled the municipality's commitment to developing new places for the homeless. When I asked why shelters became a political imperative for the municipality at that time, Andrew responded pensively, "It's because homelessness was becoming really visible." Andrew's words captured the framing of homelessness in Bucharest as a humanitarian issue linked to economic concerns about the visibility of poverty and urban blight.

Shortly after the successful opening of Second Chances, Bucharest's wealthiest sector opened its own state-funded shelter, the Backwoods Shelter. A renovated army barracks located outside the city limits of Bucharest, Backwoods slept approximately four hundred people, making it the city's largest homeless shelter. Administrators divided Backwoods's bed space between single men and women, families, and pensioners who were otherwise priced out of the city's housing stock.

Backwoods, given its location outside of the city, was difficult to access. Only a handful of pensioners living at the shelter had a car to take them to and from the city. The vast majority of residents had few options for getting around. Taxis were prohibitively expensive for residents. Over and above the issue of cost, most taxis also refused to drive to Backwoods because the long return trip back to the city center made the route unprofitable. Instead, those coming from and going to Backwoods had to rely on a single bus line that stopped just outside the shelter's gates. Although central Bucharest was less than eight miles away from the shelter, it took an hour and a half to get there from Backwoods by public transit owing to frequent bus stops, dense traffic, and long waits while switching lines.

In addition to Backwoods, municipal sectors 2 and 3 also built homeless shelters along the urban periphery, accompanied by several dozen public and privately funded soup kitchens, day centers, and health clinics. The placement of these services was striking. Like Second Chances and Backwoods, each and every one of these services was located outside of the city center.[7] Even though homeless persons frequently pace, panhandle, and sleep in the city center, no shelters were located there. Homeless persons in want of shelter services had to leave central Bucharest to receive them.

This constellation of night shelters and service providers effectively drew homeless persons away from the center of Bucharest and toward the urban periphery. This spatial arrangement raised immediate concerns among advocates and administrators alike about economic segregation, as well as larger questions about the homeless's fundamental right to access public spaces located in the heart of the city.[8] The movement of the homeless away from central Bucharest even ran counter to government workers' expressed commitment to preserving the accessibility of public space for all.

The Ministry of Development, Public Works, and Housing, for example, made it clear that they had not intentionally segregated homeless people along the urban periphery. A deputy general manager of housing policy named Radu insisted with great enthusiasm while we sat in his centrally located office that the ministry "is militant about social mixing. We are against social exclusion. We want to develop the legal tools to solve segregation in Bucharest, because we have this problem. We want to promote the moderate development of the city." Radu unflinchingly, and with great sincerity, bundled liberal democratic planning principles—economic diversity and a commitment to public space—with the future well-being of Bucharest's development. Radu's comments were, in fact, representative of a larger ethos of postcommunist rhetoric that sought to reinforce notions of democracy, civil society, and equality in Romania.[9] He even went so far as to hinge the future well-being of Bucharest on the proliferation of economically diverse communities.

Radu insisted that the increasing exclusion of the poor from the city center was an unplanned outcome of the development of infrastructure for homeless persons. Radu ascribed the problem to the municipality's land reserves—the buildings within the municipal government's control set aside for public services. To hear Radu explain it, "the municipality does not have a sufficient land reserve. It also does not have a pressure policy to encourage local authorities to purchase more land for social housing. The Ministry of Development will make improvements to the housing law, obliging [the municipality] to buy lands in order to build social housing." Dragos, a senior official in the General Directorate of Social Assistance and Child Protection, which oversees the Backwoods Shelter, echoed Radu's liberal commitments. Dragos similarly attributed the systematic placing of shelter space, and social housing more generally, outside the city center to budget constraints and the restrictions imposed by basic cost-benefit analyses. Dragos explained over coffee in his own centrally located office, "We simply can't buy social housing in the center of Bucharest because it is too expensive, and so we chose a location in another county because the price is cheaper there compared with centrally located apartments." By problematizing the placement of shelters in terms of accounting, Dragos rendered the curious distribution of shelter services outside the city center a rational outcome that expressed a utilitarian ethics. Simply put, more affordable space can be purchased outside the city in order to house more people in need. "We probably need €200 million to resolve the housing problems in this sector, and we don't have that," Dragos continued with earnest frustration. "And of course there are legal standards for shelters. The problem is, because of our tight budgets, these minimum standards represent maximum standards. But we don't have enough money to sustain even the minimum standards."

Radu and Dragos indicated that the municipal and local governments' desire to create mixed-income communities was ultimately constrained by the municipality's limited cash and land reserves. While government employees at various scales would have liked to see shelters integrated throughout the city—even in the wealthier neighborhoods of central Bucharest—the city's resources for social housing did not allow for such an integrated distribution. Subsequently, shelters and other social housing had to be placed where the city had land available and could afford to build, inhibiting the implementation of the ministry's mission to create urban communities that are, in practice, open to all.

The curious placement of shelters on the outskirts of Bucharest speaks to Michel Foucault's notion of unintended consequences, or the unplanned results of an action that nevertheless brings about a convenient end.[10] The development of homeless services along the urban periphery, where cash and land reserves allowed, had the unintended consequence of drawing homeless persons far away from the primary civic squares and public parks located in central Bucharest. Regardless of how administrators might have felt about this outcome, the placement of services along the urban periphery cleared the city center of poverty's traces and freed it for development projects geared toward more affluent segments of the population, such as businesspeople, a burgeoning middle class, and tourists. The poor, by contrast, became increasingly isolated along the margins of the city. There they found themselves far removed from the material and symbolic center of urban life.

Shelters and the Infrastructure of Boredom

"I'm bored! Very, very bored!" Ruxandra exclaimed. We sat perched atop a railing running along the Backwoods courtyard. We kept an eye on the shelter's children, who were playing soccer while we chatted. A stay-at-home mother in her early thirties, Ruxandra spent her days at Backwoods cleaning her family's room, folding laundry, and caring for her two children, among other household chores. Her husband, meanwhile, looked for day labor on the black market. In many ways, Ruxandra's daily responsibilities went largely unchanged in her family's move from a rented apartment in the city to the shelter outside of it. In both instances, Ruxandra shouldered the responsibility of turning a living space into a home, with all of the thankless drudgery that this transformation entailed. While her husband understood himself as unemployed and spent his days sitting and waiting, Ruxandra was in constant motion. She always had plenty of work to do each day. However, the displacement of that steady work from a private apartment to a room in the Backwoods Shelter rendered her daily routine unbearably boring. "I mean, what is there to do out here?" Ruxandra asked rhetorically while she removed her laundry from a clothesline and folded it into her basket. "I'm going crazy—there is nowhere to go! We're

FIGURE 2.3. Shelter hallway. Photo by Bruce O'Neill.

at the margins of Bucharest (*marginea Bucureştiului*), and that's hard for me." She pitched a towel into her laundry basket for added punctuation before picking the towel back up again and folding it neatly. "If we were in town, like how I lived for twenty-five years with my parents and with my children—I was born in the city center, you know—everything would be right nearby!" Ruxandra recounted the ease with which she could pop out to the store or catch a bus to Herăstrău, the city's main park, when she lived in her old neighborhood. She recalled feeling part of a larger neighborhood community. "But it's more difficult here," she continued. "Nothing is close by—I stay here in the courtyard with the kids when they don't have school. I clean my room, and I watch some TV. But what else can I do? Every day and from day to day, it's automatic. I'm bored!" She scooped up her basket and headed back to her room, where she intended to remop the floor.

At stake in Ruxandra's boredom was not the absence of things to do in any absolute sense but, rather, the experience of being priced out of her previously held sense of everyday life. Boredom, for Ruxandra, registered the inability to maintain her once-usual routines that cultivated a sense of belonging to the neighborhood where she had long resided. Once her husband became unemployed, and the family savings depleted, however, her family was pushed not only out of their home but also out of the community and beyond the very limits of the city. The market pressures that worked to displace Ruxandra and others from the city ran completely contrary to the socialist-era pressures on the city to incorporate the poor. At the height of rural-to-urban migration in the 1960s and 1970s, socialist-era planners sought to replace neighborhoods of privilege with highly equalized access to medical, cultural, and civic resources for all workers.[11] Under socialism, all Romanians, whether a low-skilled laborer relocated from a peasant village to the newly developed housing blocks found in the neighborhoods Drumul Taberei, Berceni, and Titan (Balta Albă) or a highly trained administrator working in a main office, could expect to access with reasonable ease the city's main parks, shops, and restaurants. Not only did such access provide things to do, but accessing these spaces allowed urban residents to feel incorporated into a larger sense of society. This is the kind of urban space in which Ruxandra was raised.

Romania's introduction into the global economy, however, changed the organizing logic of Bucharest. Rather than working to incorporate an urbanized peasantry, planners now organized urban space in ways that displaced those unable to succeed in a globally competitive market. Maximizing the value of land rents supplanted commitments to equality of access as the guiding principle of urban development.[12] Market forces now worked to place high-earning individuals in newly renovated buildings in which to live and also to socialize, particularly in historically prominent and centrally located neighborhoods such as Dorobanți, Victoriei, and Lipscani. As privileged earners gravitated toward prestigious spaces, they pushed the lower-earning and unemployed outward. The residents of Backwoods, once they had been relocated beyond the city limits, could no longer walk to a park, a grocery store, or a terrace bar. Instead, surrounding Backwoods were an empty field, a public cemetery, and a kennel that housed stray dogs, which were also collected from the city streets. A gas station was located a ten-minute walk down the road. On all accounts, Backwoods's residents described themselves as cut off from the city center. What was once a fact of everyday life—accessing the city's resources—became an indulgence that shelter residents found difficult to afford. Shelter residents, to put it simply, lacked the disposable income to get to, and then move about, the city. This became clear while speaking with another shelter resident, Lucian. A few years shy of receiving his pension, Lucian worked part-time as a security guard for a firm in the city center. His paycheck extended just far enough to cover the cost of the shelter's rent and food as well as the cost of the public transportation needed to get him to work and back. Lucian had little money left over at the end of each month for other expenses.

"Each day at this shelter I'm bored," Lucian confided while leaning against a side wall in the men's dormitory, his arms folded across his chest. "But what can I do? When you don't have what others have, it's difficult. I try to keep myself occupied. I walk around the shelter's courtyard as a way of creating something to do," he said with a shrug. "I'd like to get out of here, but to leave the shelter you have to have money in your pocket in order to get something: a cake, a drink, a coffee, or whatever," Lucian explained, equating incorporation in urban life with the ability to participate in commercial transactions. "Otherwise I sit here in this shelter, staring at the walls, and think about my troubles. And that only makes life harder." Lucian laughed anxiously. After wishing me well, he exited the hallway and began marching around the shelter's courtyard, keeping himself on the move without really going anywhere. Although Lucian would have much preferred to stroll through the park, he could not afford to go into the city on the days he was not scheduled to work. Outside of his scheduled shift, and unless he was wearing his security guard uniform, Lucian was stuck in Backwoods. It brought about an immense feeling of boredom.

Negotiating the cost of accessing the city became even more complicated for shelter residents with young children. Florin, an unemployed father of five living at Backwoods, provided a case in point. Despite feeling bored every day with life inside the shelter, Florin hardly ever left Backwoods. "Sure," Florin admitted, "I could leave this place and visit one of the parks in the city center now and again: Herăstrău or Cişmigiu. It's beautiful there. And even though it's far away," Florin added with a shrug and a modest grin, "let's be honest—I have the time." Allowing the half grin to fall from his face, Florin continued, "But if I go, I'll have to bring my kids, and then they will ask me to buy them ice cream and everything else. Kids just ask and ask and ask for things," he said in an exasperated voice. "If you walk through Herăstrău, you'll pass by go-carts, food, games, and things like

FIGURE 2.4. Tossing coins. Photo by Bruce O'Neill.

that, but you need money to buy tickets for these things. And the kids don't get that. They see the games and they want to play, and it makes me feel awful to keep telling them, 'No, not today.' If you don't have the money," Florin assessed with a tone of resignation and a shaking head, "then it's better to just stay in the shelter. Without money nothing is possible." Now placed at the margins of the city, Florin, through his own cost-benefit analysis, had arrived at the conclusion that the smartest thing he could do was to spend his days inside Backwoods's gates.

"There is nothing to do in this place but eat, nap, and jerk off (*fac labe*)," quipped Vasile, a twenty-something resident of Backwoods, while making an exaggerated jerking motion with his left hand. Amid tight budget constraints, the shelter could not afford to offer educational, vocational, or entertainment programs for its two hundred homeless residents. While shelter residents could speak to a social worker or medical practitioner on-site, there were no programs to engage residents physically or socially. Rather than educate or retrain the homeless for new types of employment, as shelters attempt to do in the United States, for example, Backwoods could offer only basic accommodation: a bed, a heated (and often shared) room, a communal bathroom, and two meals a day.[13] About five privately owned television sets existed among the complex's residents, affording a lucky few and their friends access to the Spanish soap operas and American action films from the 1980s that were broadcast each day. The majority of residents without televisions oscillated between quiet reclusion on their beds and chatting in the shelter hallway with other all-too-familiar faces. Otherwise, residents had few formal activities around which to structure their daily routines, build a sense of community, or simply stimulate themselves.

Without much distraction, residents turned their attention toward the material conditions of the shelter. Backwoods did not hold up to their intense scrutiny. The shelter, the majority of residents concluded, offended their sense of human dignity. "This [shelter] is a filthy place," Marian proclaimed while gesturing down one of the hallways. The sweeping gesture of his outstretched arm encompassed the flickering yellow lights dotting the ceiling, the mildew-stained walls decorated in children's graffiti, and the hallway's floor, dotted with spit and cigarette butts. While grateful for the roof over the heads of his wife and two children, he eagerly pointed out that the conditions beneath that roof did not meet the standards of even the oldest and most poorly maintained communist-era housing blocks located throughout the city. Those housing blocks were also places built by a state to accommodate the people, and while communist-era housing blocks may have been cramped and drafty, they nevertheless offered a sense of family privacy. They could also be kept to personal standards of cleanliness. "And check out the bathroom," Marian continued. "You'll want to vomit! It's disgusting. . . . And you eat bugs by living here. Cockroaches just walk around. Hundreds and thousands of cockroaches. These rooms are just motels for them," Marian assessed while shaking his head with disgust. His condemnation of the shelter's conditions was not without a point. Especially during the winter months, it was common to see dozens of cockroaches crawling on top of bedding, desktops, and walls. While hanging out on people's cots, these roaches would even fall off of my eyeglasses and land in my lap. "These are not good conditions, especially for children. This place just doesn't stimulate," Marian concluded with disgust.

Rather than speaking to themes of incorporation and state paternalism, as communist-era housing blocks had once done, the Backwoods Shelter detached residents from the everyday life of the city and located them in a socially and materially devalued place that called to mind images of abandonment and neglect, the proverbial "roach motel." In the absence of programming, residents spent their days "waiting" in a bureaucratically administered setting that offered little else beyond shelter.[14] This act of waiting was shorn of teleology, whereby the passage of time, no matter how slow, nevertheless brings one closer to a desired end, as breadlines had once done. Instead, one simply waited inside Backwoods for "nothing" because the room and its utilities were all that was on offer. This mode of waiting carried no sense of progress or conclusion. The rhythm of the shelter lacked a horizon against which residents could gauge progress of any kind. As the hours dragged onward, Marian, Lucian, and Ruxandra came no closer to regular employment, private housing, or an income that would allow them to advance their life narratives. Moving out of the shelter and back into the city remained as far away as ever. Instead, shelter space did little more than warehouse the poor, and being warehoused was profoundly boring.

Letting In and Leaving Out: Filtering the Shelter Population

While Backwoods residents felt stuck in place and wanted desperately to get out, Bucharest's street homeless population struggled to find bed space within it. Even though shelters like Backwoods detached residents from urban life and offered only a minimum of privacy and comfort, shelters nevertheless represented the most dynamic infrastructure for negotiating a life displaced from the private housing market. Shelters safeguarded the material well-being of residents by providing protection from the elements, a place to store belongings, and the means to prepare hot food. Shelters also provided showers and washing machines that allowed residents to maintain their appearance in a way that was not easily achieved when living on the streets. The practical material benefits, over and above their social costs, were what drove the street homeless to the shelter at a rate that far outpaced the availability of bed space. Intensifying the street homeless's search for bed space was that they had to compete with other kinds of vulnerable populations for access to government-subsidized housing. Bianca, a social worker in Bucharest, explained to me as I sat in her office, "Say we're in sector X, and they have around two hundred shelter spaces." She leaned forward in her chair as she worked through the hypothetical arithmetic with me. "Now, they also have another one hundred units of social housing, which require certain documents and other criteria to be eligible. Well, in that sector alone there are probably one thousand homeless people!" Bianca rolled back in her chair as though bowled over by the sheer numerical force. She carried on while resting in the back of her chair: "And those spaces are not only for people living on the streets. They are also for other kinds of social cases: the underemployed, the poorly paid, those living in substandard or overcrowded housing conditions." Bianca counted each additional category out on her hands for effect. Her voice grew heavier under the burden of each added category. "So there are one thousand people living on the streets, and at least another two thousand of these additional social cases competing for one hundred social housing units and two hundred shelter beds. Someone has to make a selection," she said with a shrug of the shoulder, concluding pragmatically, "And of course it's a political process."

High-level administrators in charge of Bucharest's state-run shelters readily admitted as much. Dragos explained to me, "Our sector has something like a filter where people enter directly from the street. We clean them, we offer them new clothes, we burn their old clothes because they have parasites and disease, and it is better to burn their clothes." With the apparent contagion of poverty sterilized by flame, sector officials then sent the candidate outside the city to the Backwoods Shelter. Once the candidate arrived there, Backwoods staff took stock of him or her and filtered out those expressing social and psychological problems that might overwhelm the shelter's limited resources. A high-level administrator named Mihai explained, "We see who has severe disabilities and who does not. Generally, we can send those with severe disabilities to another center. If they have severe drug or mental health problems, they do not stay here. Those kinds of severe problems are beyond our capacity to deal with. At the end of the day, though, it is the director who decides whether someone comes to this shelter or if they must go to another center." Those permitted to stay at Backwoods were then given bed space but otherwise left to their own devices. As Dragos frankly admitted, within the context of Bucharest's collapsed market for unskilled laborers, "the typical homeless are totally dependent on shelters. They don't have any social future because if they bought their apartment [just after communism] and then sold it, the state does not provide any second chances.[15] The state does not have an endless supply of apartments to hand out. Instead, they arrive at these kinds of shelters, and then they stay here." With long-term residency in mind, the shelter worked to filter out cases demanding of time, money, and other resources while letting in the self-reliant. This social and spatial strategy allowed Backwoods to place a roof over the maximum number of persons within the limits of the shelter's tight funding.

The Second Chances shelter similarly filtered its population. Reliant exclusively on private donations, it had even more stringent budgetary restrictions than Backwoods. In fact, even with the best financial management, the cost of operating Second Chances exceeded its monthly donations. To make up the difference, social workers prioritized its available rooms for homeless persons capable of volunteer work inside the shelter and of paid work outside the shelter.[16] These work obligations were particularly necessary for Second Chances as compared with American or British shelters, whose services tend to be heavily subsidized by government funding and charitable donations. In postcommunist Bucharest, however, government welfare, charitable giving, and volunteerism are new and underdeveloped practices, in part for historical reasons. The former communist government regularly conscripted people to perform long stretches of unpaid labor as patriotic "contributions to the collective."[17] As a hangover from these communist-era abuses, many Romanians continued to interpret volunteerism as a form of forced appropriations, making it difficult to establish donations of time and money as a regular feature of the postcommunist political or social landscape.

From his British, middle-class perspective, Second Chances' director, Andrew, often lamented that it was unimaginably difficult to solicit charitable donations from Romanians, even among the nouveaux riches who could afford to give. Andrew worked around Romanians' disinclination toward charity by targeting the support of Bucharest's British expatriate community. By networking with well-off British business professionals working within Romania's booming energy, real estate, and business-services sectors, Andrew was able to mobilize familiar Western tropes about charity and poverty to cover the majority of Second Chances' budget through individual donations. These donations established a baseline budget for Second Chances that covered the salary of its three social workers. Other operating costs remained, however, such as the shelter's utilities and daily upkeep. To cover this balance and to keep Second Chances' doors open, these expenses were passed on to the shelter beneficiaries themselves.

Much as was the case at Backwoods, one of Second Chances' social workers, Rodica, indicated to me that Second Chances could not accept "extreme cases" because their needs were too complex for the shelter's limited range of services. Rodica explained that Second Chances provided temporary shelter space and assistance finding permanent housing. The nongovernmental organization had neither the capacity to work with dependent persons nor the funds to provide indefinite care. Second Chances' scope was limited to working with homeless clients who were able to care for themselves, who could contribute to the cost of their shelter, and who would be able to one day move on from the shelter. These able-bodied homeless were admitted into Second Chances. Other homeless persons in need of time- and resource-intensive interventions were left out.

The filtering mechanisms at work at both Backwoods and Second Chances established a relationship between shelter space and personal responsibility in Bucharest that was the exact opposite of what has been ethnographically detailed in other prominent cities, such as Boston, São Paulo, and San Francisco.[18] In each of these cities, shelters are places where people go when they no longer function in society at large. Shelters in the American context contain the most marginal homeless persons. In Bucharest, however, the opposite is true. Shelters acted to house only a small percentage of homeless persons—those who remained relatively self-reliant and who did not require much staff attention or resources. This filtering process left the vast majority of homeless persons, particularly those "extreme cases" who were most in need of assistance, outside the scope of shelter care.

Those not accommodated by shelter infrastructure had to make their own informal living spaces. The homeless's own efforts at producing space for themselves also resulted in a marginal existence, albeit with different dynamics. The street homeless's sense of marginality was not as firmly rooted in the material dimensions of proximity and distance as it was for residents of Backwoods. Instead, the street homeless experienced marginality as a social space organized around practices of exclusion. Although the street homeless regularly passed through the city center, for example, they nevertheless felt detached from the social practices unfolding around them. Simply put, they could not afford to participate in city life as its social practices became increasingly organized around consumerism. Instead of being invigorated by their ability to physically access the city, the street homeless paced back and forth across it in a state of detachment from it.

Boredom and the Street

While those stuck in shelters could only desire the excitement of a life in the city center, Bucharest's street homeless moved throughout the city center on a regular basis. They were mobile in a way that shelter residents could only dream of. The street homeless reported walking between fifteen and twenty kilometers per day, and this movement enabled them to pass through the city's most prominent parks, such as Herăstrău and Cişmigiu, as well as some of its busiest areas—Universităţii and Unirii squares and the Gara de Nord station. Despite circulating throughout the city, Bucharest's street homeless did not feel a part of it. This became evident while I was sitting with Dinu, Gheorge, and Sorin in the parking lot of the Stefan's Place day center. They were each lifelong manual laborers in their midfifties who were now divorced. Some of their children had even moved abroad. When construction work disappeared following the financial crisis, these men quickly found themselves priced out of the housing market and without familial support to cushion the pressure. Unable to find space in the city's limited shelter system, these men did not spend their days on the outskirts of the city, as did shelter residents, but instead constructed an outdoor squatter camp near the city center. The squatter camp consisted of cardboard squares for sleeping and some plastic sheets that, when draped over low-lying tree branches, provided a modicum of protection from the wind and the rain. A fountain located a block away provided water to drink and a space for washing up. The squatter camp also provided a reasonably hidden place to sleep and to store belongings. It did not, however, provide sufficient infrastructure for them to spend an entire day there. Dinu, Gheorge, and Sorin left the squatter camp each morning in search of food and water, climate control, and the chance to make some money. Mobility was built into the street homeless's living situation in a way that was wholly absent from shelter life. Dinu, Gheorge, and Sorin, for example, awoke well before dawn and waited for work on one of the black markets in central Bucharest. On the majority of days when a contractor did not pick them up, they spent their afternoons at Stefan's Place. When Stefan's Place closed, around half past four, they then circulated between parks, main squares,

FIGURE 2.5. Late morning. Photo by Bruce O'Neill.

and the Gara de Nord train station in search of companionship or entertainment, or simply to avoid police harassment. On the coldest nights of
winter, they abandoned their encampment and instead searched for opportunities to sleep indoors, such as in the stairwells of apartment blocks, in
hospital waiting rooms, or in unused train cars at the Gara de Nord station.
Although his daily routine weaved them through the city, Dinu admitted
to feeling bored every day.

"*Mă simt plictisit* (I feel bored)," Dinu began. We sat with Gheorge and
Sorin in the Stefan's Place parking lot on a sticky summer afternoon. It had
been nearly a half hour since the previous conversation had died out. Heat,
fatigue, and a long morning already spent together made the afternoon feel
static. Tired of sitting quietly alone together, I had broken the collective
silence by asking the group what was on their minds.

"I feel bored every day," Dinu continued, "because I have nothing to do, no one to speak with, no activity or job, nothing to smoke . . ." Dinu's voice trailed off.

Gheorge nodded in agreement. "Yeah," Gheorge added, "without a job, without money to spend, I just sit on the street with nothing to do. I just have that feeling—as though everything in the world has turned gray, and there's nothing to do. It's not depression but boredom."

Sorin, who had just rolled a "fresh" cigarette out of newspaper and the unspent tobacco from a few scavenged butts, took a long drag and added reflectively on the exhale, "You see, people on the street feel bored all the time because they have nothing. There are three aspects of life in Bucharest: a home, food, and a job." Said in Romanian, Sorin's words had the ring of a communist-era slogan: *o casă, o masă și un servici!* "I mean, if you can't make a life here in Bucharest, then you are not happy with where you are. You get bored and restless and will want to go somewhere else."

At stake in Dinu's, Gheorge's, and Sorin's boredom was a sense of displacement from the rhythm of a city remade under the impress of global consumerism, more so than their present state of poverty. While communist-era austerity had been difficult to endure, one nevertheless had felt caught up in the city. State-guaranteed housing situated each person in a neighborhood, just as guaranteed employment incorporated all, to varying degrees, in the production of the urban economy; a salary enabled one to stand in line for rations along with everyone else. Shuttling between the housing block, the job, and the breadline could be miserable and tedious, but collective participation gave this routine a shared sense of meaning.

"During communism, I had a job, a furnished home, and an income. I always had something to do—I wasn't bored," Gheorge attested. "I kept very busy, and I didn't have time to think about all of the bad things in my life because I was so busy. I felt normal. I felt *human*," Gheorge stressed, locating his experience of productivity firmly in the communist past rather than in the market-oriented present. In addition to covering basic necessities, Gheorge's salary enabled him to partake in the consumption of leisure, particularly around the arts. "I used to go out all the time—to the theater, the opera, films too—I am a great lover of theater and operettas," Gheorge reflected, "but the situation is different now. In the last few years, prices have risen enormously—beyond the reach of many people." Gheorge extended his arms outward, implicating his present company. "As for me, I work whatever job I can find. But I only find low-paid work. Who wants to hire someone my age? Right now I work at a restaurant as the night watchman. You can't go to the theater on what I earn," Gheorge lamented. Unable to flourish in a competitive labor market, Gheorge no longer had the money to participate in the life of the city as he once did. Downward mobility left him to struggle with boredom as well as a diminished sense of humanity. Even though Gheorge spent his days physically in and around the city center, he felt completely detached from it. He lacked the money to engage the city. Gheorge continued to explain, "But without money it's very hard. I couldn't tell you what I do everyday. I look for more work because I don't want to beg. And there have been days where I ate nothing—three or four days pass when I don't eat anything because I don't have money. You can't do much without money."

Dinu nodded in agreement with Gheorge as Sorin began to speak. "We're in the capital of the country," Sorin explained with a note of pride in the city where he was born, "and there are many institutions here. There are many theaters and cinemas, unlike elsewhere in Romania. There are stores of another kind too—another lifestyle than you see elsewhere in the country. Bucharest is metropolitan."[19] Sorin lowered his boastful tone regarding the city's cosmopolitan amenities vis-à-vis the provinces before continuing, "But they are all for people with money. Either you have money and do what you want and walk about the capital—go to the shop or to the mall and do such and such—or you don't. You just sit around the city empty-handed and with nothing to do." Nodding in agreement, Gheorge surmised bleakly, "It's going to be another thirty to forty years before another standard of living reaches this city, but by then simple biology will have taken care of us."

Gheorge, Dinu, and Sorin were socially and economically detached from the new pleasures and possibilities that came to Bucharest over the course of Romania's troubled integration into the global economy. Their detachment cut against their expectations of heightened incorporation into new places and pleasures that had been developed and entertained before they became homeless. To be sure, these men would have liked to partake in the "other lifestyle" that Bucharest offered those who could afford it, one that took the form of lounging on newly built café terraces, watching soccer matches on oversized televisions, and perusing the Internet on pocket-sized screens. Instead of expanded incorporation into the city and the growing array of consumer practices it hosted, the opposite occurred. They experienced displacement from their long-established sources of stimulation, such as the theater or the cinema. Tickets became unthinkably expensive for their ever more constrained budgets. "It's no longer how it was before, where we woke up and had work," Sorin recalled with eyes squinting in the afternoon sun. "Many things have failed us. The government sold the factories; they made people unemployed in '90–'91. That's when unemployment started. It didn't exist in '89. Then, if you didn't have a job, the Securitate would come around and find you in the street. They would put you in jail for *six months* if you weren't working. *You went to jail for not having a job*," Sorin stressed, emphasizing that his present state of unemployment was, not so long ago, widely considered to be criminal. "Now that's not the case. The state no longer has any work. You're responsible for what you do in life. You have to find your own place to work, a house, an income." Sorin paused briefly, breaking eye contact to look off somewhere into the distance. "I don't have a job, but I dream of having one again—to have something to do. To be occupied. To help my family, my children. But for now, my dreams are shattered. . . . It's tough with this job market for us here in Bucharest," he sighed. For these men, attached to visions of "another kind of life" taking shape in Bucharest, but detached from regular economic participation and housing, time passed slowly as they came to feel permanently situated outside the action unfolding around them. Life appeared empty of all expected activities. In lieu of work, family, and the theater, these men were now at a loss as to how to fill their time as well as what to do or to make of themselves.

Invective

Detachment from the rhythms of the city went beyond the inability to buy into belonging. Detachment also took interpersonal, and cuttingly visceral, forms. Bucharest's struggling middle class regularly frustrated the street homeless's efforts to feel a part of urban life. Along the streets and on public transportation, the better-off singled out the homeless as personae non gratae. A politics of poverty and hygiene, enforced through public condemnation, worked to relegate the homeless to the margins of the city. "You find yourself on the street without possibilities," Gheorge remarked, "and that's hard. Very hard. Because other people look at you like you're shit." These unwanted stares carried the potential to quickly escalate into humiliating public scenes. This crystallized for me on one July morning when I accompanied Gabi, a thirty-something man living on the streets, to Cernica, a small monastery just outside of Bucharest where homeless persons often went for food and a night's rest.

Cernica lies just outside the city and beyond public transit lines. To reach the monastery, Gabi and I had to ride in a cramped minibus designed to seat about sixteen people. On this warm summer morning, however, the minibus held over twenty passengers. By the time we boarded, riders were already sitting on each others' laps. As a result, we had to cram our way into the aisle. A few minutes after the door closed and the minibus began moving forward, riders started yelling at Gabi. A woman in her fifties asked in a raised and disgusted tone, "Where did you stay all night? Have you been drinking? I can smell you, and you smell awful. You're stinking up the bus! Oh how awful! I want to vomit. I really want to vomit." Others in the minibus scowled and nodded in agreement as whispers and mutterings picked up volume. I stood momentarily shocked: not only because the woman was using such an aggressive and demeaning tone, but also because Gabi did not strike me as being particularly unfresh. Although it was July and one sweats constantly during the summer in Bucharest because of the hot, humid air, I knew Gabi made an effort to bathe every couple of days. He either climbed into the Dâmbovița River that runs through Bucharest or locked himself in a public restroom and washed up in the sink using the freely available hand soap and paper towels.

The public outcry continued as another man in his forties yelled, "Why did they ever let someone who sleeps in the bushes on the [mini]bus! Someone open a window! Do the windows open?" As the minibus's windows opened, riders in the middle of the minibus begged to switch seats with those sitting next to a window. "I need to change seats! I swear I will vomit if I don't change seats," called yet another woman. As bodies shifted begrudgingly in this overcrowded minibus, Gabi popped open an emergency hatch on the roof. A steady stream of air rushed from the side windows and out of the opening above. About half of the passengers cheered on as fresh air started to whip about the minibus. "Good work!" called yet another passenger. Reddening eyes betrayed Gabi's stern face; he spent the remainder of the ride silent and looking away from me. When we got off the minibus at Cernica, he did not want to talk about the bus ride and tried to act as though nothing had happened.

In yet another instance, I stood outside a donut shop with a homeless man named Crăciun. I had bought Crăciun a coffee and a sweet roll to snack on as we talked about his plans to look for work abroad the following

FIGURE 2.6. Riding the tram. Photo by Bruce O'Neill.

summer. As we leaned against the shop, a woman in her fifties started yelling at Crăciun: "Why are you here begging from a foreigner? Why aren't you working!?! Go get a job! It is illegal to take gifts from foreigners! You should be working!" The woman's diatribe picked up speed and volume and showed no signs of relenting.

I interrupted the woman's shouts to explain that Crăciun was in fact a friend and that I had invited him for a coffee. I assured the woman that at no moment had Crăciun "begged." We were simply hanging out. The woman, unwavering in her insistence, warned me in a low voice, "You can't trust these people—these beggars! They are thieves!" Turning to Crăciun, the woman again raised her voice and started a fresh round of insults: "Yes, it's hard in Romania, but I get by on my pension! I don't ask foreigners for help! You need to stop begging and get a job!"

In an attempt to calm the woman, Crăciun extended his arm toward the woman's shoulder while explaining, in a patient tone, that he was looking for work in construction but that there was none to be found. The woman, however, recoiled and shrieked as Crăciun's arm stretched toward her. She loudly declared it "disgusting" and demanded that he not touch her before turning her back on us. She continued to yell insults as she walked down the road. The words *dirty* (*murdar*), *foul* (*urât*), and *filthy* (*jegos*) echoed along the street. Passersby stopped in their tracks to watch the spectacle unfold but moved along afterward. "What the hell was that about?" I asked Crăciun with bewilderment. "That's life," he replied simply. "People don't want you around if they see you're homeless." A similar incident occurred less than two hours later at a donut shop across town while I tried to interview another homeless man.

Given the regularity of these kinds of public spectacles, Bucharest's street homeless were incredibly self-conscious about their appearance: the style and cleanliness of their clothes; the state of their hands, face, and hair; and the presence of any body odor. These were the "tells" that communicated their homelessness to the wider public. Homeless men frequently avoided public buses, main squares, or streets when they felt unsure about any aspect of their appearance so as not to be publicly berated for their hygiene. In those self-conscious moments, homeless men placed themselves in the shadows of the city center—an out-of-the-way park bench, the back corner of a Metro station—or they parked themselves in the front lot of the Stefan's Place day center. There, situated away from the condemnation of public view, Dinu, Gheorge, Sorin, Gabi, and others attested to having little to look forward to beyond "standing around," "reading a paper," or, with a simple shrug of their shoulders, "doing nothing."

The boredom described by Bucharest's street homeless has an important distinction from the boredom of alienated labor. While boredom in the workplace is well documented, from the factory floor to the office cubicle, this classical sense of workplace boredom is more neatly bound by place, time, and practice than the boredom experienced by Bucharest's homeless.[20] Workplace boredom occurs at work, during the workday, and in the act of performing repetitive or menial tasks. This kind of spatially and temporally bound boredom is a product of the enclosed institutions that defined what Foucault called the "disciplinary society": factories, schools, offices, and hospitals.[21] Alienated laborers found their respite from workplace boredom through leisurely consumption that took place before and after work, at home or at the bar, and among friends and family. Although it was grindingly dull, boring work nevertheless rewarded workers with a paycheck that bought certain escapes, stimulations, and pleasures that rendered bearable the day to come. Leisurely consumption lay at the heart of reproducing a ready and able pool of laborers.[22]

Bucharest's homeless, however, experienced a different kind of boredom entirely. Unlike the alienation of the factory or the repetition of the "bureaucratic cage," displacement from the global economy produced a boredom that was not confined to a particular time or place. Instead, this form of boredom resonated unrelentingly throughout the marginal spaces and rhythms of the city that the homeless occupy.

The Affect of Infrastructure

The global economy is facilitated by infrastructure, not only for making local connections, but also for managing the displaced. The infrastructure of displacement, this chapter has shown, is both social and material, and each works with the other to wick away discarded people toward the discarded spaces of the city. Once the unwanted are located where no one would otherwise choose to be, the infrastructure of displacement works to keep the displaced where they are, firmly pressed into the marginal spaces of not just the city but of the global economy more generally. To be sure, Bucharest's shelters provided much-needed material assistance for homeless persons. They were even developed by people with an interest in contributing to an active civil society in postcommunist Romania. The location of these shelters exclusively along the urban periphery, however, had an effect that was the opposite of creating diverse communities that are open and available to all. Rather than facilitating civic engagement, the placement of shelters removed those in need from the life of the city. Once the homeless were displaced into shelters, these institutions did little to address the social well-being of their beneficiaries. Simply put, shelters lacked necessary funding. Administrators rendered the placement of shelters, and the absence of programs for beneficiaries, not only justifiable but seemingly self-evident by foregrounding a dogged commitment to a budgetary logic of weighing costs versus benefits. The sensibility used by municipal authorities to develop shelter services along the urban periphery is a continuation of the very logic used on factory floors and construction sites to identify and discard their beneficiaries as superfluous workers. Movement to the urban margins seamlessly followed displacement from work and home and onto the streets. Rather than combating radical exclusion, infrastructure for the homeless affirmed and cemented it in place. At the level of infrastructure, shelters worked as part of the machinery that actively identified, discarded, and then systematically excluded the unwanted from urban life. The politics of infrastructure, ultimately, affected shelters' beneficiaries. As the city's devalued residents found themselves contained in the city's devalued spaces, an unbearable dullness took hold of their senses.

At the limitations of the shelter's material infrastructure, a social infrastructure mobilized a politics of harassment and shaming to subject the street homeless to a comparable end. Inadequate bed space forced the street homeless to sleep in parks and public spaces without a place to bathe regularly, wash their clothes, and store belongings. These infrastructural gaps made it difficult for homeless people to maintain an appearance that would be widely interpreted as "clean" or "put together." Instead, public sleeping and irregular washing led the homeless to be coded as "dirty," as though one "lived in the bushes" (*un boschetar*). The gaps in material infrastructure prohibited the homeless from washing away the traces of being homeless, exposing them to the ridicule of those barely better off. Unable to maintain an appearance that would allow for inclusion in basic public spaces such as the sidewalk, the bus, or the donut shop, homeless persons actively positioned themselves away from public view. Even within the geographic center of the city, homeless persons unsure of their appearance sought out the shadowy and rarely traversed spaces of alleys, parks, and Metro stations where they could avoid the public's scornful gaze.

As material and social infrastructures worked to place and then keep the homeless at the margins of the city, but also at the margins of the nation and the global economy, homeless men and women felt simultaneously attached to and yet excluded from that "other kind of life" taking hold around them. They felt the desire to shop at stores (rather than to receive donated goods), to drink espresso in a café (rather than instant coffee in scavenged water bottles), and to have a job (rather than be unemployed). These are reasonable attachments cultivated by the city's increasingly consumerist orientation, but also by the now-homeless's former history of steady participation in the city's economy under communism. Until they were displaced by globalism from work and home, these men and women experienced Bucharest as a site of incorporation. They not only worked in its businesses and industry but also made a habit of visiting its theaters, museums, and markets. It was only as the realm of possibilities for experiencing the city expanded through Romania's integration into the global economy that these men and women became cut off from the pleasures and possibilities growing within it. Not only were the homeless priced out of new malls and restaurants, but once-familiar neighborhoods and institutions similarly slipped out of their reach. At the intersection of attachment amid displacement, the homeless found themselves awash in boredom. This boredom proved to be a space where a baseline sustenance ensured that one would live another day, but only while feeling completely detached from the activity unfolding during that day.

3

THE GRAY YEARS

. . .

"I feel bored all the time at this homeless shelter (*adăpost social*). I read. I sleep. I watch TV, but I want to feel something bigger," began Tudor, a re-tired bus driver living at Backwoods. We sat in the back corner of a dormi-tory reserved for pensioner-age beneficiaries. Romania's twenty-four-hour news station recycled stories in the background, providing fodder for conversation in some moments while being completely ignored in others. Punctuating our conversation were not entirely inconspicuous sips of *țuică*. Although the shelter prohibited drinking, its staff rarely confiscated alco-hol. Instead, on the discovery of a bottle, staff would take nips themselves and offer a swig to others on shift before returning the contraband in ques-tion. To avoid the penalty of sharing his limited supply of brandy, Tudor took some caution so as not to draw attention. He spoke in hushed tones, and he tweaked the volume of his television down at the start of a noisy commercial. After taking a long, slow pull from his bottle, he passed it to me and continued reflecting. "We [pensioners] worked for twenty-five or thirty years. And what do they do with us? They throw us in the trash—or excuse me—they build us this retirement home (*cămin de bătrâni*)," Tudor said sarcastically while spreading his arms in the air like a game-show host. He held them in the air in front of me as though framing a marvelous prize. The view was of a row of aged bodies sleeping away the afternoon atop metal cots. "What enjoyment can we pensioners have in this life?" Tudor continued. "We're homeless and hungry."

FIGURE 3.1. Drinking. Photo by Bruce O'Neill.

Tudor, like other beneficiaries of a certain age, oscillated between describing Backwoods as a homeless shelter (*adăpost social*) and calling it a
retirement home (*cămin de bătrâni*).[1] Tudor's ambivalent categorization of
Backwoods is not without cause. The development of homeless services in
Bucharest coincided with efforts at pension reform that left retired workers
economically vulnerable and unable to keep up with the cost of private
housing. Once displaced from the housing market, pensioners became the
ideal candidates for placement in the city's homeless shelters. Their full
work history marked them as deserving of bed space, just as their pensions
provided a steady-enough income to cover the cost of their board. Retired
pensioners also did not exhibit mental illness, drug addiction, or so-called
antisocial behaviors that tended to absorb shelter staff's time and patience.
Pensioners provided shelters with a reasonably stable corps of "deserving"
residents toward whom to direct their limited energies and budgets. Pensioners represented the most cost-effective way of fulfilling the shelter's
mission. As a result, shelters that had ostensibly been constructed to serve
the homeless came to double as inexpensive centers to support impoverished retirees. Pensioners and near-pensioner-age beneficiaries occupied

nearly half of Backwoods's four hundred beds; they also made up a similar proportion of the street homeless beneficiaries visiting the Stefan's Place day center and of the residents of Second Chances.

The intertwining of aging and poverty in Romania makes sense when its origin is traced to governmental reforms seeking to scale back state guarantees so as to expand the role of competitive markets in providing for the general welfare. These efforts ultimately eroded two long-established pillars of support for Romanian pensioners: the state and the family. The Romanian state, for example, had a long and storied history of caring for retired workers. Consider that Romania was one of the first European countries to enact a national pension scheme, which took place in 1912. By 1933 Romania's pension system protected the entire population—a comprehensive approach to care for the elderly that was taken up by the communist government and maintained through to the end of communism in 1989.[2] This strong history of state benefits made pensioners valuable assets to the households of their working-age children. The benefits accorded to pensioners contributed to their children's households in invaluable ways. For this reason, pensioners typically lived near (if not with) their grown children and took on the responsibility for unpaid household tasks such as cooking, shopping, and child rearing.[3] These efforts freed young women to pursue paid work outside the home: for example, in an office, a shop, or a factory. In addition to performing the domestic labor of their working-age children, the pensions and food rations of grandparents contributed to household incomes. These contributions were particularly important during the depths of communist austerity. Romania's commitment to pensions, in short, enabled pensioners to exist as indispensable household resources. In return, pensioners received the physical and emotional care of being integrated into family life. It was not uncommon for pensioners to be tended to in their final years by their adult children and grandchildren. Pensions encouraged the integration of the elderly into family life in ways that foreclosed the development of the retirement centers commonly seen in the United States and Western Europe, where middle-class families largely outsourced care for the elderly during the twentieth century.[4]

After the fall of communism, and amid Romania's integration into the global economy, however, pensioners ceased to be a financial benefit to struggling households. By the mid-1990s, the real wages of pension contributors had shrunk to two-thirds of their level in 1989 as annual inflation wavered between 30 percent and 60 percent.[5] The pension system also lost three million contributors to unemployment, migration, and the informal economy.[6] At the same time, government officials had expanded benefit eligibility in pensioner schemes as a way to absorb the growing numbers of the unemployed. Between 1990 and 2002, the number of pension beneficiaries nearly doubled, rising from 3.4 million to 6.2 million, as the number of employees paying into the pension system fell below that of pensioners withdrawing from it, leading reformers to label the Romanian pensions system unsustainable.[7] As of 2006, the average pension had fallen to only 35 percent of the national average wage level, leaving 19 percent of those over sixty-five years of age in poverty.[8]

The situation grew increasingly bleak following the global economic crisis in 2008. As the Romanian government suffered further losses to its tax base, the government turned to the International Monetary Fund for an urgent cash infusion to maintain its operations. The IMF provided loans to the Romanian government on the condition that Romania's parliament enact a series of pension reforms.[9] These pension reforms, perhaps predictably, scaled back the government's entitlement programs, both by reducing their value and by ratcheting up their eligibility criteria, while shifting partial responsibility for pension provision to the private sector.[10] At the same time, the Romanian government introduced "active-aging measures," which sought to subsidize the cost of retirement through pensioners' continued participation in the labor market during their retirement years.[11]

As the absolute and relative value of pensions dipped, pensioners no longer constituted an indispensable benefit to struggling households. Instead of contributing much-needed labor and rations to the family, as they had under communism, pensioners now absorbed the resources of struggling families. Heads of households fighting against inflation and unemployment needed to make increasingly difficult decisions about whether to direct their limited means toward comforting aging parents or investing in growing children. Others, seeking stability, if not upward mobility, made use of Romania's opened borders and migrated elsewhere in Europe and the Middle East, leaving aging parents behind in the process. Amid Romania's integration into the global economy, elderly parents ceased to be interpreted as an economic benefit. Instead, grown children now interpreted their aging parents as a burden that held them down. Pensioners had become too poor to cover their own expenses when kept inside their children's homes and too costly to take along abroad. Not unlike low-skilled workers, pensioners found themselves displaced by globalism. Rather than retaining their status as privileged figures of family life, pensioners in Romania's changing economic landscape were recoded as a budgetary burden to be jettisoned. Despite having fulfilled all work and familial expectations for their lifetimes, pensioners who always thought they would be protected in their final years found themselves cast aside by both a struggling state and their cash-strapped families. At the margins of Bucharest, these costly pensioners unexpectedly confronted the gritty experience of homelessness, where they now vied with younger men and women for space inside night shelters, day centers, and hospital waiting rooms, surrounded by buzzing halogen lights, clanking radiators, and long bouts of silence. The glow of the so-called golden years was lost under layers of dense tarnish.

No Picnic

"It's a big question with a complicated answer," Tudor replied. While we were playing chess in the Backwoods courtyard, I had asked Tudor how he ended up living at the shelter. "It involves my broken relationship with my son and the size of my pension," he said. Tudor secured a full pension upon retirement, having worked as a bus driver for more than twenty-five years. He drove routes across Romania and at times beyond, connecting Bucharest and Istanbul. Tudor retired from driving shortly after the revolution. Coupled with his wife's pension, earned as a nurse, and the paycheck of his son, a medical technician, his pension allowed Tudor to keep an apartment with his son and to maintain a modest amount of savings. This arrangement broke down in the mid-1990s when Tudor's wife unexpectedly passed away. Her death took a toll on Tudor, financially; he lost the value of her pension from his monthly income. As the value of his own stagnating pension eroded amid high annual inflation rates, Tudor became concerned about making ends meet. In an effort to generate new income, Tudor responded to the entrepreneurial call of Western political and economic reformers circulating in the Romanian media. Tudor became an "active retiree": he invested his limited savings in a small business venture, opening a neighborhood corner store. His foray into business, however, did not have the return on capital that economic reformers had suggested. Instead of a new opportunity promising greater security, Tudor's fledgling effort at entrepreneurship produced only ambiguity and liability. Shortly after opening his store, Tudor received a note from a collection agency

indicating that he was delinquent on payments for a loan that he did not recall making. The letter indicated that his property would be seized. "I don't
know what to believe and what not to believe anymore," Tudor recalled to
me one afternoon while lying on his cot in the dormitory of Stefan's Place,
"but I have never taken out a loan in my life from anyone." Tudor was insis-
tent on this point. He then offered in a shaky, less certain statement of fact,
one followed by a prolonged pause that prompted me to reassure him, "And
if I had taken a loan, I would have a receipt, right? I mean there would be
some kind of papers with signatures."

Tudor's sense of uncertainty reflects Romania's rapidly changing property laws in the 1990s, which not only privatized the housing constructed
and formerly managed by the state but also aimed to return privately
held property that had been nationalized during communism. The newly
formed real estate market attracted high-interest lenders and duplicitous
real estate agents offering so-called false loans. These were loans made by
real estate agents to tenants who otherwise could not afford to purchase
their nationalized apartment units. While many of these loans were legitimate transactions, low financial literacy prevented borrowers from understanding the finer stipulations that these agreements carried, such as a
requirement that the new owner would ultimately have to sell the apartment unit directly to the real estate agent making the loan.[12] The process of
property restitution also attracted lawyers and forgers interested in making
false claims on potentially valuable properties.[13] Disputes over housing restitution were most often resolved within a Romanian judicial system that
operated within a robust economy of bribes, leading those who received
unfavorable rulings to raise not merely concerns about corruption but also
claims that their human rights had been violated.[14] Property rights, in this
moment, quickly grew "fuzzy."[15] Claims of racketeering and fraud circulated
throughout Romania as some tenants found themselves inexplicably dispossessed of apartments they had long occupied. At the exact moment in
Romania when real estate became a question, rather than a state guarantee,
pensioners like Tudor were befuddled and, ultimately, left empty-handed.

After a period of resistance, the bank confiscated Tudor's store and the
savings invested in it. He also had to liquefy additional assets, namely, his
apartment, to free up additional money to cover his debts. "I couldn't believe how many thousands of lei the bank said I owed," Tudor recalled. "The
interest was quoted to me in dollars. My son and I were tossed out onto
the street. We became homeless." The lost apartment and the accusation

of mismanaged finances strained Tudor's relationship with his son, who grew worried that his own savings might disappear along with those of his father. "After the creditors took everything, we stopped talking," Tudor explained. "He moved out on his own. I haven't seen him since." Tudor's life then unraveled with such speed and thoroughness that he could not help but wonder if he was the target of a well-executed scheme by Romania's communist-era secret police, the Securitate.[16] "The creditors knew everything, and they came and took most everything. I couldn't believe it," Tudor recalled. The one valuable possession Tudor retained was his decade-old station wagon, which soon doubled as his mobile home.

Estranged from his son and left with a diluting pension, Tudor was priced out of the housing market, and he had little hope of ever buying back into it. Even a studio apartment (*garsonieră*) on the outskirts of Bucharest proved unaffordable. To subsidize his pension, Tudor once again tried to follow the "active-aging" prescriptions. Tudor looked for work that would provide some additional income. The problem, Tudor quickly learned, was that employers were not particularly interested in offering work to the elderly. "No one would hire me at my age," Tudor attested. "Not as a driver, a security guard, or anything else. I wanted to work, but there was no work for me to do! Employers just turned me away." Too old and without the right skills, Tudor proved unviable on the competitive labor market.

After sleeping in his car for about a month, Tudor eventually headed to Backwoods, where he was offered a bed in a communal dormitory reserved for pensioner-age men. Four cots lined each of the two lengths of the wall. There were no curtains or other dividers between beds to extend a minimum of privacy, though each beneficiary received a lockable cabinet to store clothes and other belongings. "This is a miserable place," Tudor assessed from his corner bed. "It's inhumane. It's undignified. The first time I saw this room I ran away from it. I slept in my car that night. But where else can I go? If I were younger, then I would leave—I'd go to Germany or someplace like that." As much as Tudor resisted his move into Backwoods, he eventually gave in to it. He started sleeping on his cot at night while spending his day driving around town. The cost of gasoline eventually curbed his day-tripping. Like for other residents at the shelter, the cost of getting into the city became prohibitive, and so he took to staying inside the shelter. "Now I'm old and stuck here with these other guys. What shit . . . " Tudor's voice trailed off in a tone of noticeable disappointment.

Even though Tudor retained his car and could still drive into the city to run errands during the week, or drive out to the countryside to go camping on the occasional weekend, he nevertheless described life at the shelter as isolated. His roommates were older and had aged less gracefully than he. Some suffered from dementia and yelled loudly about communist-era conspiracy theories. Others were physically worn down and nearly bedridden. These roommates got up only to take meals or use the restroom but otherwise rested on their beds with their eyes closed. They spent their days half asleep. As a courtesy to the semisomnolent, Tudor had to remain constantly aware of the noise he produced while spending time in the dormitory. Tudor sat on his cot in the back corner of the dormitory wearing headphones, listening alternately to the television and the radio while he read. In moments of restlessness, Tudor paced the Backwoods courtyard or took long walks to the gas station down the road, where he could buy bottles of inexpensive wine and beer. He then smuggled his contraband past the shelter's guards and into his dormitory, where he poured the contents of his stash into old soda bottles so that he could drink in peace. "I never imagined this kind of life," Tudor admitted over Coca-Cola bottles filled with beer. "This kind of life never existed in my mind as a possibility."

In addition to consuming alcohol, Tudor found release from the shelter's boredom by ogling the custodial staff. Welcome flattery often teetered on the edge of sexual harassment as Tudor tried desperately to hold their attention. When one of the staff members named Rodika interrupted our conversation to do some mandatory mopping, for example, Tudor invited me to appreciate her "beautiful tits." As I rolled my eyes and looked away, Rodika laughed lightheartedly before warning Tudor to behave himself. When Tudor persisted, Rodika rebuked him further, using me as leverage to momentarily stop his advances. "You need to behave yourself—you're making the American uncomfortable," she chided. The custodial staff put up with Tudor's behavior for their own ends. During the slow moments of the late shift, Rodika and other women on the staff often joined Tudor on his cot to watch the news and to sneak nips of brandy, wine, or beer. These moments of companionship served as the highlight of Tudor's week and also broke up the monotony of the staff's workday.

Tudor had developed his vision for his retirement under communism. His expectations took shape while working bus routes that began in Bucharest and wound out to the countryside. "Forty years ago, I would pick up pensioners from the city and bring them to the mountains. They would spend the night up there in the mountains, and then I would take them back to town on my way back. I'd see them relaxing—having picnics (*grătar*). I've always thought that's how retirement should be. That's how I always imagined it, anyway," Tudor explained wistfully. His vision for retirement speaks to a general sense of security as much as to an ability to partake in a particular set of concrete practices. Under communism, state guarantees not only assured pensioners a stable place to live in the city, from which they could come and go, but also enough of a surplus to partake in leisurely consumption. Pensioners had the means to treat themselves in modest ways, whether that was a trip to the mountains, a night at the theater, or a shared meal with friends. After two decades of economic instability that decimated the value of government pensions, Tudor was finding that retirement was certainly no picnic in the countryside. Pensions no longer provided the security to facilitate everyday life in an apartment, much less to float a bus ticket out of town. Instead, the increasing precariousness of the golden years left Tudor unexpectedly in a shelter, surrounded by sleeping bodies on the outskirts of town, with little else to do besides concealing his drinking. Retirement turned into a prolonged exercise in keeping quiet.

While shelter boredom prompted working-age men to contemplate egress and the possibility of a better life abroad (see chapter 1), Tudor was too old to entertain such fantasies. The idea of relocation struck Tudor as desirable in the abstract but wholly unrealistic in practice. Instead, Tudor sought escape from shelter life by recalling an earlier era when his life was not so boring. "We didn't have all of this free time during Ceaușescu," Tudor assured me over a game of backgammon in the Stefan's Place courtyard. "We worked day and night. We worked hard, and then we could enjoy ourselves. You could live beautifully back then. Cafés, the mountains, the seaside . . ." Tudor sat hesitantly for a moment, aware that he was recollecting life under communism through rose-colored glasses.[17] Rather than providing a holistic assessment of life under communism, Tudor's recollections highlighted a lost sense of incorporation into the present workings of the city. After a moment's pause to regroup his thoughts, Tudor continued, "I mean, sure, life was bad back then because the lights shut down at night and you couldn't find much food"—Tudor elongated his face by simultaneously raising his eyebrows and frowning—"but Romanians got by." Young and old did without during communist austerity, Tudor admitted, but deprivation in a global economy in crisis imposed a form of deprivation with an entirely different character. Under communism, the rights to work and to housing did not always ensure material fulfillment, but they did incorporate almost everyone in the daily life of the city. In those days Tudor may have felt overworked and underfed at times; however, he never felt cast aside, like an old tool that no longer serves a use, as he came to feel while sitting on his cot in the Backwoods dormitory. Once inside the shelter, Tudor felt completely abandoned by his family but also by the state.

"Social assistance no longer exists," Tudor attested. "Under communism, the state gave you a house and free schools for the children. If you didn't have a job, they gave you one. The state was obligated. Now there are no guarantees. There is no support." It was then that I reminded Tudor that the very shelter in which we were seated, Backwoods, was a state-administered facility. While lacking the comfort of even the most modest of apartment blocks, Backwoods nevertheless provided a roof, a bed, and a warm shower. With a chortle, Tudor shot back, "You have to pay 60 percent of your pension to stay here, and after paying that, you no longer have money for food."[18] While the shelter provided two meals per day, Tudor was diabetic and unable to eat most of the meals offered at Backwoods. "The food that they serve here is loaded with fat and sugar. I can't eat any of that. It'll make my condition worse. I have to cook for myself, but I don't have the money. So instead today I don't eat, tomorrow I don't eat, and the day after. . . . You cannot compare this in any way with the social assistance offered in the time of Ceaușescu." Shaking his head, he continued in exasperation, "Now the state only disappoints. I mean, who gives you a house today? . . . Instead, the state has left me here."

Stretched Thin

"Life at the shelter is monotone, without color. Usually nothing happens here," Ana, a widowed pensioner living in Backwoods's women's dormitory, explained to me on a cold December afternoon. I sat in a chair next to Ana's bed while we watched a Spanish soap opera. Ana muted the television during a spot of commotion that interrupted the dormitory's usually "monotone" routine. A younger resident had returned from a trip to the city, where she had pocketed a set of Orthodox priest's robes from a monastery offering a free meal, as well as taking a Santa Claus beard from a Carrefour shopping center. She had just dressed herself in the two and had begun goose-stepping around the dormitory, mixing Santa's belly laugh with priestly gestures of absolution while she marched. The curious sight inspired belly laughter from everyone (myself included)—everyone except for Ana. "This place is a slum for the poorly educated," she remarked cuttingly while staring at the goose-stepping Santa-priest.

My wide smile slowly drooped agape while my forehead contorted. "Excuse me?" I asked, deflated.

"The younger ones go out and beg and steal, but they get brought back here by the police. You can imagine what kind of people stay here," Ana assessed in a low, firm tone. She turned her eyes away from the Santa-priest to the television and ratcheted up the volume in an effort to slip back into the decidedly more dubious love triangle playing out on her daily soap. When the program went back to commercials, she muted the set and continued her biting analysis of Backwoods: "The difficulty with this place is that I have these colleagues, but I'm always alone. That's the hardest. If we were on the same wavelength, if I had something in common with these people, then time would pass more easily, more pleasantly." Several of "these colleagues," in fact, sat listening to our conversation. Their presence did not seem to blunt Ana's assessment of Backwoods. "But as it is I feel bored each and every day that I am here," she concluded.

Ana, like Tudor, never imagined that retirement would take the form of the Backwoods Shelter. She had earned a full pension serving as an accountant for a construction firm from the mid-1960s to the early 1990s. As a former administrator, Ana understood herself to be on another wavelength entirely from her neighbors at the shelter who worked, when the opportunity presented itself, as security guards and custodians. The difference in occupation, in Ana's reckoning, was not horizontal but hierarchical. As an educated administrator, Ana understood herself as part of another, higher class of people entirely, compared to the unskilled workers who surrounded her, despite their shared economic condition. None of Ana's neighbors in the dormitory questioned Ana's claim to rank. Even her youngest and least reverent roommates addressed Ana as either Ms. Ana (*Doamna Ana*) or even Madam Colleague (*Doamna Colegă*). With her status came certain privileges. Almost everyone in the women's dormitory took turns making Ana coffee throughout the day. They also delivered meals from Backwoods's kitchen to her bed, and they shielded Ana from the indignities of bumming cigarettes by asking around on her behalf. Ana accepted these honorifics without a word of gratitude, both out of a sense of entitlement and also out of need. In her early sixties, Ana was skeletally thin with cancer and easily became exhausted. She rarely got out of bed. In exchange for these acts of assistance, Ana ajudicated disputes in the women's dormitory.

She also extended invitations to watch television to those who helped her out—a coveted offer since she owned the only set in the room.

Ana's sense of privilege developed under communism, where she enjoyed what she described as "another kind of life." She lived with her husband, who also worked as an administrator, in Militari, a neighborhood in western Bucharest that developed rapidly after the revolution in 1989. "We lived on the third floor, and it was very good there. We stayed a great way off the road with trees and a garden. . . . It was a beautiful place to live. Life was secure then," she recalled. Ana's sense of financial security, however, began to unravel during the early years of Romania's transition; as her story makes clear, even skilled office workers found themselves struggling to find their footing in the new economy. Heightened market competition also recoded midlevel administrators of a certain age as redundant and unnecessary. "A private company bought the firm where I worked," Ana explained. "My post got restructured, and I was fired at the age of forty-eight." Although Ana's twenty-five years of service granted her a full pension, she was not eligible to begin receiving payments for another decade. Too young to retire, Ana sought other work without luck. "I couldn't get hired," Ana attested. "After the revolution companies looked only for the young: girls and boys they could train.[19] They didn't want to deal with people like me. A lot of computers also came into operation, and I don't know how computers work. Time and again, companies saw me walk through the door, and they just looked the other way." Although Ana was competent working the literal books, her extensive work history under communism left her ill prepared to navigate a computerized, postcommunist office environment. As office technology upgraded beyond her comfort zone, Ana became an unhireable job candidate. Unable to find new office work, she lived simply on her husband's salary while she waited for her own pension payments to begin on her fifty-eighth birthday.

In an effort to free up additional money, Ana and her husband sold their apartment in 1995. They planned to bank some savings after moving to a smaller, less expensive apartment elsewhere in the city. Their financial plan unraveled, though, when they fell victim to a housing scam. They signed away the deed to their apartment without receiving any payment in return. "We were tricked by gypsies," Ana assessed, using the ethnic slur to refer to her defrauder.[20] Given Ana's overt racism, though, it is unlikely that she would ever have initiated such a transaction with an ethnically Roma person.

"At least we still had my husband's salary," Ana recalled reasoning. "We could still rent at that point, but it was tough." Ana ultimately lost her tenuous hold on housing when her husband passed away a few years later. "After my husband died, I had no other possibilities. Even when my pension started I didn't have the funds to live in a studio apartment. My pension is very low—about 40 percent of my old salary. You can't live on that—you need two pensions just to cover everyday needs." To substantiate her claim, as much as to demonstrate her affinity for numbers, Ana took out a piece of paper and pencil from underneath her pillow and began to account for typical monthly expenses. In one column, she listed the items "rent," "utilities," "medication," "food," and so forth. In another column, she estimated the expense for each budgetary item in the old Romanian currency (the ROL), which, owing to the effects of hyperinflation, had been abandoned over half a decade previously. "Rent, even in the cheapest apartment, costs three to five million ROL ($100–$150)."[21] She continued to work down her list, assigning a value to each item. Quoting prices in the old, hyperinflated currency had the effect of dramatizing the unaffordability of everyday life in Romania. "What pensioner can afford to pay five million a month in rent? And that's before you pay for the lights and the heat or whatever. I certainly can't afford it—and my situation is probably that of 90 percent of pensioners," she insisted.

While the value of government pensions dipped, Ana could not turn to family to support her in the way she had supported her grandparents under communism. Like in many Romanian families of that generation, her maternal grandmother had lived in Ana's childhood home, and when Ana's parents grew old, Ana had extended the same invitation to them. Although her parents ultimately kept their own house, Ana maintained a close relationship with them. "Every week I brought the three grandchildren with me to visit them, so there was someone there to help the time pass. We visited for a bit, and then everyone had their own life. They did not want to leave home, even when they were old. They said it felt good to stay in their house, alone. They were independent people." Ana explained that the possibility of remaining at home and near family at the same time was possible because of a robust set of state services. "During Ceauşescu's time, pensioners were able to live decently. Unlike now, the government helped pensioners, and pensioners could help their children. Pensions made us providers for the family. But now it's the inverse. We are completely dependent. Pensioners can't get by without the income of their children," she explained bitterly.

Unlike Tudor, Ana had remained on good terms with her children; she spoke on the phone with them regularly. Her children, however, were no longer in Romania. As Romania integrated itself into the global economy, its once-closed national borders opened up. When market reforms stalled rather than thrived, ambitious Romanians sought opportunity elsewhere in Europe, rather than waiting for conditions to improve at home. As Ana summarized, "After the revolution, it was a moment of chaos. The government sold off the heavy industry, factories and so on—and the people who worked were left without jobs. Money lost its value. There just aren't any opportunities here anymore." Ana's three children joined millions of other Romanians migrating en masse away from Romania.[22] In search of higher wages and a better standard of living, her children moved to Cyprus. There they married and found work as bank tellers. "They have a great situation," Ana assessed with pride while smoking a cigarette atop her cot. "They are skilled workers. They know Greek and English. They earn well."

Although Ana's children managed to cultivate comfortable and stable lives abroad, their success in Cyprus did not translate into remittances to Ana in Romania. To be sure, sending remittances is a common and widely expected practice for Romanians working abroad. Around this time, Romania was one of the top receiving countries for remittances, which increased in value from $96 million in 2000 to over $9 billion in 2008.[23] Indeed, a few hundred euros a month would have been a sufficient addition to Ana's pension to allow her to secure a studio apartment in the city. Entire Romanian villages, in fact, survive on such remittances.[24] This strategy, however, conflicted with Ana's sensibility of the direction in which financial aid should travel within a family. While it may be common for Romanian husbands and sons to send remittances to support their families back in the countryside, it was not universally accepted for adult children to send money to aging parents, particularly if these migrants had children of their own in need of care. Such an arrangement conflicted with the way Ana and others believed resources and care should be directed within the family. The resources of parents, Ana firmly maintained, should flow downward to support their children; the resources of children should not flow upward to support their parents. An upward flow of money, to Ana's mind, made no sense. "My children have offered to send me money," Ana continued, "but I don't want it. They have their own difficulties. They pay for housing and food, and their children are in college, and paying tuition is not easy." Ana stubbed out her cigarette in her ashtray and adjusted the pillow supporting her back before continuing in a firm voice, "I have my pension. That should be enough to live on. That is the way it is supposed to be. Why would I ever let myself be a drag on my children? If I can't afford to help them, the least I can do is not drag them down." It was a principled stance that Ana cultivated over the course of her relationship with her own parents. "My parents had enough left over from their pension to help me with money. They also helped me to raise my children while I worked, and, in exchange, I helped them around the house when they got older. I did some cleaning, and I cooked some meals, but I *never* gave them money," Ana emphasized. "I did not ever contribute a single dime to support their material needs. Ever since I had my children, my parents were always the ones that helped me. And that's how it should be. That's how I should be able to help my children," she explained.

The remittances that Ana's children have offered to send home represented the kind of familial support that would have allowed Ana to live that "other kind of life" located beyond the walls of Backwoods. It was the kind of independent life that Ana believed was befitting her education and status. Instead, Ana lived at the shelter to avoid absorbing resources that Ana's children would otherwise have directed toward themselves and, ideally, Ana's grandchildren. The sort of help that Ana was prepared to accept—such as help preparing meals, cleaning, or going to the store—her children were unable to perform from Cyprus. They also did not visit Bucharest regularly. "Why would they?" Ana rebuffed my question in a curt tone, one that suggested a visit home would be an unthinkable waste of her children's time and money.

Despite Ana's bleak assessment of life in Romania, two of her grand-daughters had recently chosen to enroll at the University of Bucharest. Ana now had family in the city who could perform the kind of occasional household care that Ana found it appropriate to have flow up the family ladder. Ana refused, however, to let her grandchildren visit the shelter (much less clean her living space within it). Instead, on the rarest of occasions, Ana rode the bus an hour and a half to meet her grandchildren in the city center. Not only was the journey long and expensive, but, given Ana's failing health, it was also physically draining. "I don't bring my family here," Ana affirmed to me. "When they want to visit, I meet with them in the city.

They can never visit me here. For most of my life, I had another level of living, but now it's pretty bad. I don't want them to see me like this."

Much like the offers of remittances, Ana waved away offers of visits from family that would have been punctuated by small gestures of care. Rather than be a drain on her family's resources, Ana much preferred to make do by mobilizing a sense of class privilege over her roommates at Backwoods in order to obtain help around the dormitory. It was a self-conscious act of familial estrangement that allowed Ana to perform, in the limited way still available to her, the role of grandmother-provider in a moment where she had little with which to provide. Each day that Ana spent at the shelter, where she did not want to be and where she was surrounded by people with whom she did not wish to associate, became Ana's gift to her children and to her grandchildren. It proved to be a profoundly boring way of fulfilling her familial obligations. The gift of not taking from her children left Ana little to look forward to. "I'll spend the rest of my days here," Ana told me one afternoon. "Eventually I'll close my eyes. That's my future."

Overexposed

"My head is saturated with boredom," Victoria, a homeless woman in her late sixties, explained to me. It was a few days before Christmas, and we were sitting inside a toolshed situated in the back of the Stefan's Place parking lot. Stefan's Place made the shed available during the winter months because the main building lacked a waiting room where the homeless could sit protected from the elements. While it kept out the rain and the snow, the shed was neither heated nor insulated. Gaps between the boards allowed gusts of wind to whip through it. No-smoking signs hung on two of the four interior walls. Homeless men with construction backgrounds spent their afternoons sitting inside that shed questioning its moral, as much as its structural, integrity. "If they actually gave a shit," noted one man, "it would be pretty easy to seal those gaps. All you have to do is wrap this box with a plastic sheet." "They could also run an electrical cord from the main building so we could have a space heater," commented another as he lit a cigarette in disregard for the signs. Eye rolls and indignant laughter ensued when one of the center's staff popped his head in through the door to enforce the no-smoking policy. "Trying to keep the place tidy?" the man quipped as he stepped out of the shed to finish his smoke. "The whole thing could catch fire," the staff member insisted curtly as the door shut behind

FIGURE 3.2. The shed. Photo by Bruce O'Neill.

them. The apparently flammable toolshed served, quite literally, as a winter storage unit for homeless people.

"There's nothing for me to do in this country—I no longer want to live here," Victoria continued. "I'm bored through and through!" Victoria had good reason for feeling this way. She had lost her hold on housing shortly after the fall of communism and became part of Bucharest's first wave of homeless persons. She had been living on the streets of Bucharest for nearly twenty years. Unlike Tudor and Ana, Victoria had never married. She did not have children, even estranged ones, who could be called on as a potential source of support in her old age. Victoria also did not cultivate a formal employment history, and, as a result, she did not qualify for a government pension of any kind. Instead of being underprotected by governmental and familial support, as was the case with Tudor and Ana, Victoria found herself overexposed to the precariousness of aging. It left her chronically homeless.

To be sure, Victoria had worked intermittently throughout her life. She waited tables here and there off the books at neighborhood restaurants. Victoria worked only part-time because she spent much of her adulthood performing the unpaid work of caring for her own aging mother. Familial obligations prohibited Victoria from cultivating the twenty-five-year work history needed to receive a pension. "My mother wasn't well. She had a weak heart, so I helped around the house, helped her to make food, to clean, to wait in line. She needed help all of the time. I helped her around the house like that for sixteen years until she finally died. It was its own full-time job," Victoria explained. "We had an apartment with a yard in Uranus," a neighborhood in western Bucharest. "I planned to stay in the apartment after my mom's death. I was going to keep working at the restaurant and live simply. That was enough for me. But the restaurant folded, and I got thrown out onto the street." When I asked Victoria why she did not inherit her mother's apartment, she shrugged her shoulders and explained hurriedly, glossing over the sticky details, "My name wasn't on the housing contract, and so I got cheated out of the apartment by some gypsies. They took all of my things and threw me out. . . . Now I've been on the streets for twenty years." Like Ana, Victoria did not attribute her homelessness to general economic instability, a fuzzy legal and political landscape, or diminishing state protections. Instead of being pressed by shifting historical and economic forces, Victoria made sense of her descent into homelessness by mobilizing a familiar racism directed toward the Roma, the so-called gypsies.

Without a pension and working-age children to rely on, Victoria got by from day to day with a smaller social aid payment from the state, which she supplemented by visiting homeless service centers offered by a constellation of nongovernmental organizations, Orthodox monasteries and Catholic churches, and hospitals located across the city. These services did not operate every day, nor did they coordinate with one another. For those wholly dependent on them, the piecemeal coverage of services for the street homeless created a temporal experience of homelessness distinct from that of homeless shelter residents or the younger street homeless who occasionally earned money on the black market. While shelter residents, such as Ana and Tudor, could rarely guess the day of the week, with their Mondays looking much the same as their Fridays, Victoria maintained strong distinctions between the two. This is because Victoria had to access everyday necessities like meals, medicine, and shelter in different locations each day. In the moments when services were not available, such as on a Saturday morning or late at night, Victoria sat in the park. During rainy weather or in the depths of winter, she sat on public buses and circled the city again and again. Once a week, Victoria also visited her sister, Nicoleta, who also lived in Bucharest. While an invaluable friend and source of the occasional warm meal and hot shower, Nicoleta could not offer to house Victoria full-time. Nicoleta, herself a pensioner, and her husband had their own precarious financial and familial difficulties to manage. They lived in a studio apartment with their children and grandchildren. The three generations piled together in one room to stay afloat. Although she would have liked to offer Victoria a place to stay, Nicoleta lacked the extra money and additional space to accommodate another family member.

Instead, Victoria made use of the city's freely available food, shelter, and medicine. She moved between these different resources slowly and arduously. She walked with a cane and, owing to a lack of storage space, carried with her almost all of her personal belongings in two overstuffed duffle bags. Each time I helped Victoria with her baggage, my considerably younger and better-rested body found them to be of a formidable weight. After a few minutes of carrying them, my shoulders ached and my arms shook. I would have to set the bags down regularly to regain my balance and rub away the burning sensation left by the straps digging into my hand. Unsurprisingly, under the weight of such baggage, Victoria missed any and every bus interchange, which only further slowed her movement across the city. To compensate for her labored mobility, Victoria scheduled plenty of time to get from one service provider to the next. The stakes of her travel provided ample motivation. If Victoria did not pay attention to the clock, then she would miss out on meals or a comfortable place to spend the night. Otherwise, unlike those who occasionally found day labor on the black market, Victoria did not have much cash on hand to buy food or to pay for a bed in a shelter. Victoria stayed attuned to the time. She regularly asked social workers and friends to check their watches for her, seeking clarification down to the exact minute.

Victoria's hyperscheduled relationship to time shaped her sense of boredom. While the vast majority of Bucharest's homeless described boredom as an experience of time without borders, marked by empty hours and undifferentiated days, Victoria's weekly calendar was punctuated by events and transitions. With meals to catch and warm seats to reserve, Victoria had a sense of forward progression that others on the street felt no longer existed. Her schedule was also difficult to keep, focusing her attention at all hours of the day. Nevertheless, Victoria understood herself as overwhelmed with boredom. This is because boredom, for homeless persons, does not express a lack of things to do or places to be in an absolute sense.

FIGURE 3.3. Worn out. Photo by Bruce O'Neill.

Rather, boredom for the homeless is an affective state that registers temporally the experience of displacement to the margins of the city, but also of the global economy. The experience slows the rhythm of life to a crawl. Victoria's days may have unfolded along a clear sequence of events, but those events were composed of painstakingly slow treks across the city followed by hours sitting in the waiting rooms of various institutions. These sequences of walking and waiting became a part of Victoria's routine only because of her loss of stable housing and because of the absence of government protections. Otherwise, Victoria would have spent her time in other places doing different things with other people. To be sure, insult was regularly added to the indignity of trekking back and forth between the marginal spaces of the city.[25]

"Yesterday," Victoria explained to me as we sat in the shed of Stefan's

Place, "I was on my way to the hospital when I lost my shoe in the snow. It got stuck in a snowdrift. Some guys saw me struggling to get it free, and they started laughing at me. I felt terrible." Amid Victoria's difficult act of balancing herself on a cane while searching for her shoe, all while hoping that her overstuffed bags would not spill over, cackling onlookers layered shame onto the very real danger of a frostbite injury. Once Victoria regained her shoe and her composure, she made the slow trek to the waiting room of a public hospital to warm up. "My feet were cold and wet. Luckily I had some extra money from begging in the Metro," she continued, "so I bought a coffee at the hospital to help me warm up. I sat on the hospital radiator all night to warm up." Victoria paused momentarily, allowing the image of nights spent sitting on a hospital waiting room's radiator to take hold. "This is why I tell you and tell you of my boredom in Romania. The boredom is great here because there is nothing for me. Unless I'm going to a free meal or a warm room, I don't even know in which direction to walk." Displaced from regular membership in the city, Victoria squatted in a string of nonplaces avoided by all those who could afford to be elsewhere. In between disposable Styrofoam bowls of watered-down stew and nights spent sleeping upright in waiting-room chairs, Victoria and her struggles attained public recognition only as a joke to the better-off. "You make all of the effort to go somewhere and then nothing happens. And along the way some guy is always putting you down. If it's not someone laughing at you, then it's those bastards from the police. They're always accusing me of stealing. You can't make anything of yourself in this place," she continued, referring as much to the social service providers as to the city and the entire country. Victoria might have had places to go, but her grinding schedule was composed of people and spaces that actively affirmed her nonbelonging in the city. Rather than providing a sense of meaning and incorporation, the day-to-day grind of accessing homeless services made it clear that, in a city organized around consumer practices, there was nothing for the person with nothing to spend. Homelessness left Victoria with little else to look forward to aside from hurrying between institutions, only to commence waiting for the next move.

In search of relief, Victoria retreated into fantasies of a capitalist elsewhere—one that would identify and fill, in vivid yet cruelly intangible ways, the gaps differentiating those that belong in a global order from those that do not. Sitting in the shed of the Stefan's Place parking lot, talking over water bottles repurposed as mugs for the instant Nescafé packets that I regularly carried with me, Victoria explained, "I want to move to America—to California—and live there." Victoria's specification of California, the place I had identified as "home," spoke to a desire to tap into the possibilities of mobility and consumption that I represented to her. "I think about what I will do once I get to California a lot. I won't come back to Romania, that's for sure!" she said with emphasis. With a smile warming her face, Victoria continued, "I'll go to California, get hired as a cook, find a home, and never come back to this boring life. And you can come visit me at home, Bruce. We can sit and talk and drink coffee together. I'll make you a mug."

Importantly, Victoria's vision of another kind of life, one understood as meaningful rather than marginal, was organized around the very same activities in which we found ourselves engaged, namely, sitting, talking, and drinking coffee. What differentiated Victoria's vision of the good life from the boredom of living at the margins was not the realm of possible activities but the way in which they unfolded. Victoria dreamed of drinking coffee at her apartment (rather than a shelter) out of mugs (not water bottles recovered from the trash) and acting as the provider of coffee (instead of perpetually enacting the role of grateful recipient). Caught up in these material distinctions are cultural ones that differentiate between incorporation and displacement, hospitality and charity, leisure and boredom.

Victoria's imagined new beginning in California was, of course, wholly implausible. She lacked the cultural and economic capital to secure a tourist visa, much less to make the trip over to the United States and become a permanent resident.[26] Instead of encouraging an unreasonable fantasy of the good life, I asked Victoria how she might improve her living situation in Bucharest. I suggested that she apply for space in one of the city's homeless shelters. While unsatisfying in its own way, a shelter would at least afford Victoria a steady place of her own and the opportunity to sip coffee with neighbors out of ceramic mugs. Waving away my suggestions, Victoria spoke with great confidence: "It's different when living abroad," she lectured with authority. "In Romania you can't do anything. When you want to sit somewhere or want to eat something or to work a job, you're not allowed. So how can you make money for your cigarettes, for food and for coffee? That's why I want to go to California and get a house with my own food, television, phone—that's everything that I could want." In the unbridgeable gulf between the good-life fantasy projected on life abroad and the materiality of the toolshed in which Victoria and I sat in the parking lot of Stefan's Place, boredom took hold.

"In sector 1 there are sixty thousand pensioners. In all of the social assistance units in all of sector 1 there are four hundred pensioners. So four hundred people out of sixty thousand is very good," explained Dragos, a senior official for the General Directorate of Social Assistance and Child Protection, in an optimistic tone. We sat in his office in the city center. "Pensioners have other services too: a senior's club with activities, legal services, health counseling, and if they're old enough to be a pensioner, then they can stay in a retirement center (*azil de bătrâni*)." He listed the services with a reassuring smile.

There is a certain truth to Dragos's optimism. The local authorities administered around 1,600 beds in various institutions for the elderly. Dragos's optimistic tone, however, elided the long waiting list for a bed in such a place, which exceeded 2,800 names.[27] Dragos did admit that there are also conditions as to who is eligible for bed space, and when that eligibility begins. "To get a bed, a person needs to have earned a full pension, and they need to be pensioner aged." Excluded by these conditions were a large number of Romanians who earned their daily wage through under-the-table arrangements in restaurants (such as Victoria) and other day labor markets. Although these men and women working off the books spent their productive years laboring, their informal contracts did not pay into the pension system. As a result, they were detached from the security of receiving a pension at all, even a heavily devalued one. Rather than staying in their homes, these aging workers ended up in squatter camps and homeless shelters, which, in turn, came to look a great deal like underfunded retirement centers.

"And we know there needs to be pension reform," Dragos continued, with his optimistic tone turning pragmatic. "There is discussion about a private system or a vocational pension scheme to subsidize state pensions, but it is not a very promising idea because the salaries in Romania are so low. The minimum wage in Romania is 900 lei, or about €200," Dragos admitted with a wince. "How much can you contribute to a private pension when €200 is not enough to get through the month? And that is the reality of the vast majority of the people."

As government administrators searched for market-based solutions to support an aging population with an evaporating purchasing power, aging and poverty grew ever more tightly entangled. Rather than a temporary stopgap, homeless services became a critical source of support for Bucharest's pensioners. The infrastructure of homelessness absorbed an elderly population left in the void created by the diminishing value of government pensions, stretched familial relations, and an absence of infrastructure devoted specifically to their needs. Pensioners, faced with few other options, got pushed out of their homes and were swept into shelters and day centers. Sitting on cots in communal dormitories, men and women who had fulfilled the work obligations of their lifetimes sat side by side with those struggling, perhaps with futility, for the opportunity to do the same. In a global economy in crisis, the distinction between pensioner and pauper grew indistinguishable. Whether used up or unusable, the economically superfluous were cast aside to the same place. In the absence of robust state guarantees, Tudor, Ana, and Victoria could no longer act as generous providers for family and friends as pensioners did under communism and as they had expected to do themselves. Simply put, they now lacked the funds to do so. Rather than actively contributing to the life of familial households, economic pressure now compelled pensioners not to act at all lest they absorb the limited resources of the next generation. This recasting of the elderly heightened intimate feelings of social estrangement and physical inactivity. To avoid slipping into an unshakable boredom, pensioners made their escape by recalling other times when life was not so gray and imagining other places where it might be different. This was one of the few indulgences they could still afford.

4

BORED TO DEATH

. . .

"Boredom is the hardest," Adrian—a forty-something homeless man living in the waiting room of the Gara de Nord—started with a heavy sigh. On a winter night, we stood in a corner of one of the station's side entrances. We loosely cupped our hands around exposed hot water pipes while we chatted. "I leave the station, I walk around, I look for something to do and clear my thoughts, but it's hard. All these people, this entire atmosphere, all of this day-to-day. . . . You get bored with life." Adrian's confession was interrupted by a security guard making his rounds. The guard wanted to shoo us away from the pipes, but Adrian's mild protest to let us linger for a few minutes longer to warm up elicited a sympathetic nod. Turning back to me, Adrian continued, with another heavy sigh, "This boredom is a state where you get this feeling of 'Enough—I want to put an end to this life!' You just cannot live day to day to day anymore. It's like you've been put in a coma, you've lost your memory, you leave a critical state, you lose vision and patience—you just get so bored that you want to kill yourself. No one understands."

"But there's got to be something for you to do," I prodded with American optimism.

Adrian shrugged his shoulders and rolled his eyes. "Perhaps I can go to another country and clean," he offered. "I'll even buy my own mop. Maybe then I could have a salary and something to do." He let go of his hot water pipe and headed out toward the short-term parking lot of the station,

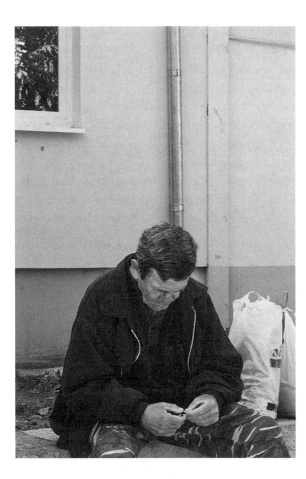

FIGURE 4.1.
Afternoon. Photo by
Bruce O'Neill.

where he hoped to earn some quick money helping travelers load and un-
load baggage from the trunks of their cars.

Biding his time in the little-noticed corners of Bucharest's main railway station, Adrian not only lacked a steady job and a salary to spend in
the present but had no hope that his circumstances might ever improve
in the future.[1] He could no longer envision, in any believable way, regain-
ing a foothold in Romania's struggling economy and earning the kind
of salary necessary to participate in the life of the city, much less attain
a European standard of living. Such participation would include, for example, reestablishing the fundamental infrastructure of everyday life in the
form of a rented apartment and a sufficiently full refrigerator to support
himself and eventually a family. At stake were also the little pleasures that

make up having "something to do" in the city, such as visiting friends at a café, going to the movies, or running to the store. Stripped of any expectations of a recognizably meaningful existence, Adrian's life now unfolded in a state of constant attrition that extended as far as he could see. Basic self-maintenance became the dream, but one that was so ungraspable that Adrian could only imagine its realization in a distant elsewhere—in an unnamed country where custodians were in demand and paid a decent wage. In an era of global capitalism when acceleration is life, Adrian's displacement from the market pressed him into a space that resonated with Lauren Berlant's notion of "slow death," in which the physical wearing out of a population is the defining condition of its experience and historical existence.[2]

This chapter, then, is not about suicide or biological death as such; rather, it is about enduring social death and the widely shared structure of feeling brought about by having to live through the prolonged experience of one's own "dying out."[3] The homeless's state of being "bored with life" provides a window into the affective dimensions of biopolitics amid a brutally competitive global economy. *Biopolitics*, Michel Foucault taught, refers to the logic and practice by which governing bodies cultivate certain population segments through investments in health, education, and security, for example, while pruning those other segments perceived as internal threats to society's flourishing.[4] *Pruning* here refers to efforts made (and not made) to expose the unskilled, the elderly, or the otherwise superfluous to foreseeable hardships that ultimately bring about an early death. In sharp contrast to an execution, where the condemned is the subject of immediate sovereign power, those exposed to a biopolitical state of "letting die" are simply ignored.[5] Chronic neglect may be a passive act, but it nevertheless holds a fatal power. Letting die is capable of effecting an early death on the scale of a population, such as the homeless. Of critical importance is that the slow, drawn-out trauma of letting die does not generate social concern the way that sudden catastrophes such as an earthquake or a tsunami might. This is because letting die unfolds along an almost imperceptibly slow horizon, one that becomes synchronized into the everyday rhythm of life.[6] Biopolitical decisions to underproduce public housing, restrict participation in the labor market, scale back government protections, or limit family care, for example, do not kill the unproductive and unwanted in sudden, eye-catching ways.[7] These decisions instead open up spaces where deterioration becomes the defining condition of everyday life.[8] Living through the wearing out of life is an excruciatingly slow affair, one that affects the senses in this moment of global consumerism in deathly dull ways.

Bored with Life

"I'm bored—everyday I'm bored with life," Anton lamented distantly. We stood at the bus stop located next to Backwoods. Anton would soon have to vacate the shelter because he had reached its newly implemented six-month residency limit. In his early fifties, Anton was too young to receive a pension, but his body was too old and too worn for him to land a day's work on the black market, much less a stable position in the formal economy. Still, on the advice of a social worker, Anton planned to take a bus into the city to see if he could drum up any leads. He was not at all optimistic. "I don't have anything, no relationships, I don't know anyone. One of the social workers asked if I had family in the countryside who would take me in and find me some work, and I don't even have that. If, God forbid, I die tonight, no one would look for me—no one would be interested in me. *I don't have anyone,*" Anton stressed, his voice rising to shout over the sound of a car rushing past. Anton had become estranged from his family three years earlier upon divorcing his wife. As was common among Bucharest's homeless, Anton left the house and half of his savings to his ex-wife and children. The divorce did not leave Anton with much with which to re-establish himself. As work became more difficult to find in the aftermath of the financial crisis, Anton started living on the streets. "I have no pension, I have no job, I have no place to stay—and that's the most painful," Anton admitted, shifting his gaze down the road, presumably to see if the bus was coming. Instead, a string of cars came up on the horizon. "There is nothing for me anymore," Anton continued, his eyes following the cars as they whipped past. "I really think I should throw myself in front of traffic to just finish with this life, because I have nothing to do in what's left of it. I don't know what to do or even what else I can do. When I look at a road, I don't even know which way to go because it doesn't matter. I am completely demoralized, ruined, finished." He continued to stand waiting for the bus to pull up.

Like for Adrian, Anton's state of being "bored with life" was punctuated by violent language of death and self-destruction. It was a state of being that captured the internalization of the homeless's exclusion not only from the present but also from the foreseeable future and from all social mediums that would otherwise provide, in the words of Pierre Bourdieu, "recognition, consideration, in other words, quite simply, reasons for being."[9] Displaced from all but the most marginal vectors of Romania's new globally oriented economy, homeless men and women like Anton came to feel dead not just to the city surrounding them. These men and women had been squeezed out of participation in the market-driven activities that now animated so much of city life. The homeless no longer worked, as their upbringing under socialism had ingrained in them that they should, nor did they partake in the pleasures of consumption that the heightened consumerism of postsocialism celebrated. In the absence of a job, and the steady income that comes with it, these men could not support a family household, and they struggled to sustain long-established friendships. Instead of being energized by the New York minute that incorporated Bucharest's upwardly mobile, homeless men and women who had been dumped by globally competitive markets instead drifted down along their city's streets, feeling completely estranged from their surroundings.

A conversation with Costel, a low-skilled laborer in his late forties, on a hot July afternoon illustrated as much. Sitting on a stretch of lawn in the courtyard of Stefan's Place, in the shade of some brush, Costel explained matter-of-factly: "Believe me, my life is saturated with total boredom. I no longer have desires. I mean, it's hard when there's nothing to eat. If I had a piece of bread or sausage or a can of something, I could take pleasure in knowing that I won't have to sleep with an empty stomach." Costel trained his eyes on his hands as he rubbed them slowly together, intermittently clapping them softly before rubbing them together again. "I avoid most of my old friends. What are we even supposed to talk about? When you have a job you always have something to sit and talk about over a beer or a coffee at a terrace bar or whatever. But what am I supposed to do now? Go and tell people that I'm homeless—tell my friends all about my problems? That I can't even afford to buy the drink that's in my hand?" Costel asked rhetorically while lifting the cold bottle of cola that I had bought from a nearby kiosk for him to drink while we chatted. After a pause to gather his thoughts, Costel continued, "As it is, I go to the park, sit on a bench, and stay there all day sitting on my ass. This is the most boring thing one can do, so I read a paper, and then another, and then I finish them all. I read each paper that I find from cover to cover." Costel chortled when I asked what he did next. "I read them again. What else can I do? This boredom is a state—a situation in which you have nothing to do and nowhere to go." Costel turned his focus off into the distance. He narrowed his eyes, and the faint grin fell from his face. He continued in a more solemn tone, "It makes you want a sudden death or, if I could, to die by a lethal injection so that I could just be done with this life." He took another sip from his cold drink before returning eye contact.

Costel's description of boredom gives credence to quotidian phrases like *deathly dull* and *tortuously dull*, and it marks out a literal core of lived experience otherwise used in hyperbolic sentiments, such as being "bored to death"—exaggerations so often expressed by the middle class when meetings drag, planes are delayed, or the Internet cuts out. His description also shows how boredom can be a kind of traumatic suffering that is difficult to convey and the remedy for which seems entirely out of one's hands. As opposed to the bombastic utterances of bourgeois ennui, Costel articulated through boredom the inwardly felt harm of radical displacement not only from the urban and the national economy but also from the global economy. This is a kind of harm to which Costel was subjected externally through the logic of competitive labor markets, the politics of distribution in a consumer society, and the imposition of austerity measures that limit how long can be spent in a shelter, for example, but also through personal choices motivated by the shame of homelessness.[10] For his part, Costel actively chose not to maintain certain friendships because he lacked the money to buy a beer at the bar, as well as the work-related stories these friends would expect him to tell while drinking that beer. Rather than trying to maintain his relationships by organizing get-togethers around ostensibly free activities, such as strolling through Herăstrău Park or hanging out at the Gara de Nord, for example, Costel allowed his friendships to slowly dwindle alongside his cash reserves. As familiar faces drifted away, a deeply alienating sense of boredom set in.

Victor, a manual laborer in his late sixties, echoed this sentiment. While standing in an underground pedestrian passage in central Bucharest sipping instant Nescafé from a grab-and-go kiosk, Victor admitted to me that his daily routine left him feeling bored with life. When unsuccessful at landing day labor on the black market, which was the case most of the time, Victor spent his days circulating between the waiting rooms of institutions whose services he did not require. After giving up on the black market in the morning, for example, Victor would move to the parking lot of Stefan's Place for the remainder of the day, then along to the train station for the evening, only to spend his nights sleeping on a bench in the hospital waiting room. These places offered warmth, water, and restroom facilities. These spaces also enabled Victor to stay seated for long stretches of time and provided reasonably convenient locations to meet up with other acquaintences living on the street. These venues were also good for the occasional free meal. However, living out one's life in a series of institutional waiting rooms lent itself to an existential crisis. Victor described a persistent state of boredom that elicited fidgeting at some moments and long, glassy stares at others, as well as, in quieter moments, questions as to whether life itself was worth living at all. Victor stated, "It's a permanent boredom from having nothing to do—there is just nothing to do here in Romania. Sometimes I think it would be better to throw myself into the river and be done with it." The specific image of drowning in the Dâmbo-vița River, which passes through central Bucharest, gained added salience a month after our conversation when Victor confided to me that his youngest daughter had drowned accidentally a few years earlier while swimming in those waters. She had just graduated from college. "Now I walk the city. I steal some things and try to sell them," Victor explained unapologetically. "I looked for work, but no one wants to hire a sixty-seven-year-old. Believe me, I tried. The truth of the matter is that life in Romania is just somber, grim, dark. We are all beaten to the bone." With that he tossed his now-empty cup of Nescafé onto the floor and made his way to the train station.

In a state of being bored with life, Bucharest's homeless spent their days waiting for biology to mirror their social status. Bucharest's homeless lived as though dead to the city because they lacked the means to participate in the market-oriented practices that now organized it. Boredom with life affectively registered the homeless's radical social displacement from a consumer society. This state of being bored with life took on an indefinite quality as the homeless came to understand themselves as unwanted by global circuits of production and of consumption, not only in the present but also for the foreseeable future. These men and women were, in the words of Zygmunt Bauman, redundant, and redundancy carries far different connotations than does mere unemployment: "Where the prefix 'un' in 'unemployment' used to suggest a departure from the norm—as in 'unhealthy' or 'unwell'—there is no such suggestion in the notion of 'redundancy.'... 'Redundancy' whispers permanence and hints at the ordinariness of the condition."[11] Low-skilled manual laborers who were needed under communism no longer had a viable foothold in a moment of brutal, market-driven competition—and it was highly unlikely that their labor would ever be re-absorbed into new capitalist sectors of growth, such as business services or retail work.[12] Not only had Anton, Costel, Victor, and others outlived their utility to production, but they were also unnecessary to satisfy the demands of global consumerism. These men were superfluous to the needs of global capital, and as such, they had been discarded as the waste of a bygone era.[13] No further investment was made into their well-being.[14]

Redundant

"We are the sacrificed generation—those born in the fifties and sixties," Costel started, his hand hovering above his eyes in an effort to ease his squinting from the summer sunlight. Our regular meetings at Stefan's Place afforded us ample time to reflect on Romania's changing economy. "We did all right until communism ended in '89–'90," Costel continued. "Now we wait at churches and nongovernmental organizations for a plate of food. And that's all the help we get. We cannot speak of social aid from the state," he added disappointedly. Too old to compete in the global economy but not old enough to qualify for a pension, Costel was at a loss as to how to support himself. Lacking market value and social protections, this cohort of men had been pushed onto the street without any clear idea of how to get back into regular work and housing. Once they had been cast aside, life became infinitely more precarious: "A lot of people come here from other cities like Constanţa, Timişoara, Braşov, to find work," Costel elaborated, noting that the capital had long served as a place of incorporation into the Romanian economy. "And so Bucharest is a very crowded city now. There are too many people looking for work and not enough jobs. It's almost impossible to find work here." The problem, Costel went on to admit, was larger than simple arithmetic. Aside from a swelling pool of low-skilled workers aggregating in the capital and tilting the labor market in Bucharest to the employer's advantage, there was also a larger shift in the type of work on offer. Heavy industry—the base of urban employment under communism—collapsed after the revolution. "I mean, look around you," Costel continued, "the work we were accustomed to under Ceauşescu no longer exists. Back then you had a job, you had a salary, and you had them indefinitely. You were not at a loss for work. Everyone had his fate, and he went about his day, with a purpose." A manual laborer under communism, Costel was always in demand. The Communist Party, after all, structured

FIGURE 4.2. Squatting in an abandoned building. Photo by Bruce O'Neill.

the economy around universal employment, reflecting the sensibility that all labor is useful. In that spirit, central planners flooded factory floors and construction sites in an effort to maximize the availability of productive labor. There were idle moments during communism, to be sure, when there was not enough work to go around during a particular shift, but this down-time was momentary and passing. It was an idle period in which those not immediately needed stood on reserve before being called back into the service of production. "That's not the case anymore," Costel assessed. "The passing from communism to capitalism was sudden—my generation got caught staring into the sun. Many companies changed hands, and jobs disappeared, factories disappeared. My job disappeared. Many places that used to hire aren't anymore," Costel added grimly.

While deprivation in earlier modes of production served to exploit labor, dangerously limiting personal consumption in order to pressure laborers into performing dirty, underpaid, or otherwise undesirable work, Bucharest's homeless needed no such encouragement.[15] Shaped first by twentieth-century socialism and then by twenty-first-century neoliberalism, these men had a thoroughly ingrained labor fetish. Their sense of masculine self-worth was tied up in their brute capacity to dig, push, and lift day in and day out. Simply put, these men believed in the importance of hard work, and they were not afraid to get their hands dirty. The problem, however, was that there was little need in Bucharest for the long and grueling low-skilled manual labor that they were primed to perform, and it is not at all obvious that one-time brick polishers and cement mixers could be retrained to have the cultural capital necessary to sell sweaters at the mall or serve espresso at a terrace café. Deprivation, in this moment, did not discipline labor to work longer or harder, or to do dirtier work, but rather punished those workers for lacking the youth and the varied skill set presently prized by the market. Conversations with Victor, Mișu, and Anton confirmed as much.

"I was a mechanic during communism," Anton explained while perched on a park bench. "I worked in a Dacia [car] factory in town. Work was never a question. I always had work, but then all of those factories closed down. Life got harder, but I could manage odd jobs here and there," he explained with a sense of pride in his ability to scrape by through tuning engines here and there while laying bricks on the side. "But then the [financial] crisis hit, and now it's impossible. My social worker told me to go to an employment center to see if there's a job somewhere for someone with my specialization. I went, but there were about fifteen other guys looking for the same kind of work. And, anyway, there are few companies that need a machinist like me. What are my chances of finding a job that actually uses my expertise?" he asked with exasperation. His fingers grew antsy and drummed the seat of the bench. "So I no longer even look for the specialized kind of work I'm trained to do. Now I don't even know what to look for. I just take what I can get."

As work opportunities contracted, and as production shifted away from the factory floor, the manual labor jobs that remained became increasingly "flexible." Factory and construction work ceased to be stable, full-time occupations; instead, industry moved toward more short-term contract work. While regular employment continued to be a normative expectation for this aging cohort, it became increasingly difficult to find. While those with a pension exited the labor market, aging workers unable to retire and failing to compete found their expectation of regular employment cutting against the experience of redundancy. This state of redundancy, in day-to-day life, meant living through the inability to act out one's expectation of regular work. Whatever activities Costel did undertake as he passed the time registered as doing nothing at all. Unpredictable periods of short-term work provided brief moments of relief from being redundant. Costel explained, "Now there is very little work, and the work you can find is for a definite period—a few days, a week, maybe a month. If you get a month of consistent work, then enjoy it, because otherwise there is no continuity. You no longer have certainty about tomorrow or the day after."

Younger workers shut out of the formal economy merely reoriented themselves toward the black market. Contractors extended fairly regular work to those with young backs and fresh knees who were willing to put in an elongated day for a substandard wage. This option was not available to this older cohort of men, however. Even on the black market the older cohort remained uncompetitive and unwanted, making the difference between redundancy and relegation to the informal economy ever more palpable. Limiting Costel's, Anton's, and Victor's ability to find work was not only that their skill set has fallen out of demand, leaving them to fight for only the lowest-paid and most menial of jobs, but also that their bodies were interpreted by employers, and now by themselves, as physically spent and unable to be retrained. Costel elaborated, "I know I have to adapt. I readjusted myself, and I try to learn new things along the way. I'm trying to reapply my knowledge elsewhere, to change my entire mentality. I cannot expect something from above. I don't want to sit around all day and do nothing. I'm tired of waiting. I tell you, it's the most boring thing one can do." Costel shifted his weight from side to side as he collected his thoughts, gingerly extending out his hip in an effort to work out a knot in his lower back. He had been sitting most of the morning on a curb without any support. "But what other opportunities do I have?" he continued. "At my age, who wants to hire me for physical work? You have a better chance of getting work if you're under fifty. Even if you're educated, employers prefer the young."

Mișu agreed. In his late forties, Mișu was also regularly passed over on the black market in favor of his younger counterparts. While smoking a cigarette in the Stefan's Place parking lot, Mișu admitted, "Every day I wait for work at the black market. I have to wait two or three days on average to land a day of hard work. For example, I might get hired to lay some tiles. And that pays very little—fifty lei ($15). And at this age, and with this crisis, I don't expect my situation to improve. Life in Romania is just shit—it only whips you down." Anton expressed the same sentiment, albeit in more brutal terms: "No one wants to hire me. My legs aren't well—I have water in my knees. There is no work for me to do. At fifty-three my life is over. There's work for a handful of younger men, but the rest are finished."

Costel, Anton, and Mişu confirmed all too well Bauman's observation that "for anyone who is once excluded and assigned to waste there are no obvious return paths to a fully fledged membership. Nor are there any alternative, officially endorsed and mapped roads one could follow (or for that matter, be forced to follow) towards an alternative title of belonging."[16] Once one has been displaced by the state and the globally competitive market alike, there is no forum for return. Instead, one enters into a state of letting die where living life becomes synonymous with life's attrition. "If I go to a hard day's work, then sleep on the street, I can go back for another day, maybe two. But if I do that for a full week, I fall down exhausted. It's cold at night, you only sleep three to four hours. And then you have to get up and work construction?" Mişu asked rhetorically while shaking his head and clucking his tongue. "No, sir—it's impossible. And if you don't have work, you still have to spend the whole day walking: to churches, foundations, and food pantries. Run over here and then run over there to eat. Even that takes it out of you. Even at the end of those days I'm still dead tired, but I don't get paid for all of that effort!" he exclaimed. "You can keep up that kind of routine if you sleep in a house, have heat, eat three meals a day on time, go to the bathroom on time, but otherwise you wear out quickly." And wear out they did, underfed, underrested, and overexposed to the summer heat and the winter chill. The competitive global marketplace did not reshape these laboring bodies to be lean and mean. Instead, it left these unwanted workers haggard.

In a state of redundancy, Romania's oldest cohort of street homeless men existed not as a reserve army of labor to be recycled and folded back into production in any substantive or permanent way but as the living remnants of another era. Costel, Anton, and Mişu had been displaced onto the street in a state of letting die. "There is no security anymore, no sense of where food might come from tomorrow. I have no perspective on the future. There is nothing else for me to do but sleep, sit, and walk the streets," Costel admitted with a matter-of-fact tone. Not only did the trauma of letting die wear away their sore joints, breed infected wounds, and promote persistent hacking coughs, but it also became embodied through the senses as an unshakable monotony, a loss of direction, and the emptiness of unmet expectations. Letting die proved to be not only a social and material condition but also a structure of feeling that grinded away at people's sense of what it means to have a life.

"Let me give you an example of what I mean," Costel began in response to my prompt to describe what being bored with life was like. "You wake up at six o'clock at a mission. You eat, you drink a coffee. In exchange for your stay, you have to do some cleaning, so you grab a broom or a mop and make the place clean. At eight o'clock you have to leave. You're not allowed to stay any later, but where are you going to go?" he dramatized by rolling his eyes back and throwing his hands in the air. "You look this way and then that way, and then you slowly move where your eyes settle, because there is nowhere else to go. If the weather is all right, you find yourself at a park. Again, you look left, and then you look right. You read the newspaper all the way through, and you smoke some cigarette butts you found on the sidewalk. At some point you see what you can do for food." The strategy, Costel explained, shifted during rain and snow, but the affect remained roughly the same. "When it rains or it's bitterly cold in winter, you can sit on the bus while it circles the city, or you can just stand in a Metro station. Sometimes I pace in the supermarket, not that I have the money to buy anything. But you just do that while you wait for night when you can head back to the mission, if you have a spot, or you find a stairwell in a[n apartment] block to spend the night. The next day you have to do the same thing. It keeps going on and on like that," Costel lamented.

Anton described a similar experience of days reduced to aimlessly pacing the city: "I walk through the city every day, and every day I'm bored with it. I probably walk ten kilometers a day, but what else can I do? I walk here and there and try to forget my problems. I try to imagine my family, a place to stay . . ." Anton's voice trailed off as he pursed his lips. "But wherever I go my problems follow me. My entire day is spent walking like this. And it leaves me so tired. At night, I fall down from fatigue and sleep like a log."

Stripped of the bourgeois connotations expressed in Walter Benjamin's flâneur, this endless walking served not as a distraction, a mental stimulant, nor even as an example of "passing the time," but as an embodied expression of displacement.[17] It contributed to, rather than relieved, the homeless's sense of boredom. The redeeming quality of this walking was that it brought about sleep—an inanimate state in which existence was, quite mercifully it would seem, likened to wood. In this state of displacement, the world slowed, conjuring thoughts of death. Costel attested, "Your life gets spent waiting unendingly. You begin to walk slower and slower, up to a point when you get so bored that you want to leave the world. You know that life on the street has made you into something other than you were. That's it, and that's not good for anything—not for your mind or your body."

Like a still-functioning typewriter in the digital age, it was not quite clear to these men, much less to their potential employers, what purpose they still serve. Their apparent irrelevance to the urban, national, and global economies was confirmed by the fact that no one is investing in them: not the state, not private corporations, not even their families. Displaced to the margins of the city, these men had little to do beyond living through the slow attrition of whatever remained of their life.

The Social World of Social Death

Bucharest's homeless described the state of being bored with life in stark terms of disconnection, inactivity, and isolation. The way Costel, Anton, Adrian, and others narrated their boredom suggests that letting die is an asocial experience—one somehow situated within a vacuum of social relationships and practices. These narratives, however, belied the intensely social process of letting die, for just as boredom registered disconnections from work and home, family and friends, for example, boredom also captured the proliferation of alternative sets of social relationships. These included relationships with other homeless men and women, aid workers, contractors, religious figures, and the bureaucratic institutions within which all of these actors were situated, such as monasteries, day centers, shelters, and construction sites. These relationships tended to drop out of the homeless's narratives on boredom because, quite simply, they were the wrong kinds of relationships. The social attachments forged once a person became homeless did not support a return to any recognizable vision of the good life to which these men ascribed, visions marked by incorporation into the life of the city and of the global economy rather than expressing displacement from them. The attachments that proliferated in homeless shelters, day centers, and black labor markets instead had a way of bringing into view the clear detachment from work and home, but also an urban life organized around practices of consumption.[18]

Time and again, the homeless's boredom narratives treated the social and material space of the margins as though it were a photographic negative. When taking a snapshot, Walter Benjamin observed, one "manages only to register the negative of that essence on photographic plates."[19] A snapshot, then, not only creates a photograph that indexes the people and places that fall within its frame, but it also records a negative image. The negative is a liminal space hidden away in the nonplaces of darkrooms and film canisters that reveals a world inverted, one where presence appears as absence just as light appears as darkness. To make sense of the homeless's boredom narratives, which were marked by claims of totalizing social disconnection over and against their observable connections forged at shelters and on black labor markets, it is productive to view the ethnographic record as a negative. This means interpreting boredom narratives as the taking of a snapshot, one that records an inverted social world, whereby the present actors and activities serve as a dark background against which the displacements and disconnections that make up the homeless state of being bored with life are brought to light.[20]

A SNAPSHOT

I met Costel and Sorin around five in the morning at the black market, where they waited in the hopes of landing a day of construction work off the books. About twenty men in total gathered at the square that morning. They scattered into a series of small circles of conversation. I joined Sorin in a group discussing various construction sites around town. One man pulled out a plastic water bottle filled with brandy and took a gulp before passing it around. As the bottle circulated, he bragged that it was "good clean *țuică*" that he had been given while visiting family in the countryside the week before. After taking a hearty sip, Costel went off to a corner store down the block to buy a round of Nescafé for himself and two others. When he returned from the store, Costel did not collect money for the coffees because he owed his two colleagues from the day before. The men alternated drinking coffee and *țuică* as they chatted. The combination of caffeine and liquor had the desirable effect of numbing us to the autumn chill without leaving anyone drowsy.

A loud and barrel-chested man in his thirties, who went by the nickname "the Bear" (*ursul*), joined our circle. Bear had an uproarious laugh

FIGURE 4.3. Standing around. Photo by Bruce O'Neill.

that quickly followed friendly digs directed toward Costel and other familiar faces. Bear held a two-liter bottle of beer in his hand, which he extended in offers of apology when his pointed efforts at poking fun missed the mark and came across as needling. When Costel introduced me to Bear as his "American friend," Bear's eyes lit up. "Americans have money!" he exclaimed with a wide grin and a belly laugh. He took his rucksack off of his back, set it on the ground, and opened it so that I could note its contents. It was filled with illicit goods. "You see, I'm like a bear in the woods," he explained with a rolling chuckle. "I take what I need to survive!" Those listening laughed aloud as Bear handed me his bottle of beer. I took a swig while he laid out his lifted wares: a bottle of cologne bearing a Carrefour sticker, a knockoff Nokia cell phone peddled in Metro stations at the time, a windbreaker, and a pair of women's heels in a shoebox marked size 8 narrow. He asked if I saw anything that I liked, assuring me that prices were negotiable. I politely declined while those watching continued to laugh. Bear collected his wares and took back his bottle of beer, promising to let me know if he came across anything more interesting. The other men carried on mixing alcohol and caffeine in an effort to ready themselves for a full day of manual labor on empty stomachs and without much sleep.

At about half past seven, a contractor drove up to the square in a black van. When the contractor exited and made his way toward the waiting men, the small circles converged into a single crowd. Each shouted their credentials in an effort to appear part of the reserve army of labor rather than the lumpen proletariat. The contractor shouted above the clamor that he needed three people for a weekend's worth of work at a construction site in Moldavia, a morning's drive away. For all of Bear's early morning antics, he turned rigidly serious when listening to the job opportunity. While the contractor spoke, Bear gave me a nudge. He showed me the calluses on his hands while he whispered to me, "I can move twice as much as anyone here." He then stepped forward. Bear's formidable size and known reputation for consistently hard work made him a regular pick for contractors visiting the square. The contractor looked Bear up and down before nodding approvingly in his direction. The contractor then charged Bear with the task of picking two others to join him on the trip. A number of men pleaded with Bear to come along, mobilizing tones of interpersonal familiarity in the hopes of tilting Bear's judgment in their favor. One voice even reminded Bear of the thirty-cent coffee he had just bought him that morning. Costel, by contrast, turned away from the sudden commotion. When I later asked why he was not hustling for Bear's attention, Costel offered a dramatic eye roll before explaining to me, "They'll drive you all the way out there to work and then not pay you. Or even if they do pay you, they probably won't drive you back to Bucharest. These guys are going to earn just enough to pay for their bus ticket back to Bucharest. I don't trust it." While Costel chafed, Bear had little difficulty identifying two others willing to make the trip. The chosen three crawled into the back of the contractor's van. When the doors shut, the van's tinted windows rendered them instantly invisible.[21] The rest of the men continued to wait at the square.

At about eight o'clock, with the likelihood of additional work offers dwindling by the minute, Sorin and Costel invited me to head over to Stefan's Place with them for the rest of the morning. We walked through central Bucharest to a major intersection to catch the bus. We arrived at Stefan's

Place about half an hour later. Roughly a dozen men and a few women were already waiting to be let into the courtyard when Stefan's Place opened at nine. Some claimed to have arrived hours earlier to ensure their place for the evening meal offered on Fridays. Stefan's Place could guarantee a plate of food only to the first twenty names on the meal list. While waiting for Stefan's Place to open, Costel exchanged light chatter with a group of men who had set up a squatter camp nearby, while others eavesdropped. Those listening quietly to Costel shook their heads knowingly as he described the bleak morning on the black market and sympthetically when Costel recounted the suspect offer to work a weekend in Moldavia. Sorin, for his part, paced along the far side of the street with Ion, a man who squatted nearby. The two searched for discarded cigarette butts in order to harvest any usable tobacco that might remain.

Iulian, an administrator, opened the front gate of Stefan's Place just after nine. Homeless beneficiaries filed into the parking lot and quickly formed a single-file line. Iulian took down names on two separate lists: one for the evening meal and another for those requesting to use the Stefan's Place shower. The line dispersed once the available slots for both had been taken. Costel and some others left immediately after registering for the meal, planning to return at four o'clock to receive their servings. In the interim, this group headed toward the Gara de Nord, where an evangelical minister offered a noon meal near the station. Others, like Sorin, who wanted to take a shower or speak with a social worker or health-care provider, sat atop the retaining wall in the Stefan's Place parking lot to wait their turn. Some read tabloids, while others chatted among themselves. One by one, beneficiaries cycled through the medical clinic, exiting with pocket-sized wax paper bags containing donated vitamins and expired pain relievers. They also rotated through the shower facility. Sorin smoked the tobacco he had recovered earlier from off the ground, which he had rerolled in some newspaper. He gave the second half of his hand-rolled cigarette to Dinu in exchange for the second half of Dinu's bottle of cola.

Around ten in the morning, Iulian dragged several black plastic trash bags out of storage and set them next to the parking lot. The bags contained clothes donated by a pentecostal church in Florida. Iulian stepped back from the donated bags and invited the two dozen beneficiaries present to search through them. Those in the lot quickly crowded around the free clothing, weeding through the bags for useful garments in a relevant size. Boots were the first to be taken, then coats, sweatshirts, and heavy socks, and finally unstained T-shirts and underwear. Odd-sized or stained items were left behind. Iulian consolidated the uncollected articles into a single trash bag and returned them to storage. Iulian later assured me that every item gets claimed at some point.

The showers closed at noon; however, those who had registered for the evening meal continued to wait at Stefan's Place until half past four, when it was served. A few napped in the shade while others read and reread the paper. Men chatted about where they had worked the last few days and where some additional jobs might be found. The effects of the morning binge on brandy and Nescafé had long dissipated, leaving Sorin in the lurch. Talk of boredom abounded as those in the parking lot spent another day waiting. In search of something to do, Sorin took a push broom out of a storage closet and swept the parking lot of fallen leaves and the remnants of discarded cigarettes. In exchange, Iulian offered Sorin his gratitude.

The food, donated by a nearby restaurant, arrived at four o'clock, as did those who had spent the day at the train station. Even those who did not make it onto the reservation list returned in case there were extra portions of hot food to be allocated (which there were not). Iulian offered an additional five people tubes of crackers from Stefan's Place's store of donated boxed foods. After the meal, men and women drifted off in small groups, heading toward the transit stations, parks, and monasteries for the night.

I joined Sorin on his way to the Gara de Nord station. A bar located inside the station made a single television visible from the hall, giving non-customers an opportunity to watch something while they waited, ostensibly for a train. Sorin and I joined a group of other homeless men (several of whom had been at the black market earlier that day) in the hall to watch a soccer match. Bottles of brandy and beer circulated cautiously so as not to draw the attention of the station's private security guards. At the end of the match, Sorin headed into one of the station's twenty-four-hour fast-food restaurants, where he spent the equivalent of half a dollar on a cup of coffee. He was less interested in the hot, watery liquid than the cup and the receipt that came with it. These objects evidenced to the private security guards patrolling the restaurant that he was a paying customer allowed to sit at a table and to use the bathroom, as opposed to a loiterer to be pushed out. Sorin claimed a seat in the back corner. Although the spot was brightly lit and situated beneath a speaker playing loud American pop music, Sorin chose the table because it was the most secure. Sorin tucked his bags into the corner, and he folded his receipt neatly and put it in his chest pocket

FIGURE 4.4. Railway station bar. Photo by Bruce O'Neill.

for safekeeping. He then positioned his purchased cup of coffee conspicuously in front of him before lowering his head onto his folded arms. He closed his eyes and hoped for sleep. Loud pop music and bright halogen light showered down from the ceiling above him, doing their best to keep Sorin awake.

READING THE NEGATIVE

The picture that emerges from a snapshot of Sorin's and Costel's day is both decidedly active and social: they were enmeshed in a dense constellation of relationships organized around informal institutions such as the black market, central city landmarks such as the railway station, transnational aid organizations such as Stefan's Place, and the local and transnational businesses and churches that donate to them. In these places, Sorin and Costel affirmed relationships with other homeless men mediated by gift exchanges of mundane commodities like beer, coffee, and tobacco purchased in kiosks and grab-and-go stores but also homemade brandy procured from relatives in the countryside. They watched soccer matches on flat-screen televisions with friends, and they patronized fast-food restaurants. They even acted as entrepreneurial subjects who sought to contract out their labor and who exercised discretion in deciding to pursue (or not) offers to work.

The ethnographic record posits a subject that, far from being inert and awash in solitude, as the talk of boredom suggests, was embedded in a variety of activities, interactions, and relationships. The ethnographic fact is that as Sorin and Costel became displaced from home and work, family and friends, they also became entangled in alternative ties with people, places, and things. These alternative ties were made durable through daily enactments of looking for labor, contributing to economies of favors, and bartering, but also through more mundane practices like reading, pacing, scavenging, smoking, and drinking. Even when conducted alone, these mundane social practices nevertheless provided a means for Sorin, Costel, and other homeless men to participate in the global consumption chains of a number of commodities—from tobacco to news media to donated food, clothing, and pharmaceuticals. These practices connected the homeless to people and places at a variety of scales, from the immediacy of the Stefan's Place parking lot, to the local restaurants that donated meals, to family members in the countryside who supplied bottles of brandy, to middle-class American churchgoers who offered up their unwanted Gap branded clothing, to the foreign nongovernmental organization that administered Stefan's Place and the corporate donors that filled the shelves of its storage closet. It would not be ethnographically inaccurate to sit those who purport to be bored to death down and point out a basic contradiction in their worldview: although these men experienced homelessness as a deeply felt boredom tied to the withering away of social relations, they were, in fact, thoroughly engaged in the production of a dynamic set of alternative relations that stretched throughout the city and the country, as well as across borders and oceans. They were, in an ethnographically observable way, fully caught up in a global order.

Such an analysis bends toward the optimistic by focusing on the productive agency of a vulnerable population as a way of foregrounding the homeless's endurance, creativity, and empowerment. This decidedly etic perspective, however, stands completely at odds with the structure of feeling under which these global relations unfold. Rather than being stimulated, Sorin and Costel were bored, and rather than being immersed in a richly complex social milieu, they insisted that they were cut off. By foregrounding a politics of activity, this ethnographic record misses the point of the homeless's existential angst. These men were not bored because they failed to see the people with whom they engaged or the places and things with which they interacted on a daily basis. Rather, their boredom was tied to concerns about the many ways in which they were inactive, and the long-held relationships they could no longer afford to maintain but would otherwise enjoy. An ethnographic analysis that bends, ever so optimistically, toward themes of alternative production and entanglement over and above the politics of inactivity and disconnection has the unwanted effect of talking over the very concerns that organize the homeless's engagement with globalization. Such an approach infuses the homeless's sense of emptiness with a meaning and purpose that they themselves neither celebrate nor recognize.[22]

The homeless's emic sense of a troubling absence of activity begins to make sense only when the ethnographic record is viewed as a negative, so that actually present attachments serve as a backdrop against which the displacements organizing their world can be brought into view. For example, the relationships forged in the early hours while waiting for work off the books have a way of reminding a working-class sensibility that one is in fact not stably employed. Offers of a weekend's worth of employment get interpreted as a mirage, an opportunity to work for money when there is no intention on the part of the employer to actually pay it. Trash bags filled with donated sweaters, as well as restaurants that give away food, served in parking lots on thin and buckling paper plates, call to mind one's inability to shop in a store for the clothes one needs or to order off a menu the food one actually wants to eat. A soccer match observed while standing outside a bar only underscores these men's inability to walk through the door, order a beer, and take a seat, just as a night spent sleeping on a fast-food restaurant's table stiffly conveys that there is no home with a bed to sink deep into. The social world in which Bucharest's homeless partook was so thoroughly detached from the coordinates of work and home established over a lifetime of steady employment that the new coordinates produced once they were living on the streets failed miserably to measure up by comparison. These new attachments to people, places, and activities were, from the homeless's perspective, not worth acknowledging. Contrasted with the expectations of a working-class life that one believed should be obtainable (but that was not), the social connections that were forged while managing, with limited success, the hunger, harassment, and other symptoms of life's wearing out rung hollow. Time and again, rather than revel in a social world on the streets, Bucharest's homeless were most deeply affected by the troubling absences and deafening silences of what was not present in their lives but ought to have been. Rather than the melancholia of loss, boredom took hold as the newly homeless wrestled with their displacement from their enduring attachments to the people and places that constituted their sense of what it meant to keep on living.[23]

Boredom and the Continuum of Violence

"Everyday I feel bored with this life. And so twice I tried to kill myself," Mişu started to explain. We leaned against a retaining wall at Stefan's Place one morning in early December, watching the snow fall around us. Mişu's head was wrapped in bloodied bandages. He had suffered an accident while working off the books at a construction site a few days before. While Mişu had made it to the hospital on his own, he could afford neither the prescription painkillers to manage his aches nor a supply of fresh gauze to keep his injury clean. I sat with Mişu while he waited at the day center to have his injury re-dressed. "Once I tried to hang myself, and the other time I tried with pills," he recalled. "I mixed fifty-six pills with alcohol. Do you understand what that looks like? I grabbed a handful of pills and then took a mouthful of vodka, and then another handful of pills and then more vodka. I drank half a liter before I fell into a coma. I spent three days in that coma, and I don't remember anything from those days. Only the tubes—there were infusions to clean out all of those toxins." After a short pause, with the snow still swirling around us, Mişu started again: "I tried hanging myself two years before that. I hung myself, but some friends found me shortly after and cut me down. When they found me I only had a few more moments to live." With a sarcastic snort, Mişu noted, "I've learned that if God doesn't want to take you then you cannot die. Twice I tried and failed. . . . I was tired of living in this world."

Boredom emerged for Bucharest's homeless as a traumatizing social relationship born out of having been cut off from sites of meaning making and excluded from participating in all but the most marginal dimensions of the city but also of the global economy. Rather than maintaining households

FIGURE 4.5. Contemplating. Photo by Bruce O'Neill.

established during a communist past, or partaking in a European standard of living consisting of IKEA furniture, smartphones, and evenings spent drinking at terrace bars as middle-class Romanians now aspired to do, the homeless understood themselves as sitting empty-handed (*stau degeaba*). Without recognizably meaningful ways of passing the time, the homeless internalized as a profound boredom what it meant to lose their foothold in a competitive global economy.

This state of being bored to death that was described by Mişu, Costel, Anton, and others calls to mind a thickening literature in anthropology that documents the human misery built into the regular workings of every-day life.[24] Captured by terms such as *structural violence* and *social suffering*, the distress and affliction of marginalized groups are linked to the violent consequences of political-economic processes like heightened market competition, unemployment, lack of opportunity, and downward social mobility.[25] At the heart of this line of research is a desire to override liberal approaches to injury, suffering, and responsibility, which frame conversations about marginalized actors at the analytical scale of the individual, in order to bring the role of historical forces into view. This includes, for example, economic instability, the scaling back of government protections, the introduction of a competitive labor market, shifts in the forms of labor in demand, and the commodification of social belonging. These historical forces render some people superfluous, displacing them from everyday life and into social spaces defined by the dynamics of letting die. These are physical, and highly marginal, places in the city where the unwanted and uncompetitive must live through the regularized harm and persistent suffering of redundancy.

What a detailed description of being "bored to death" clearly illustrates is how social suffering unfolds within what some have called a "continuum of violence": the overlapping structural, symbolic, and normalized acts of violence that wreak havoc on the everyday lives of the vulnerable.[26] To be sure, the trauma of letting die leaves its mark on the body: underfed, exhausted, and overexposed to the elements, Romania's homeless suffered from malnutrition, gangrene, and tuberculosis, among other ailments.[27] Yet, as Bucharest's homeless testified, poverty also devastates inner worlds. Social exclusion, unmet desires, and ultimately social death corroded all that once animated the homeless's sense of personhood. In a moment of heightened global competition and consumerism, living through the wearing out of life left the homeless feeling bored through and through. Some escaped the affective toll of homelessness through fantasies of drowning and lethal injections; for others, this unending boredom prompted physical movements toward ropes, pills, and liquor. In both instances, boredom proved to be both a symptom of structural violence—a mode of being that was brought about by a distinct set of economic and historical circumstances—and a conduit of structural violence in its own right. Boredom itself became its own torment, an acidic inner state marked by the pronounced lack of even mundane distractions, leaving the affected fully trained upon themselves and their situation within the grim circumstances of poverty.

At its depths, boredom proved to be a place where the inflicted entertain death. After all, as Costel, Adrian, Anton, and others insisted, there did not appear to be any meaningful social obligations for them to meet with what remained of their lives. In the absence of a steady income, these men could not participate as recognizable members of society, and they did not reasonably expect they would be able to obtain a steady income in the future. A competitive market places little value on the labor of aging manual laborers, and these men knew it. "My life is a disaster. It's humiliating," Costel assessed. "The world looks at you, everyone sees that you don't have money, good clothes, a place to wash up, and it changes a man. You come to understand that there's no God, you don't feel anything—pure and simple. You feel nothing but boredom." Redundant in the present, and with no hope of reincorporation in the future, Bucharest's homeless lived as though already dead to the city, the country, and the global order.

This affective suffering is not inflicted by spectacular trauma but was wrought through the mundane (yet persistent) grind of life without work, without home, and without the ability to participate in a social world that increasingly unfolds through practices of consumption. Importantly, the brutality of "letting die" is not a state of exception set apart from society. It is part of the everyday logic of globalization, where heightened market pressures discard the redundant.[28] As the slow wearing out of life became indistinguishable from efforts at reproduction, the homeless felt mired in a dense fog of boredom, and this boredom left them questioning whether their foreseeable future was worth living.

5

BORED STIFF

. . .

To counter the abomination of being poor, why deny it,
we are in duty bound to try everything, to get drunk on anything
we can, cheap wine, masturbation, movies.
—LOUIS-FERDINAND CÉLINE

"Before the crisis, I worked all the time on the black market," Constantin
said. We sat on a bench near a Metro station in Bucharest, Romania, watching professionals come and go at rush hour. Horns honked and tires spun
as anxious drivers waiting through a red light hurried to get back up to
speed once the light turned green. "I put up walls. And I paint and tile too.
But now there's no more work on the black market—there just isn't any
demand for me. And so life is hard. Very hard." Unable to land consistent
work in the city, Constantin had had to give up his studio apartment and
start sleeping on the floors of friends and family. "I no longer have anything to do here in Romania. It's an ugly life. I mean, you can't even go
out on the town and cruise [for women] without money in your pocket,"
Constantin explained as he leaned forward on the bench. "I don't have a
lot of options. I talk on my cell with family and friends for hours on end."
Constantin was not exaggerating. His cell phone bill averaged out to over
five hours of talk time per day. "But at some point I get bored of all that
too, and so I head to the Gara de Nord to fuck hookers (*dă-le în pula mea
de curve*)."[1]

FIGURE 5.1. Morning rush. Photo by Bruce O'Neill.

A few weeks later, down the stairs of that very same Metro station, sat Adi. "I got nothing to do," Adi muttered. "I've been here six hours, and I haven't made any money." As he spoke, Adi folded the bottom of his T-shirt up over the top of his chest to keep cool but also to showcase his core. Barely twenty, Adi started living on the streets shortly after moving to Bucharest. He had arrived a few years earlier after aging out of a Moldavian orphanage. When Adi could not land a job in a factory or on a construction site, he headed into the men's room, where he sold sex to gay Romanian professionals and foreign tourists. Although the work paid well, it was intermittent. Hours, sometimes days, passed between clients. During these stretches of down-time, Adi earned pocket change by servicing Constantin and other home-less men. "I haven't had sex all day," Adi mumbled, "and I'm not looking to get laid. I want money. Money for food. For cigarettes. And I want to have fun too—to go out to the clubs and maybe wear some Adidas. . . . But today there's nothing for me. Just terrible boredom." He sat with his head in his hands as departing passengers hurriedly marched up and out of the station.

Boredom, more than sex, bound these two men together. They were, this chapter argues, bored stiff. By this I mean the ethnographic fact that the politics of social exclusion, and ultimately of social death, unfolded in Bucharest through the inability to participate in consumer practices. This chronic underconsumption left the homeless bored, day in and day out. In an effort to counteract the slowing down of their worlds, men displaced from work and home headed into the bowels of the city's transit hubs in pursuit of a rush. There they organized a market for sexual favors, commodifying *la petite mort* as part of a wider effort to combat the dull but deeply felt sense of *la mort sociale*, if only for a moment.

In Search of Release

DOWNTIME AND FAST MONEY

"Three days ago I had too much money," Adi bragged. We sat at the top of a stalled escalator that led down into a Metro station in the city center. Aloof students gathered nearby, burning the time between classes by sipping coffee, chatting with one another, and perusing rows of kiosks selling used books. I kept Adi company, sitting off to the side while he solicited potential clients. He otherwise spent these moments of self-advertising alone. "There was an Englishman the other day—I got 600 lei ($200) from him right here in this toilet. He gave me €70 and 300 lei in cash after he came!" We sat just above the free public toilet where Adi conducted much of his business. "It only took me two or three minutes, and then I had all this money," he continued to boast while affecting a blasé attitude. "And a few days before that, I found a doctor in the bathroom stalls who gave me another 200 lei ($60) right then and there. The money just comes so quickly." Adi sounded not unlike the kind of get-rich-quick testimonial that is usually heard on Sunday morning infomercials. "And it's so easy! They look at you, and then you make eyes back. And then you ask what they'll pay. If they say 100 or a 150 lei ($30–$45), then let's go!" Adi's bravado crested and then began to break. His grin started to thin, and his voice downshifted. After a pause, Adi shrugged, "But today there's nothing. No money, no clients,

FIGURE 5.2. University Square. Photo by Bruce O'Neill.

nothing. Just terrible boredom." In an effort to shake free from boredom, Adi wiggled his shoulders back and forth in an exaggerated fashion so that his arms danced about like wet noodles.

Despite the heavy foot traffic on this afternoon, Adi did not generate much interest. Hours spent catcalling, flaunting, and preening did little to coax those passing through into the nearby bathroom stalls and to put money in Adi's pocket. "I just want a distraction. Something to smoke, something to drink," Adi explained as the afternoon wore on. "When you drink a cold beer or two, it's like 'another kind of life.' I just want to make enough money to go to a terrace and drink tonight. Instead, I'm stuck here. It makes my head just ache with boredom. It sucks not making any money . . ." Adi's voice trailed off.

Shifting abruptly from the intimate to the explicit, from the earnest to the self-alienating, Adi stopped killing time with me and refocused on the hustle at hand. Emboldened by my company, as both an audience to humor and a foreigner whose presence kept the police at bay, Adi slipped off his T-shirt and started to strut back and forth. He called out loudly to a middle-aged woman walking up the stalled escalator's stairs, "What tits you have! Beefy! (*Ce țâțe ai! Cărnoase!*)." Adi publicly pitched his product to women in an effort to avoid a violent response from an intensely homophobic Romanian public. While Adi directed his catcalls toward women, their sensational content attracted the attention of almost everyone in earshot, providing Adi with an opportunity to catalogue his services to anyone who would listen: "If you got money, I—can—do—all—kinds (*pot să fac orice*)," Adi announced loudly and slowly. He overenunciated each adjective when describing the kinds of sex on offer: "anal, oral, all kinds!" The woman's face began to approximate her scarlet red dress. She shot Adi a disgusted look and hurried past. Some onlookers shook their heads disapprovingly; others chortled and turned away, while a small number laughed aloud and continued to watch in anticipation of what Adi might say to the next round of passengers exiting the Metro station. One twenty-something-year-old man in particular, idling at the base of the escalator near the men's toilet, met Adi's gaze with a prolonged smile. Encouraged, Adi glided down the escalator steps to offer the onlooker a more personalized proposition while I took note from my perch. Moments after Adi's approach, though, the young man's amused face fell flat. He shifted his weight anxiously between his feet and shook his head "no" definitively. Adi turned away and headed back up the escalator steps. "He's just waiting for a friend," Adi explained. After registering a brief but palpable moment of disappointment, Adi continued with his catcalling. "How hot! A woman of the world! Are you *Italiană*?" he hollered to another lady walking past. Adi's eyes avoided the woman's heated face entirely and instead darted back and forth among the onlookers staring around her as he attempted to sort out the amused from the potentially aroused.

Adi and other men in their late teens and early twenties paraded their bodies and whistled in and around transit stations in the hope of securing the attention of a gay foreign tourist or wealthy Romanian professional. A casual encounter with a well-off customer held the potential to generate fast money: windfalls of cash earned in a few frenzied moments in a bathroom stall. On a good day, Adi could earn more in a couple of minutes with a single client than he could from several days of hard labor on a construction site. With a rapidly filled wallet in hand, Adi then had the means to spend the next few days at a bar, a club, or one of the many local casinos found in any neighborhood in Bucharest. Higher-paying clients also raised the possibility of work that extended beyond the restroom stall. Adi boasted to me on another summer day, "Tomorrow I'm going to the seaside with a Frenchman, and I'm going to make money! The last time we went to the seaside together he gave me fifty euros. I also earned more on the side because there were a bunch of other foreigners there too!" Beyond the immediate possibility of a night on the town, the right john also carried the potential to transport Adi from Bucharest to the seaside, from bathroom stalls to hotel rooms, and from the company of homeless Romanians to that of comparatively wealthy foreigners. Adi spent his fast money almost as quickly as he earned it. In these moments, hopping between clubs and beach hotels, Adi got his taste of that "other kind of life" that he imagined as normal among his Western patrons and that Bucharest's aspiring middle class struggled so desperately to emulate. Adi took full advantage of the consumerist rush that fast money made available. This was an experience Adi enjoyed only if and when he made himself available to the right benefactors.

Adi's tales of life in the fast lane, however, belied the crushing downtime that occurred when the turnaround between high-paying clients stretched into hours and, most often, days.[2] Simply put, well-to-do clients were few and far between, and these customers did not stick to a reliable routine. As a result, Adi regularly waited ten to twelve hours a day, for several days in a row, before coming into his next windfall of so-called fast money. Perhaps ironically, his brief forays into middle-class consumerism ultimately contributed to and intensified the crushing sense of boredom that Adi experienced during these moments of downtime, which he spent leaning against the mildewed corner of a Metro station unaroused, idle, and, most troublingly, unpaid. Encounters with that "other kind of life" heightened Adi's attachment to all of the consumer pleasures that were unfolding around him but were otherwise inaccessible in his day-to-day existence. Boredom took hold in the gaps, absences, and silences of a life excluded from consumer stimulation.[3]

When downtime dragged on alarmingly long, leaving Adi without the money to pay for a minimum of food for the day ahead, he directed his attention to other homeless men waiting at the Gara de Nord. The few dollars that Adi netted from servicing the down-and-out covered a diet of packaged snacks, instant coffee, and cigarettes. Otherwise, Adi preferred not to work at the station. Although it was a considerably busier market, the clientele did not pay well. "I work the Metro because I can make a lot of money off one client," Adi explained. "There aren't as many clients here, but if you catch one, they give you 100 lei ($30). At the station," where homeless and working-class men tended to gather, "you have to catch ten people to make 100 lei." Rather than undergoing the alienation of poorly paid but steady labor, Adi's strategy was to wait for hours on end between quick bursts of cash. Friendship was critical to managing these yawning stretches of downtime, when Adi had little to spend on distractions such as drinks or media. Ideally, Adi endured his downtime by hanging out with his friend, Răzvan, a petty drug dealer whose clientele partially overlapped with Adi's. They first met while living in the waiting room of the Gara de Nord. Adi had recently started to pool his earnings with Răzvan in order to rent a studio apartment near the station. Tall and spindly from a diet consisting predominantly of cigarettes and coffee, Răzvan accompanied Adi at the Metro when not working his own hustle. The two would sit just outside of the station sipping instant Nescafé procured from a nearby vending machine, smoking cigarettes, and reading *Click*, Romania's free daily tabloid. Adi, the more lucrative earner of the two, floated their consumption of stimulants and magazines with his own earnings. While providing the snacks and cigarettes proved to be a drain on Adi's bottom line, Răzvan's companionship made the endeavor of getting through the overwhelming downtime of Adi's workday bearable.

On one afternoon, Răzvan and I sat outside the Metro while Adi performed a set of celebrity impersonations. He parodied the singing of American pop stars, combining intentionally off-key falsettos with clownish dance moves, at one point vigorously waving his shirt over his head while inviting onlookers to check out his body. The mix of scandalous sneers and bemused laughter encouraged Adi to carry on with his antics. As Adi started to transition into a new "song," Răzvan interrupted the spectacle to ask Adi to buy another bag of pretzels from a nearby corner store. After only a mild protest, Adi put his shirt back on and ventured off. Răzvan's once-encouraging grin quickly fell flat. "You know he grew up in an orphanage in Moldavia," Răzvan disclosed quietly and a bit unexpectedly. "From the age of five he has had no parents, and you know, back then, orphanages didn't have the conditions that they have now," Răzvan explained, referring to Romania's orphanage scandal that unfolded immediately after the fall of communism. Romania's gut-wrenching austerity coupled with draconian restrictions on birth control had pressured impoverished Romanian families to leave their children in the care of underfunded state institutions. At the fall of communism in 1989, an estimated 753 out of every 100,000 Romanian children resided in state-run orphanages with deplorable conditions.[4] Images of skeletally thin children left bruised and naked in overstuffed dormitories circulated through the international press, evoking widespread condemnation.[5] Răzvan was concerned that my observations of his friend's catcalling and parodying would reveal only a caricature of Adi, one in which Adi actively presented himself to me and to customers, in his pursuit of fast money in urine-stained stalls, in a seemingly uncomplicated move toward the good life. While Adi made every effort to appear to float above the gritty conditions of his hustle, Răzvan wanted to bring into view the humanizing pain that lay beneath the surface of Adi's playboy persona.

When Adi returned from the corner store, I asked about his memories from the orphanage. At first taken aback by the line of inquiry, Adi chewed on a pretzel for a moment to gather his thoughts. "I was small," Adi began. He spoke matter-of-factly as he chewed, but he stopped making eye contact. Instead, he stared into his bag of processed snacks. "I was afraid of the others at the orphanage. They were all bigger than me. A lot bigger. They would cover my head and beat me," he confided. "There were others who were frail like me. We got beaten every day by the bigger kids. And the people working there weren't any better!" he exclaimed. He returned to making eye contact and spoke with animation. "So, for example, when I was young, I used to suck my thumb. The workers would hit me upside the head and scream at me to stop. But when that didn't work, they rubbed hot peppers on my hand so that I would burn myself if I sucked my thumb. It was like that every day. It was awful." Adi continued to speak of the regular abuses he weathered at the hands of older orphans but also at the hands of the staff charged to protect him.

At the age of twelve, Adi moved from the orphanage to a foster home. It provided a comparatively higher degree of stability than the orphanage, at least up until his eighteenth birthday. "After I finished school, it was time for me to leave. My foster parents sent me here to Bucharest to work at a bread factory, but the contract didn't come through, though." Adi soon found himself on his own in the capital without a place to stay and with no money in his pocket. Too lanky to thrive in construction on the black market, Adi made ends meet by heading to the toilet to perform what the public health literature refers to as *survival sex*, a term that foregrounds immediate economic need in the selling of sex coupled with a disavowal of desire for or pleasure in the sex itself.[6] Adi remained adamant that, had other viable opportunities been available for making money, he would have pursued them over and above selling sex. Somewhat ironically, though, while poverty pushed Adi into sex work, sex work facilitated Adi's upward mobility. The fast money earned from well-paying clients made sex work incredibly lucrative. While most of the money was spent at clubs and on clothes, Adi pooled the remaining fraction that he saved with Răzvan's earnings from the latter's own petty hustles. The resulting sum was enough to enable the two to stop sleeping at the railway station and to rent the modest studio apartment nearby.[7]

As talk of Adi's upbringing dwindled, along with the reserve of pretzels and cola, Răzvan grew restless. Without snacks, much less the prospect of a new client and another windfall of cash to hold his attention, Răzvan indicated that he would leave Adi to return to the Gara de Nord to see if there was any excitement unfolding there. After all, Răzvan did not earn his money at the Metro, and once the goods Adi laid out were consumed, Răzvan saw little reason to stick around. He simply felt that there was no longer anything to do in the Metro, evidencing that friendship amid downtime had its own cost. In these moments when Răzvan roamed elsewhere, solitude impressed itself on Adi. On another late night, when I unexpectedly came across Adi waiting alone in a central Metro station, he responded to my friendly greeting with bitter curses, "Răzvan is being a cocksucker (*un bulangiu*)!" Adi exclaimed. "When I have money he hangs out with me, and I spend all my money with him. Now look! I've run out of money, and he left me again. That cocksucker left me with nothing but terrible boredom!" Without the defense of mundane stimulants like caffeine and nicotine, and the companionship that these stimulants mediate, boredom ground away at Adi. Adrift in downtime, he thought about the past pleasures of fast money, knowing that such pleasures continued to exist all around him, if only he had the means to tap back into them. Rather than indulge, all he could do was speculate as to when the opportunity to shift back into high gear might return. For the moment, the next rush of

FIGURE 5.3. Gara de Nord railway station. Photo by Bruce O'Neill.

fast money felt impossibly far away as Adi sat alone on the Metro stairwell, with his chin resting on his folded arms and a glazed expression on his sagging face.

THE DAILY GRIND

Augustin and I leaned against a wall near the ticketing room of the Gara de Nord station on a bitterly cold winter night. Augustin kept his eye on roughly a dozen men, all of whom were silently vying for his attention. While it was a well-known place to meet male prostitutes, the ticketing area of the train station was by no means a sanctioned market where propositions could be made openly. Instead, interested men did their best to attract Augustin's attention discreetly. They lingered in the hall of the station without making any pretense of purchasing a train ticket. They intermittently cleared their throats and forced coughs, and they tried to make eye contact when Augustin looked their way. Otherwise, the men paced back and forth, scuffing their feet in place and rubbing their hands together in an effort to keep warm. The unheated station provided only a partial reprieve from the below-freezing temperature outside. Some of the faces I recognized from homeless shelters and black labor markets around town, but others, adorned in fitted leather jackets and heavy boots, were of another social class entirely.

The bathroom stalls of the station where Augustin worked offered plenty more clients than did the stalls at the Metro. Several dozen men gathered to buy sex at the station on any particular night. Given that most of these clients were homeless and unemployed, however, there was not much money to be made providing it. The busyness of the station required homeless sex workers to exercise more craft than in the comparatively quiet market at the Metro. At the station, Augustin and the others had to assess not only who was interested in buying sex, and who was just waiting for a train, but also what price buyers could afford to pay. The added calculation, however, did little to alleviate the sense of boredom framing the production of sexual services. Just like Adi at the Metro, sex workers at the station found themselves adrift in downtime while they held out for the best offer. In these moments, Augustin felt bored not because of an absence of immediate activity (everyone inside the ticketing area, after all, needed to be evaluated) but rather because of his displacement to the most marginal dimensions of the economy. Time moved as slowly as the trickle of pocket change accumulating in Augustin's pocket. "There's no construction work anymore. We just stand around and talk, we walk about the street, we look for a place to watch a football match," Augustin said with a shrug. "Well, and any man wants to have fun, to have a lady (*gagică*)—a girlfriend, you know?" Augustin continued. An eavesdropping teen near us elaborated, "To hook a lady (gagică)—a gay." The teen was maintaining his own watch on the milieu before him, trying to hold the gaze of the better-dressed while avoiding, if only for the time being, eye contact with the rougher-looking. "And so we wait for someone to be interested," the teen continued, linking, as if it were self-evident, the recognizability of personhood with a sufficiently high disposable income. The homeless and unemployed lingering about, by contrast, continued to be regarded as nobodies within this sex market.

While a number of homeless men were looking to buy time with Augustin at that very moment, Augustin avoided making eye contact with them, holding back to see if he could land a better-off client. Like Adi, Augustin hoped to earn big by hooking a single wealthy john rather than grinding out a modest wage with several homeless clients. As with Adi, the attraction of this line of work was not the sex but the money. For both men, the approach to the workday was to maximize fast money while performing a minimum of sex acts. These sex workers constantly made their own calculations. "How much you earn depends on how poor the person is," Augustin explained bluntly. "If you can catch a foreigner on his first time here, and he doesn't know the prices, then you can make a lot of money. Others pay well—doctors come here, lawyers, someone from the American embassy too." Unprompted, Augustin substantiated his claim by fishing a stack of business cards out of his wallet. Still keeping an eye on the men before him, Augustin continued, "Otherwise, I get five to ten lei ($1.50 to $3) each time." Augustin's earning spectrum with clients at the station placed the value of his efforts somewhere between a can of beer and a pack of cigarettes. While he made only pocket change, his earnings went untaxed. This sex economy, as well as other small-time hustles happening around the station, was not overseen by any kind of organized crime. As one close informant explained laughingly, "There's no mafia regulating business here at the station. There isn't enough money to be made here to interest a mafia. You keep what you earn, and anyone can earn. If you want to get to work, then go ahead. Get to work. No one will stop you."

The kind of sex exchanged in these stalls depended on the amount of money offered. Most of the time, though, Augustin emerged from the men's room chewing gum and spitting compulsively. "It's not good money," Augustin admitted, "but there's no other work available to me. Every other kind of job requires a high school diploma. Otherwise, you wouldn't see me waiting for men. I want a woman—a *family*." About a decade earlier, Augustin's parents had pulled him from school so that he could help contribute to the household income by working odd jobs. This short-term strategy to negotiate Romania's troubled economic transition left Augustin completely irrelevant to present opportunities in retail, much less business services. Unable to flourish within Romania's increasingly competitive job market, he turned to marginal hustles in the station's informal economy. There Augustin negotiated the precariousness of poverty by instrumentalizing his body.[8] Compared with directing traffic in the station's parking lot, carrying passengers' bags to the train, or stocking small vendor kiosks in and around the station with soda, sex work proved the most lucrative option available to young homeless men. Augustin, however, remained firm that he found no excitement in his evenings spent having sex with strangers. He identified as straight, and the paltry sums he would accumulate by the end of an evening's shift having sex with other men left him with not much disposable income. Subsequently, Augustin felt like a nobody. "At the end of the day, you just feel bored with life in the sense that you have become completely saturated by poverty. You can't afford to do anything that you need to do, much less what you want to do." Unlike Adi, who sought respite from downtime by rapidly spending his earnings, Augustin endured slow days for the sake of family betterment. Augustin gave his younger brother a portion of his earnings to subsidize his education. Augustin wanted his brother to earn a diploma so that he could access a wider set of opportunities that had been denied to Augustin. "Every little bit helps," he reasoned optimistically.

Aside from the impoverished customer base that allowed Augustin to generate only the meagerest of earnings, he was also subjected to harassment from the station's security services. While informal hustles abounded at the station, often unfolding in plain sight of private security guards and uniformed officers alike, they were not always tolerated. The police regularly cracked down on such entrepreneurial activities when they generated complaints from ticketed travelers. This included sex work in the station's bathrooms but also less taboo hustles such as offering to carry bags for passengers getting on and off a train or selling available parking spaces in the otherwise free pickup and drop-off lot immediately outside the station's ticketing area. On these occasions, police officers and private security guards would ask Augustin to show a valid ticket stub to indicate that he was waiting to travel. When, predictably, Augustin could not produce a ticket, the police would fine Augustin for loitering and demand that he leave the station. At other times, the police would offer to waive the fine and allow Augustin to carry on working in exchange for a bribe. On more than one occasion, when Augustin refused to pay a bribe, he faced physical violence at the hands of the police. This became apparent when I found Augustin one morning with his left eye blackened, his jacket torn, and his scalp bloodied and bandaged. "The police beat me," Augustin explained. "I got a fine, but for what? Because I couldn't justify my presence here in public? Because I had nowhere else to go? The police yelled at me to 'get out of here!' When I stuck around to find a client, they took me downstairs [into the bathroom]. They handcuffed me to the radiator and started beating me. Not with their batons but with their fists and with their legs. Then they drove me out to the edge of the city and left me in the forest. I had to walk all the way back here. Now look at me." Others working the station reported similar stories of being picked up by the police and dropped off in a forested area outside the city. There they described being punched, kicked, and pepper-sprayed and then left by the police in the woods without food, water, or money. The walk back to the Gara de Nord is over ten kilometers.

Augustin's and Adi's precarious foothold in the informal economy grew ever more tenuous with time. As the spring rolled around, a new crop of young men in their late teens had arrived at the station. Like Augustin and Adi before them, they were fleeing the depressed conditions in the Romanian countryside in the hope of finding greater opportunity in the capital; like their predecessors, these new arrivals found fast money to be made in the station's bathroom stalls. In their effort to overcome a crippled economy and potentially near-permanent unemployment, these teens gelled their hair and sported tight jeans and even tighter T-shirts. "I don't need school," one teenage newcomer loudly lectured me, "because there's money here in the Gara!" As fresh faces started to monopolize the attention of higher-paying clients, Augustin and Adi found themselves becoming displaced from the informal sex economy by heightened competition. The depths of the financial crisis gave little reason for optimism that their circumstances might turn around. "I'll wait for the end of next month, and then I'll look for some more construction work—sandstone, tiling, that sort of thing. I just haven't been able to find any because of this crisis," Augustin concluded grimly. "I wait with nothing, and each day I feel so bored and empty." As the logic of displacement grew ever more pervasive, he struggled to adapt further. "I have to find a guy to sponsor me, to keep me in an apartment. I just don't see another way." As Augustin's vision for the future shifted from being a family man to being a kept man, he continued laboring in bathroom stalls in an unending battle to keep time from slowing down further, or even coming to a dead stop.

THE JOHNS

"When you don't have money, life sucks (*viaţa e naşpa*). It's a beautiful life, though, when you have money," Constantin began as we strolled through central Bucharest. We passed by quaint cafés and stationery shops frequented by university students. The sweet scent of pastries wafted out of bakeries all around us. "When I had money I went to clubs every Saturday. There you could pick up 'real women' (*femei adevărate*). . . . But all of that money ended," Constantin lamented, "and now it's as you see because I haven't found any work." An occasional customer of Adi's, boredom and sex had also become entangled for Constantin amid Romania's depressed economy. Constantin could no longer afford to go to his usual haunts for entertainment. And, to be clear, Constantin had a longtime habit of paying for sex. Before the economic crisis, Constantin regularly picked up what he called real women at bars and nightclubs, covering their bar tabs and even offering to pay for hotel rooms in exchange for a casual encounter. Once he was no longer able to find steady work, trips to the club, much less the hotel parties afterward, became unthinkable. The economic downturn cut Constantin off from established modes of entertainment, leaving him with the dreary sense that nothing much happened anymore. Constantin now spent his days and nights observably and self-consciously bored. Nicotine and coffee provided a certain degree of relief in the day-to-day, but sex provided a totalizing release. For those few fleeting seconds, Constantin did not feel stuck but rather caught up in a rush. As another homeless john explained to me with an oversized grin, "every man wants to have fun—to get laid now and again, you know?"

Sexual relationships were otherwise difficult to sustain on the streets. As formerly working-class men became down and out, casual girlfriends redirected their affections toward stable, if not upwardly mobile, men. Even the most committed wives rarely stayed out on the streets for long. Instead, wives returned to their parents' homes (if they were young) or moved in with their grown children (if they were older). Time and again, women proved more adept at mobilizing networks of family and friends to regain a roof over their heads. Much of their success owed to cultural assumptions about the place of women being in the home.[9] Family and friends, by contrast, left men to reconstruct a life for themselves on the street, either formally divorced or estranged from their wider family. In need of a rise, homeless men first turned toward themselves, as many men quipped to me during my research: "When I got nothing to do, I jerk off (*fac labe*)!" . When regular masturbation turned into stimulation without satisfaction, homeless men collected what money they had and turned their attention toward sex workers.

Dozens of female prostitutes worked in and around the Gara de Nord station, and the homeless men regularly ogled them. However, the services of these women were outside the regular budgets of homeless men. This is because female prostitutes could reliably secure working-class and middle-class clients. "I have at least one and a maximum of three clients a night," Elena, a sex worker in her twenties at the Gara de Nord, explained to me. "I make between 200 and 400 lei ($60–$120) a night. *And I get taken to hotel rooms*," she emphasized with sass. These were unthinkable sums for men like Constantin to pay.

Unable to maintain a steady relationship, and too poor to afford the services of a woman, some homeless men opted to buy and sell time with other men. Male prostitutes, simply put, cost a fraction as much. "It's not the same as taking bitches (*curve*) to a hotel," Constantin admitted, "but then again, I don't have to pay all that money. I can't afford it. I don't always have money for cigarettes, and women expect a hotel room? So instead, I buy some time with a bitch (*curvă*) like Adi." Like the majority of homeless men frequenting the bathroom stalls, Constantin did not identify as gay. He referred to Adi and Augustin using the feminine form of nouns (*fată, curvă*), and he would correct me for referring to these sex workers as men (*bărbați*). Constantin also regularly spoke of dating "real women" during better economic circumstances, as did others. While Constantin admitted that sex workers like Adi were "not the same" as "real women," sex in the men's room stall nevertheless provided Constantin with the rush needed to overcome the restlessness evoked by time detached from the club, the hotel, and "real women." This makes sense within the context of working-class masculinity, where sexual identity is more closely linked to the role performed during sex—whether a man is *active* (*insertive*) or *passive* (*inserted*)—than to the gender of the partner.[10]

"Fun otherwise doesn't exist for us," Eugen, a homeless man in his forties, said to me on Christmas Eve. We were standing around the largely vacant train station and drinking bottles of beer that I had procured earlier from a grab-and-go market as a means of marking the occasion. Most of the others in Eugen's network had cleared out for the holidays, joining a housed friend in their apartment or traveling to family in the countryside to spend the holidays indoors. Those few who remained on the street over Christmas were the most vulnerable and socially disconnected. Eugen was the kind of impoverished, homeless client that Augustin and Adi avoided unless they were in desperate need of pocket change. "I'm bored all the time. I leave the station, I walk around, I clear my thoughts, but there's nothing to do here. I can't celebrate the holidays. I haven't celebrated Christmas or New Year's since I arrived at the station years ago." Originally from Moldova, Eugen had lived with a long-term partner in the beach town of Constanța. When the relationship ended, Eugen headed to Bucharest in search of work and a new home. Given Eugen's older age, selling sex was not an option for him. There were too many young, manicured teens for him to compete against. Instead, Eugen performed low-paid manual labor around the station. "Everyone comes to Bucharest through the station, but I stuck around. I make money doing odd jobs—carrying bags, directing traffic in the parking lot, that kind of thing. I grind out an existence, but it's a pathetic one," Eugen stated grimly. "You see that we are unwashed, unshaven, *nothing*. And you sleep with the worry that someone will come and take what little you do have. I can't even afford the bribe at a night shelter." Eugen paused while we both turned away from a blast of cold air whipping down the terminal. When the gust subsided, he concluded flatly, "This all makes for an enormously boring life." Displaced from family and friends, work and home, Eugen sought relief from that terrifying silence of having nothing to distract him from life's wearing out. He headed into the restroom stalls. "The only thing fun about life at the station is those teenage prostitutes over by the bathroom!" he exclaimed with a howling laugh before heading off in their direction.

The Gara de Nord's toilets provided a sense of release for homeless men; they organized much of the nightlife for those living in and around the station. Eugen spent almost every evening hovering near the restroom entrance along with about two dozen other men. On the nights when Eugen could not afford the five lei ($1.50) minimum for a trick, he could still take nips from the bottles of beer and *țuică* that the better-off passed among the johns. The men circulated the bottles cautiously, balancing the desire to create a festive atmosphere against the danger of attracting the police's attention. After the police walked past on their rounds, *manele* music would start playing through cell phone speakers, only to be silenced when the phone's owner expected the officers to loop back around.[11] In the police's absence, men eyed each other and joked about the people and pleasures waiting in the bathroom. In those moments, belly laughter paused just long enough for them to take a pull from a two-liter bottle of beer. "It works like this," Eugen explained while passing me a bottle of țuică. "You can make an arrangement with someone standing around up here. If you agree on a price, you both pay a leu ($0.30) to use the bathroom. You then just head [past the turnstile and down some stairs and] into a stall. Otherwise, there are also some more men standing around in the bathroom. You can bargain with them too." Consuming sex shifted homeless men out of long stretches of downtime and into a rush of titillation. Alcohol, music, and, ultimately, climax filled the void left by the absence of work, as did the mundane pleasures of sugary snacks and cigarettes. The men's room also brought Eugen into contact with another class of people entirely: gay professionals, both foreign and Romanian, who were also looking for cheap tricks to escape from a very different kind of boredom.

FIGURE 5.4. Toilets. Photo by Bruce O'Neill.

"This is where you cruise," explained Franco, who was holding court in a sit-down bar at the Gara de Nord. He bought rounds for those with whom he wanted to chat. Romanian by birth, Franco earned his money as a waiter in Greece during the tourist season. Solidly middle class by Romanian standards, Franco resided in a small village outside of Bucharest during the winter so as to stretch out his summer's earnings. Franco dressed well and made the trip into Bucharest by first-class train specifically to find one-night trysts with young men at the station. After picking his partner, he took him to a low-cost motel for the night. "Otherwise, there are a few gay bars in Bucharest, but they are only open on Friday, Saturday, and Sunday," Franco explained in near-perfect English while music videos from American pop stars looped on a flat-screen television behind his head. Like other gay professionals, Franco paid a premium for sex at the station, owing to a lack of alternatives. Highly taboo under communism, homosexuality was decriminalized in Romania only in 2001.[12] An openly gay community—complete with bars, clubs, and restaurants—had yet to take shape in Bucharest.

Like the others at the station, Franco linked his participation in the sex economy to an overall sense of disenchantment with life in Romania: "Life is otherwise boring here in Bucharest. It is as if you don't have any chances. As if you are cut off from the opportunity to work," he explained. "Sure, all is well when you have euros in your pocket. Everyone in Romania wants to get rich. But when you don't have euros, for the people of Romania, life is very expensive. . . . So I come here to cruise whenever I can, but it's not as good as in other cities I've visited such as Athens, Budapest, Amsterdam, or Berlin." Franco bought a fresh round of beers, including one for me, while he recounted his escapades abroad.

Like Augustin, Adi, and Eugen, Franco spoke of being bored in Romania. Franco's subjective malaise had an entirely different set of temporal and spatial characteristics owing to his relative affluence. As for the homeless men at the station, Franco's boredom was spatial: life was not boring in and of itself. Franco found life in Athens, Budapest, and Amsterdam, for example, to be quite extraordinary. Indeed, his travels provided the comparative framework that led Franco to code life in a Romanian village as "cut off from opportunity," lacking in "anything to do," and, ultimately, "boring." However, unlike Constantin and Eugen, Franco's class standing gave his battle with boredom clear temporal boundaries. For Franco, boredom would pass with time. Dreary winters in a Romanian village might feel mired in a dense fog, but winter would give way to summer just as the slow village routine would give way to the excitement of euros, tourism, and Athens's comparatively robust nightlife. Franco merely had to bide his time at the station until the next season of adventure began. Franco's homeless counterparts, by contrast, were stuck at the station. Rather than waiting for the onset of the summer tourism season, the only relief these homeless men had in sight is the occasional trip to the men's room stall.

Male Intimacy

I tried to find a woman to see—to see if we could live together. But women, if they see you don't have a job, that you don't work, that you make nothing and that you don't have money, then they don't stay.
—TOMAS

"At one point, I had a girlfriend," Augustin emphasized as we sat on the steps of the station. We watched another group of homeless guys from the station directing traffic in the parking lot. They stood in open spaces and waved to oncoming traffic to turn in, relinquishing the space in exchange for a small fee. "To be clear, these things we do in the restroom we don't like to do, but we do them because of the poverty. That's all. If it wasn't for the poverty, you wouldn't see us hanging around here. But these are the kinds of jobs we have available to us in this country." Adi expressed a similar sentiment, albeit in less dejected terms: "It's not about getting laid. I don't want sex. I want to make money. And it's not about guys or girls. I'll have sex with anyone to make money."

While regularly selling sex to other men, neither Augustin nor Adi ever identified as gay in any cultural sense. To the contrary, Augustin and Adi maintained a heteronormative masculinity, one that emphasized their capacity to earn money, support dependents, and dominate women. Augustin in particular also regularly voiced aspirations to start a family in the future. To be sure, a certain tendency among impoverished men, and ostensibly straight men, to engage in sex with other men is not a new observation. Social scientists have long documented a prevalence of intimacy in predominantly male settings such as homeless encampments, prisons, and the military. "[A] considerable lack of repugnance to homosexual practices may be found among the lower classes," wrote Havelock Ellis at the start of the twentieth century, citing accounts of soldiers having sex with other men for money but turning to women for pleasure and relationships.[13] At the same time, historical records show that working-class families, who expected children to contribute to the household income, often pushed young boys to seek out profitable relationships with older men.[14] While moral reformers cautioned against the dangers of sex on the streets, working-class boys themselves were likely to point to factories as places of danger where equipment accidents routinely led to the loss of limbs and life.[15] Nels Anderson, who wrote prolifically in the early twentieth century on so-called hobos and tramps, adds that "sex perversion is very prevalent among the tramp population. . . . [I]solated [the tramp] must seek elsewhere for his sex expression, which is substantially what all womanless groups have done. He substitutes the boy for the woman."[16] Anderson notes that street-savvy men, termed *wolves* and *jokers*, sexually dominated less savvy *punks* and *lambs* for both pleasure and economic gain.[17] These early attempts at making sense of why ostensibly straight working-class men had sex with other men pointed to close living quarters, the absence of impoverished women, and the inability to court the better-off.

This male intimacy did not mark its participants as necessarily effeminate or homosexual, a cultural category that, as Michel Foucault argued in *The History of Sexuality,* gained saliency only with the second half of the twentieth century.[18] This is because, in the early 1900s, a traditionally masculine identity for working-class men was simply not tied to the sex of one's partner. Instead, men cultivated their masculine personas by embodying certain attributes, values, and behaviors.[19] Working-class men earned their masculinity by garnering the approval of other men through hard work and the capacity to dominate others, regardless of the dominated person's gender. It is a theme carried into more recent work on male intimacy generally and male prostitution more specifically.[20] Working-class men who are "active" during sex with other men often assert a fully heteronormative masculinity without a sense of contradiction.

Both Adi and Augustin maintained that they were not driven to the bathroom stall by a desire for men. Nor did they claim to take pleasure in their labors. As Augustin attested time and again, he headed to the station owing to dire economic circumstances. Although he would rather have worked in construction, he could not find a reliable job tiling floors or painting walls. "We have nowhere to wash up, nothing to eat," Augustin explained. "Unless God grants us a piece of bread, I might die of hunger tomorrow or the day after." Blending market pressure with ethical concern, Augustin based his decision to sell sex on a moral high ground, arguing that sex work was preferable to engaging in more aggressive, criminal acts to generate money. "It's just better to do this kind of thing—sell sex for money—than to mug someone and risk hurting them," he reasoned.

While Augustin and Adi framed their participation in the station's sex economy as survival sex, the high-earning clients that they targeted described another kind of encounter entirely. "The station is a safe place to find or meet people," Franco explained. "In Romania, it is very difficult. This is not America. There is not much activity in the gay community—there is 'Accept,'" a nongovernmental organization working for the protection of sexual minorities, "but there isn't an outstanding figure that stands up and says, 'I am gay.' This is the problem in Romania," Franco assessed over lattes at a café near the railway station. For Franco, Romania's stagnant economy was not the problem that it was for Adi and Augustin. Franco was not displaced by the global economy, as so many of those spending their time at the Gara de Nord were, but rather empowered by it. Franco was the kind of well-educated and flexible laborer that the global economy rewarded. His college degree, and his proficiency in English, Greek, Russian, and German, gave Franco mobility and access to opportunities across the European Union. Franco shifted out of boredom by staying on the move.

He enjoyed fast times earning more waiting tables in cities from Budapest to Berlin, Athens to Amsterdam, than he could expect to earn by staying in Bucharest. While riding the heights of the summer tourism industry did not allow Franco to live abroad full-time, it did provide enough savings to live comfortably in Romania for the rest of the year. The acceleration that Franco enjoyed each summer was, however, foreclosed to people like Eugen or Augustin, who lacked the cultural capital bestowed by formal degrees and the ability to speak multiple languages. Rather than his own immediate economic need, Franco held a different set of stakes in the station's sex economy, ones surrounding questions of identity and acceptance in a country where communist-era prohibitions on homosexuality were quietly and informally maintained. Despite a decade of decriminalization, homosexuality remained heavily stigmatized in Romania, stifling the development of openly gay neighborhoods and nightlife.[21] As a result, Bucharest's gay scene remained (at times literally) underground. The basement bathrooms of transit stations and the secluded areas of Opera Park (Parcul Operei) became popular locations for gay Romanian men to find partners—often for a relatively small fee. The demand for sex in Romania's underground gay scene drew and sustained the attention of the unemployed and homeless like Augustin and Adi.

That members of the middle class would seek out sexual partners among the down-and-out turning tricks at the station is also not without historical precedent. Middle-class men have long directed their affections toward men of a lower class. During these encounters, the better-off enjoyed the added confidence of class privilege when engaging poorer partners, for example. The trip across the tracks also gave well-off gay men a reprieve from restrictive middle-class norms.[22] The presence of significant class differences also provided an additional level of discretion, for their wider social networks were not likely to overlap with one another, allowing married lawyers and "celibate" priests, for example, to find company in the station's stalls at night without much worry of bumping into that partner later that week while on the street, at the office, or at home. This was (and is) especially true in Eastern Europe, where, following the end of communism, Western middle-class tourists enjoyed a significant economic advantage over Eastern European men. Westerners found an abundance of men willing to have sex in exchange for "gifts" (as opposed to cash payment), blurring the line between sex work and noncommercial trysts altogether.[23]

Long-standing questions about sexual orientation and identity abounded at the station: who was gay and who was straight; who was buying and who was selling; who found pleasure in the transactions, and did anyone really not; and what would that mean for the sexual identity of those involved? Running through these questions was a resounding sense of boredom, one that not only linked each and every participant with each other but also positioned them all within a local, national, and global economy. For those stuck at the margins, sex provided a sudden surge of relief, even if it ultimately left the relieved exactly where he started.

Laid Bare

Time slowed for men like Adi and Constantin, Augustin and Eugen, as they were displaced to the margins of the city and cut off from established dynamics of recognition.[24] These newly homeless men no longer worked, as Romanian socialism had encouraged, nor did they avidly consume, as capitalism celebrates. "If you have money, you get to live," Augustin observed while striking a philosophical tone. "That's why I want to find a job that will last every day for my entire life. . . . Because if you don't have money, you just sit and wait to die of hunger. And that's incredibly boring." Displaced to the most marginal dimensions of the global economy, these men lived through the slow wearing out of life, even as others in the city around them appeared to gain speed. To overcome the sense of time dragging while being stuck in space, these men sought out stimulation. The homeless gathered in the largely ignored corners of transit stations, where they drank beer, listened to music, and bought and sold sexual favors, giving flesh to Gabriel Tarde's testament on the importance of idle hours to the development of markets.[25] The transaction of sex provided displaced persons with an illicit venue to pursue the widely shared value of consumerist pleasure.[26] Inside bathroom stalls, men forged new social relationships across class divides, connecting the homeless and the housed in unexpected and otherwise absent ways. These relationships opened up new money-making opportunities that brought about new modes of being beyond the boredom of displacement. Instead of boredom, these men enjoyed short bursts of excitement and acceleration. Calling to mind Jean Baudrillard's observation that "it is in the consumption . . . of a superfluity that the individual—and society—feel not merely that they exist, but that they are alive," men discarded from a hypercompetitive global economy sought to overcome the slow wearing out of life through the consumption of overwhelming stimulation.[27] For buyers the pleasure was immediate, converting the tedium of life without mundane distractions—food, cigarettes, music, and movies— into titillation, while for producers sex provided the opportunity to earn in restroom stalls what they could no longer expect to make on the factory floor, much less selling sweaters at the mall. The cash on hand opened up new parts of the city otherwise foreclosed to the unemployed, such as the cafés, restaurants, and casinos that dotted the city center. Whether buying, selling, or just hanging around for the free beer, those who participated in the sex economy were offered a window into that "other kind of life" that globalization had promised all Romanians but that always remained out of reach for so many: a life sped up by the stimulation of market-driven production and consumption.[28]

The homeless's turn toward sexuality, from autoeroticism to commercial exchange, to manage the subjective and affective dimensions of displacement provided momentary relief to the economically and sexually excluded. However, this turn toward sexuality was not without its own sense of danger, in the Foucauldian sense that all things are dangerous.[29] To be sure, there were the dangers of interpersonal violence that pervaded the unregulated markets where marginal actors scrambled for meaning and subsistence.[30] These men also confronted the practical public health concerns surrounding prostitution in unsanitary conditions.[31] But there was also a larger and more abstract danger in this turn toward the sex trade in that it marked a flaccid response to the intensifying politics of inequality in Bucharest. Rather than mobilizing the men politically to challenge a logic of displacement, one that identifies and discards people as superfluous, the sex economy reproduced its logic through a constant reaffirmation of inequality between those who could consume and those who could not. In the most marginal corners of the city where the displaced looked for release, recognizability as a "someone" still hinged on distinguishing between who could afford to have sex (and who could not) and who was able to sell sex (and who could not). Instead of experiencing collective solidarity, these men came together in relationships marked by individual exploitation. Framing the ostensibly festive atmosphere of sex, money, music, and beer found late at night at the Gara de Nord station was a raw sense of vulnerability opened up by the politics of displacement, and everyone knew it. A widely suppressed class of gay professionals headed into underground meetups not just to pay for pleasure but also to avoid verbal abuse elsewhere in the city, just as homeless men made their bodies available in the hope of securing a baseline subsistence. Amid the exchange of money and pleasure, the boundaries between those who had and those who had not grew ever more rigid, leaving the homeless, in turn, ever more open to exploitation. "With money, you can do anything here—you can buy anything and do *anything*," Augustin explained with emphasis. A recurring lament among Romania's homeless, the observation gained poignancy when voiced by men laid bare by the pressure of a brutally competitive economy.

6

DEFEAT BOREDOM!

. . .

A college student sits on a bench with a half-zipped hoodie, a few days' stubble, and a pile of books. Groups of students gather around nearby him to chat with their friends. He sighs, not because he is half-awake or aloof or even alone, but because he is bored. The television advertisement, moments later, explains as much. To beat back boredom, the student pours Nescafé instant coffee into his life. A catchy pop song drops with his first sip, propelling the student off the bench and into the quad. His excitement proves contagious. How could it not? His classmates shoot to their feet, forming a well-choreographed flash mob. An impassioned voice-over then closes the commercial: "Învinge Plictiseala! Alege Pasiunea! Alege Nescafé 3în1!" (Defeat Boredom! Choose Passion! Choose Nescafé 3-in-1!).

In Romania, during the summer of 2010, the Nescafé brand battled boredom: "Învinge Plictiseala!" "Boredom is, for many Romanians, one of their greatest fears," the campaign's creative director explained to me. We sipped espresso in the agency's in-house café in central Bucharest. "They are not worried about their career, or even about money, but about being bored. And they want to eat so much, to consume so much, that every pause causes them boredom." "This is why," he continued while skimming the screen of one of the two smartphones he had laid out, "we positioned the product as a stimulus, like a spark, that helps you avoid those awful pauses that lead to boredom." And what a consumerist spark did Nescafé ignite. The Nescafé Corporation paired its coffee product with regular drawings to win Nokia smartphones and €1,000 cash prizes. Hugely successful by industry standards, the promotion solicited 1,700,000 entries over fifty-four days.[1]

Away from the commercial's studio set, and about a twenty-minute bus ride from the University of Bucharest, where students can be seen milling about with their own cups of Nescafé between classes, Sorin stood in the Stefan's Place parking lot. "What else can I do?" Sorin responded rhetorically when asked how he fights back against boredom. "Whatever I have on me I consume: beer, cigarettes, coffee." Sorin held up a stash of Nescafé 3-in-1 packets from his backpack as he spoke. Packets in hand, Sorin headed to just beyond the parking lot's entrance, where a patch of grass collected trash that had been chucked from the windows of passing cars. He picked up a green plastic bottle and, with his nose scrunched, gave the mouth a quick sniff to test its freshness. Reasonably satisfied, he headed into the Stefan's Place bathroom and filled the bottle halfway with lukewarm water and then dumped in the contents of his three Nescafé packets. "It's better to drink them all at once," Sorin explained as he shook the bottle vigorously. "It makes for its own kind of distraction." Sorin then drained the bottle's contents in a rapid sequence of large gulps. Moments later, supercharged with caffeine and sugar, Sorin grew animated. He laughed loudly and easily while chatting with a group near the entrance of the parking lot, only to whip toward the back to retell the funny anecdote to those who had been out of earshot. When *manele* music began to play on an onlooker's cell phone, Sorin snapped his fingers in the air and shuffled his way into the lot's center while others laughed and clapped in encouragement. For a few blissful hours, a burst of Nescafé transformed into full color a world otherwise experienced in shades of gray.

In the battle against boredom, Nescafé offered itself to Romanians as their first line of defense. It was a product pitch that Romanians were eager to accept. Purchase, drink, and discard—the instant coffee product promised to jolt the young and the restless through life's quieter moments by initiating a wave of sugar and caffeine, if not companionship, music, and dancing. It was a promise of engagement that proved highly attractive in particular to Bucharest's homeless men and women. Cast aside to the margins of the city, the homeless were cut off from the consumer-oriented spaces and practices that were now central to the rhythms of everyday life.[2] Their exclusion from mass consumerism left the homeless bored day in and day out. In response, the homeless strategized and saved in an effort to buy into a relationship to the city, and to the global, beyond the margins.

FIGURE 6.1. Coffee.
Photo by Bruce
O'Neill.

By entering into highly caffeinated inner worlds or strolling through newly constructed megamalls, for example, the homeless did their best to "Învinge Plictiseala!" (Defeat Boredom!) by participating in the pleasures and possibilities of mass consumerism that were otherwise denied them. It was a consumer-driven response to marginalization that was fraught with tension.

Beyond the Marginal

"Could I have another 'Nes' and a cigarette?" Clara asked. She had found me sitting on a shaded stretch of pavement behind the Backwoods Shelter's communal dormitory. I often retreated there in the early afternoon to jot notes while I ate my lunch. Clara directed her request to me, in part, because I had gotten into the habit of offering these items when collecting life histories. Although I initially conceived of coffee, cigarettes, and chocolate as token gifts, I was immediately struck with how homeless men and women accepted these items with a rush of enthusiasm. They often eagerly asked, even during a chance encounter on the street, whether I had anything in my book bag or in my pockets that I might be willing to pass along. "Sorry," I replied, "but I've given them all out. I don't have anything left." She stared back skeptically. Prompted by her unwavering gaze, I showed Clara the interior of my empty backpack to prove my claim. Clara nodded hesitantly. After silently standing for a moment, she politely asked if I would take the bus to the gas station down the road to buy some chocolate or a soda for her. Factoring in the wait for buses, the proposed round trip would have taken about forty-five minutes. Besides the inconvenience of running such an errand, I was concerned about the precedent that it would set. While entirely happy to balance out the tediousness of the anthropologist's many queries with something sweet, I did not want (nor could I afford) for every conversation to be framed by the constant provision of desired things. The shelter, after all, had nearly two hundred beneficiaries, all of whom observed me closely. Beneficiaries kept note of how much time I spent with whom, where, and what (if anything) I made available during a conversation. These tidbits of information filled countless hours of idle chatter in the shelter's hallways. Cold shoulders and whispers of favoritism quickly followed me if I happened to share a chocolate bar while chatting with one person but did not have something similar to share with another the next day. Given that much of shelter life is defined by the absence of this kind of mundane consumption, I also wondered if regularly circulating such items obscured the very social world I was trying to understand. "Sorry, Clara, but I can't go to the store right now. I'm in the middle of something," I explained apologetically. I returned my attention to my notebook while she continued to stare.

After registering a moment of disappointment, Clara changed tactics. She quietly turned on her heels and walked back into her dormitory, only to return moments later with some personal items she had stored in her locker: an umbrella, a ballpoint pen, a coffee mug. She asked if I wanted to buy any of them. The price that Clara set for each object happened to be equivalent to that of an inexpensive packet of cigarettes. The transaction would have secured Clara some spending cash while alleviating the need for me to do any of the provisioning. Struck by Clara's persistence, I again apologized, explaining that I did not need any of those items and that even if I had, I did not have any money in my wallet to buy them from her. In fact, to politely avoid constant requests for money, I deliberately emptied my wallet of all but a few small banknotes before heading to the shelter, the day center, and the black market. With narrow eyes, Clara exclaimed in frustration, "But Bruce, a coffee, a cigarette, some chocolate—these things are all I have to look forward to each day! I'm just so bored! There is nothing else to do here but sleep!" When I asked Clara how much she slept each day, she paused briefly to calculate. "Well," Clara continued tersely, "last night I slept fourteen hours, and I hope to sleep another two hours this afternoon." Pushed to the margins of the city, and without any means of stimulation, Clara's world slowed to a deep sleep. Taken aback by her somnolent escape from shelter boredom, I shook out my pockets and rummaged through my book bag. I found just enough coins to buy Clara a coffee from the Nescafé vending machine located at the shelter gates. I packed up my things so that we could walk over to the coffee machine together. "Now it's like I'm at a café," Clara said as she accepted the dispensed plastic cup of "Nes" with a smile of relief as much as gratitude. She then walked off on her own away from the front gate and across the Backwoods courtyard. She took a seat on a bench in some shade, where she then slowly savored each sip.

While the condition of homelessness was rendered visible by the inability to attain the minimally expected levels of housing, food, and hygiene, homeless men and women made daily efforts at consumption that were not wholly preoccupied with attaining absolute material necessities. For shelter beneficiaries such as Clara, the Backwoods Shelter's heated dormitories, hot meals, bathrooms, and medical clinics assured their baseline subsistence. These resources protected the homeless from utter deprivation. To be sure, conditions were far more precarious for those living on the streets. The street homeless dedicated long hours each day to shuffling between, and waiting at, a constellation of disparate and uncoordinated services scattered across the city. Days could lapse between hot meals, and winter nights were commonly spent huddled in the unheated stairwell of a housing block underneath layers of donated blankets. Despite these unforgiving conditions, the homeless's adept efforts at provisioning were generally adequate to secure the minimally necessary bread and donated clothing for them to make it to tomorrow, even as the hardship of homelessness ground years off their lives.

Beyond the pursuit of absolute necessities, consumption for the homeless was also a social practice, one with the powerful potential to move homeless persons beyond the margins and to incorporate them into the pleasures and possibilities of global consumerism. Clara's dogged persistence in seeking mundane commodities like coffee and cigarettes, colas and chocolate, is a case in point. These items allowed Clara to partake in the ambient stimulation that global consumer chains made readily accessible to other Romanians but that generally eluded her. These forays into mass consumerism, limited as they were, were not a matter of sustaining life and avoiding death so much as of negotiating a place of incorporation within the city, within Europe, and within the global economy. Being awash with consumer stimulation opened up a space for Clara to be something other than excluded and bored. Consumption enabled Clara to join in the places and practices that now made up so much of the urban imaginary.[3]

Consumer practices move the homeless beyond boredom and into two different kinds of "places." On the one hand, acts of consumption physically took the homeless out of the marginal spaces of the shelter and the squatter camp, for example, and into the cafés and shopping centers where the working and aspiring middle class actively choose to spend their time and money in the city. These were environments shaped in the tradition of carefully constructed commodity displays, store designs, and soundscapes, which were all directed toward exciting people to engage with mundane goods.[4] Take the gas station down the road from Backwoods, where Clara and other beneficiaries went for the occasional beer or cigarette. In addition to selling gasoline, the station operated a café that made an effort to look slick. Customers entered through automatically sliding doors and were greeted by a wave of air-conditioning that washed over them. The floor was white and glossy, and pop music played overhead. Advertisements and music videos alternated on a series of flat-screen televisions hanging from the ceiling, while the attendant served an espresso macchiato in a ceramic Nespresso-branded mug for the equivalent of $1.50, nearly four times as expensive as drinking a Nescafé instant coffee packet out of a repurposed water bottle in the shelter dormitory or the Stefan's Place parking lot. But the espresso and the trip to the café, even one located in a roadside gas station, were still a luxury—one that even the homeless could save up to afford. While the station served small coffees designed for drivers to throw back before returning to the road, Backwoods residents took their time. My own downing of espresso shots elicited raised eyebrows when I visited there with Backwoods residents. "Are you in a rush?" they would ask with

FIGURE 6.2. Gas station. Photo by Bruce O'Neill.

a hint of confusion. Instead, shelter residents slowly sipped their coffees while relaxing into the café's brightly colored faux-leather chairs, which were gently lit by copper lighting fixtures dangling overhead. Backwoods residents paid the premium not to get the coffee but to take in the café experience, as the sound of pop music and the whoosh of foaming milk proved more inviting than the mildewing walls and echoing corridors that they otherwise had to confront when stuck at Backwoods. Even the banal roadside espresso opened up a space for the homeless to escape the boredom of shelter living, a space where they could buy into the pleasure of a consumer experience.

On the other hand, consumption also facilitated movement toward another kind of place. Consumption allowed the homeless to escape into mental worlds shaped by the hyperstimulation of mass consumerism.

Clara's solitary cup of Nescafé in the Backwoods courtyard evidences as much. Consider how, during communism, coffee was scarce in Romania. Romanians could acquire coffee only by receiving it from family or friends living abroad or by paying smugglers a premium to sneak a packet across the border from Hungary. As a result, in the communist era, coffee was a luxury reserved for important holidays or used for bribing officials.[5] It was only after the fall of communism, and through Romania's integration into the global economy, that Romanians could consume coffee regularly. Coffee was now inexpensive and ubiquitous in Bucharest: instant espresso machines were located in nearly every Metro station, corner store, office building, and public park. The postcommunist subject in Romania was highly caffeinated, and all of this coffee stimulated the imagination as much as the body. The homeless sought out highly caffeinated inner worlds in the hope of being transported from shelters and day centers to an ever more captivating capitalist elsewhere taking shape in their interiority.[6] Whether headed physically into the café, or flooded with caffeine and sugar to facili-tate the fantasy of being at one, the homeless turned toward mass consum-erism in an effort to get up to speed. These acts of consumption represented the clearest way of staking a claim to belonging to the city but also to par-ticipating in European-style consumerism more generally.[7]

Places of Consumption

"Hey, Mr. American—get over here!" I turned around to see who had hailed me from across the park. I saw Anghel and Victor waving from a bench. We had spent the predawn hours together at a black market, where they had waited unsuccessfully for some work off the books, before parting ways for the day. I hurried over to say hello and to hear how they had spent their afternoon. Since the early morning, they had changed out of their blue workman's overalls, which were now folded neatly into the oversized bags containing the rest of their belongings that they always lugged around with them, and were now wearing regular street clothes. "We've done nothing but sit here all day and read the papers," Anghel began. "We haven't had anything to eat except for this." Anghel held up a cheap loaf of the bleached white bread sold at every corner store in Bucharest. Even when money is at its tightest, the homeless could generally find the single leu ($0.30) necessary to buy one. While neither particularly satisfying nor nutritious, it was good for quieting a growling stomach. "We're thinking of going to the Mac[Donald's], though. Come join us!" Grateful for the invitation, but not having enough money in my wallet to float the trip, I explained that I had only enough cash on hand to pay for a coffee. "Okay," Anghel replied as though to a non sequitur. He put away his paper and gathered his bags.

We walked out of the park and made our way toward a nearby McDonald's. This particular McDonald's occupied two levels within a larger shopping complex. In addition to the standard restaurant, it featured a McCafé and a PlayPlace. A guard from a private security firm stood just outside the entrance. "Go get your coffee," Anghel instructed once we were inside, "and we'll set our bags down at a table upstairs and get some food." As instructed, I went to the café portion of the store, ordered my coffee, and then headed back through the main restaurant and to the upstairs seating area. I was momentarily surprised to find Anghel and Victor already seated with full trays. It was only after I sat down and noted their trays' contents that their timely turnaround made sense: several partial bags of fries, the syrupy bottom of a melted sundae, the final bites of several different kinds of sandwiches. "The food's still good," Anghel insisted after catching my curious stare, "and it's better than another loaf of that bread!" "Mmmm hmmmmm," Victor moaned and nodded in agreement as he scooped up the last, fudgy spoonful of ice cream and chocolate sauce from a plastic parfait glass and slurped the bottom of a cola.

As the two ate, they kept watch over the seating area, taking note of what careless and carefree teenagers left behind on their tables before heading back in to the mall. When an abandoned tray caught their eye, Anghel would get up to bus the table, collecting the tray and discarding the empty wrappers into the trash but holding onto the leftover food. To the half-observant, Anghel appeared to be overcommitted to good manners rather than scrounging for a free meal. After the two had their fill, we continued to relax in our seats. We chatted about the day's tabloid headlines and listened to the pop music playing overhead. We also watched with amusement the other families around us playing in the arcade. We had been there for well over an hour when an employee interrupted. "This area is now rented out for a birthday party," the employee said flatly. Anghel and I nodded understandingly and stood up to leave. As we collected our belongings, though, Victor could not help but notice that none of the other customers appeared to be stirring. "They do have kids with them," Anghel replied generously to Victor's halfhearted protest. The McDonald's employee looked on as we cleared out of the area.

From coffee machines to fast-food restaurants, homeless men and women across Bucharest fought back against boredom by trying to move into a place beyond the margins. They strategized ways to incorporate themselves within the consumerist spaces and practices of the city. Risking public insult from private security guards and underpaid employees, as well as cold stares and visceral comments from middle-class customers, Anghel and Victor left a park bench for a fast-food restaurant. They cobbled together a meal out of chocolate parfaits and packets of French fries, and, for that moment, McDonald's delivered to these men a momentary glimpse into that other kind of life located beyond the margins, even if the food was secondhand. With stomachs sated, they stuck around the dinner table to chat and to take in the communal spectacle of family and friends laughing and children playing in the arcade. It was a desire for incorporation that took the homeless to unexpected places throughout the city.

"Have you ever been to IKEA?" Ion, a barrel-chested day laborer in his fifties, asked me. We were sitting in the Stefan's Place parking lot along with Anghel, Victor, and Bogdan while we waited for the Friday dinner to be served. I used the downtime as an opportunity to learn where else in the city people can go to find a hot meal. The group first listed a handful of monasteries and other nongovernmental organizations before bringing up the Swedish-based home furnishing store, which had recently opened a branch on the outskirts of Bucharest. IKEA struck me as a curious point of reference given that the men reported living on less than five dollars per day and all lacked homes of their own to decorate. I admitted to visiting IKEA on rare occasions—generally about once a year in the autumn. "That's it?" Ion asked with raised brows. "I go there as often as I can! I hop off the bus, and I head straight for the ice cream—it's only one leu ($0.30) for a cone. I'll eat two or three straight away!" he explained with growing excitement. "Then I buy a coffee mug—you can refill it as many times as you want, you know. And I have all the coffee that I can drink. I even fill my mug with soda." Ion's efforts to dodge a separate charge to buy the bottomless soda cup by reusing his bottomless coffee mug set the group laughing and nodding knowingly. "And there is *every kind* of soda," interjected Bogdan. "I bring (empty plastic) bottles in my backpack, and when no one is looking, I fill them up with different kinds of soda and coffee!" Bogdan simulated his technique, pretending to take a sip from a cup, only to lower it discreetly underneath a table and carefully empty its contents into an awaiting water bottle. The others continued to laugh. "And the hotdogs cost only one leu ($0.30) too," Bogdan stressed while holding his index finger in the air for added effect. "I only need *five lei* ($1.50) to fill up on whatever I want!" Deploying tactics similar to those of Anghel and Victor at McDonald's, bussing abandoned trays with unfinished plates provided Ion and Bogdan with the opportunity to sample IKEA's wider menu, such as meatballs and salmon, at no additional charge. These men recounted the experience of visiting IKEA as a bountiful banquet.

Intrigued, I asked the group what they did once they were done eating. "I head to the showroom and find a nice-looking sofa, somewhere quiet, and I go to sleep," Bogdan replied with a wide grin. He laid down on the Stefan's Place parking lot and, with a gesture that called to mind Garfield the cat, patted his belly and grinned widely. "The air-conditioning feels *won-der-ful*," Ion added with emphasis, "and no one there bothers you." The others laughed. "It's the best," Bogdan agreed.

To be sure, Ion and Bogdan were not drawn into IKEA by its affordably priced, modern home designs. Instead, they gravitated toward the plates of nearly free food and bottomless cups of sweetened, caffeinated beverages that IKEA sells to keep middle-class customers in the store and energized to shop. For the cost of a packet of cigarettes, homeless men could fill their bellies, not to mention their backpacks, any day of the week with coffee and soda, ice cream, and hotdogs. The low prices enabled the homeless to buy into the same constellation of food options enjoyed by IKEA's better-off customers but, more generally, to also share in the middle-class experience of eating and drinking until one's belly was taut and one's heart content. The IKEA food court, ultimately, afforded these men the opportunity to engage in the gluttonous pleasure of any big-box store: hyperconsumption.

With stomachs stretched, these men turned to the IKEA showroom, where they saw their own sitting and pacing in an entirely different light than when they were stuck in the marginal space of the shelter or the day center. The very practices that expressed brutalizing boredom at the margins were reconstituted within the space of IKEA as the pinnacle of leisure. Ion, Bogdan, Anghel, and Victor strolled about countless home interior mock-ups. They marveled at the extravagance of the displays, with beds layered with white linens and striped duvet covers, then piled high with brightly colored pillows. They tested the cushiness of the couches and the firmness of the mattresses. Conscious of the air-conditioning blowing on them, they found a quiet corner to nap the afternoon away in total comfort. In such blissful moments, the unbearable boredom of the streets felt miles away.

Managing the Pecuniary Divide

To be sure, Bucharest's homeless would rather spend their days eating at McDonald's and napping at IKEA than sitting exposed to the elements at Stefan's Place and munching on loaves of white bread from the corner store. Unlike middle-class patrons, however, the homeless cannot visit these retailers whenever they like. Simply put, the visibly homeless are not welcome inside them. Private security guards police the entrances of these upscale developments to prevent loitering, just as working and middle-class patrons single out and publicly humiliate the smudged and unperfumed on buses and along the street (see chapter 2). Not only do these efforts work to filter the homeless out of the city's central consumer spaces, but they also become entangled with a diffused public shaming as a way to keep the homeless firmly pressed into the city's margins. To penetrate this filtering process, and to access the pleasures and possibilities of consumer spaces, the homeless must make a conscious effort to not look homeless. It is a performance that requires those living on the streets to close the divide between the homeless and the housed by identifying and managing the visible markers of sleeping outdoors.[8] The battle over boredom, as the homeless make clear, begins with the rigorous self-management of one's personal appearance. When successfully accomplished, those living on the street can pass anonymously through the public's gaze and head straight to the food court.

The Stefan's Place day center was a critical staging site for scrubbing away the markers of homelessness. The day center provided its beneficiaries with otherwise rare access to the infrastructure needed to manage both body and dress. This became evident on a warm summer morning when I found Nicu, a homeless day laborer in his forties, sitting in the shade in the Stefan's Place parking lot. With his left hand inside his left sneaker, he meticulously observed the heel, sides, and top of his shoe, burnishing any blemishes until the faux leather gleamed bright white. Noticing my stare, Nicu smiled awkwardly. "I'm heading to the American Mall," he explained. Located fifteen minutes away from the Stefan's Place parking lot on foot, the American Mall was an 818,000-square-foot development oriented toward

FIGURE 6.3. Mall atrium. Photo by Bruce O'Neill.

Romania's aspiring middle class. It featured over three hundred stores, including prominent Western brands like Zara and The Gap, Starbucks and Paul's Bakery, as well as a multiplex cinema, an indoor ice-skating rink, and a pond with bumper boats. College-educated Romanians point to the development as evidence that world-class shopping had come to Bucharest, while the very elite chafed at its offerings. Instead, the very well-to-do insisted on filling their wardrobes by taking annual shopping trips to Italy or France.

Beyond the sparkle and shine of the American Mall's oversized window displays, music floated down the mall's climate-controlled corridors, which were dotted with plush sofas. As Nicu insisted, the comfort, sights, and sounds of the American Mall were preferable to spending the day sitting on a hard park bench underneath the hot sun.

To gain access to the American Mall, Nicu scoured away. With the sweaty labor of shoe shining completed, Nicu headed into the Stefan's Place public shower, which was free for anyone to use once per week. The public shower was staffed by an administrator, Leonard, who recorded Nicu's name under the day's date and checked the shower log to confirm that his name did not appear within the last seven days. Satisfied, Leonard then handed Nicu a complimentary razor, a shampoo packet, and a mini bar of soap, the kind typically found in a discount motel. Leonard also reminded Nicu that he needed to be out of the shower area within the next ten minutes. While Leonard wanted to conserve hot water and speed up access for the next user, the tight time limit meant that Nicu had to be efficient to wash and get out on time. "It can be done in the summer," Nicu explained to me afterward, "but it's a hassle in the winter. It takes almost ten minutes to take off and put back on all those layers of clothes. That doesn't leave much time to actually wash and dry off."

After a shower and shave, Nicu replaced his clothing. He handed his shirt, pants, and socks over to Leonard. Leonard set aside reusable items to be washed on-site and discarded the threadbare. Nicu then picked through Stefan's Place's cache of clean clothing to assemble a new outfit. Although stored in black trash bags, the clothes were by no means trashy. Donated from the United States, England, and France, among other places, these clothes featured labels from The Gap, Levi's, and H&M. While the items were a few years out of date, and at times oddly paired or sized, homeless men could nevertheless assemble reasonable outfits. When the store of donated clothes ran low, beneficaries simply scrubbed clean their existing clothes in the shower using the remaining bits of their complimentary bar of soap. In the warmer months, wet clothes regularly hung to dry from tree branches in the parking lot. On a hot summer day, even thick socks or pants would dry in a matter of hours.

An economy of toiletries circulated outside of the public shower, enabling the homeless to access a full array of grooming items that, individually, they otherwise could not afford to buy or to carry around. Nicu, for example, gave Ion a packet of Nescafé in order to borrow his fingernail clippers. He also took a few swipes of Anghel's deodorant in exchange for a single cigarette. Nicu then cleaned up his hair. He paid Andre, a homeless man in his late fifties who had worked as a barber under communism, three lei ($1) for a trim. Andre took out his shears from a bag and sharpened them on the street curb before getting to work.

FIGURE 6.4. Shower. Photo by Bruce O'Neill.

After a morning spent at Stefan's Place, Nicu had groomed away many of the common identifiers of homelessness: sweat-glazed skin, unkempt hair, scuffed shoes, and dirty fingernails. Once fresh and wrinkle-free, Nicu and other homeless beneficiaries were able to walk away from the day center not looking homeless. Stefan's Place's public shower allowed Nicu to pass through the doors of the American Mall without raising any attention from the security guard or better-off patrons. Once inside the mall, maintaining one's appearances grew easier. The mall made freely available to its customers invaluable infrastructure that was otherwise difficult to access on the street. Rather than walking along hot and sunny sidewalks, for example, Nicu strolled in air-conditioning; instead of sitting in a shaded patch of grass at Stefan's Place, he rested on plush sofas. Just being inside the mall curtailed sweating and helped to keep clothes from getting stained. Nicu also did not have to scrounge for money to buy a loaf of bread as he might when spending a day in the park. He simply headed to the food court, where abandoned trays offered plenty on which to snack. Family restrooms further enabled Nicu, and others, to refresh themselves throughout the day. "Best part about the American Mall are the handicapped bathrooms," Ion explained half-jokingly while we chatted at Stefan's Place. "Those bathrooms have big sinks and the liquid soap is never empty. I wash my underarms, spare socks, underwear, and shirts there. You have to be quick, though," Ion made a rapid scrubbing motion with his hands to illustrate. "Once you close the door, you only have about five minutes before someone starts knocking."

As Ion's comments underscore, these escapes into the mall, as invigorating as they were, were intertwined with a twinge of anxiety. While Ion or Nicu might pass anonymously by security, they worried while in the mall that their actions might call attention to themselves. While not looking homeless, these men nevertheless remained homeless, and for the sake of continuing to enjoy the mall and its amenities, they could not afford to be found out. As they cautiously cycled between abandoned food trays, timed themselves in the restroom, and scrutinized the state of their clothing, the homeless took to the mall as though trying on a donated glove rather than resting in their own skin.[9]

Carnivalesque Consumption

The homeless's presence in higher-end consumer spaces such as IKEA and landmark McDonald's restaurants did not always go unnoticed. Unless the line between the public shower, fresh clothing, and the shopping center was direct, negotiating the gap between the homeless and the housed became nearly impossible. A night outdoors, a shortage of donated clothes, or the inability to shower away the previous day's work on the black market all took their toll on the homeless's carefully orchestrated passing aesthetic. Stained clothes and a sneaking, pungent odor attracted the disciplinary gaze of security guards and the rolled eyes and sharp tongues of solidly middle-class shoppers alike. The heightened scrutiny became a barrier to incorporation into the resources of consumer spaces. As the material consequences of homelessness tilted the battle against boredom ever further in boredom's favor, the homeless, at times, changed tactics. In these moments, rather than trying to obfuscate their low class status, the homeless actively and strategically drew attention to it. Homeless men farted loudly, catcalled women, and spat indoors, for example. Rather than engaging in protracted efforts to purify the body, the homeless turned toward the profane and reveled in bodily processes. These crass antics cleverly evoked what Mikhail Bakhtin calls "carnivalesque laughter," an uproarious cackle that temporarily suspends hierarchical rank, privileges, norms, and prohibitions.[10] Carnivalesque laughter served as a weapon of the weak,[11] one the homeless mobilized in order to temporarily shift class anxiety off of themselves and onto the better-off. Carnivalesque laughter enabled the homeless to take aim at the middle class's own anxieties about respectability and turn them into a foil against which homeless persons undermined the very people, places, and social processes that systematically excluded and confined them to the margins of the city.

The turn toward the carnivalesque came into clear ethnographic relief on a rainy autumn day spent with Emil, a skilled construction worker able to find work most days on the black market. Although Emil maintained a small home and plot of land in the village where he was raised outside of Bucharest, he was unable to live there year-round. Simply put, there were no jobs to be had in his rural village. "You can't eat the house," Emil explained to me bluntly that morning. "And when winter comes, the cold wind could give a fuck about you. It only gives you snow. So I have to go find work here in the city to pay for the groceries, the electricity, the hot water back in the village." To earn enough to get through the winter, Emil and his wife, Eveline, slept in a squatter camp near Stefan's Place from early spring until the very end of fall. "During each of these months, I need twenty-four days of work in Bucharest to make it through the winter in the countryside. And to be clear, if I could, I would never come to the city if I didn't have to. Why would I want to? It's a hard life here in Bucharest. Some days you have money and eat and then for two days you don't. It's bullshit. I'd stay in the country all year if I could," he said flatly.

This particular day, much to Emil's frustration, did not count toward his monthly work quota. He had arrived at the black market before six o'clock and had waited there for two hours without seeing a single contractor. By eight o'clock, Emil decided to cut his losses. He made an early exit from the black market to meet his wife, Eveline, at Stefan's Place so the two could register for the free meal offered later that evening. Once their names were on the list, however, the two had seven hours to burn until the food was actually served. In the interim, Emil, Eveline, and the others were invited to

FIGURE 6.5. Country home. Photo by Bruce O'Neill.

wait in the parking lot. It was there that I found the two and joined them on the lot's curb. We watched the other beneficaries alternate between sitting and pacing, chatting and staring blankly into the distance. Several men recovered pieces of cardboard from the Stefan's Place dumpster, set them in the shade of some bushes, and laid on them in an effort to sleep the hours away. As we watched people fidget and nap, Emil rubbed the back of his neck red. He lamented to me, "I should be out there working hard, earning money—not sitting here all day doing nothing." Noting the pained expression on Emil's face, I asked if he was doing all right. "I'm fucking bored," he replied curtly. Emil continued to squirm in place, bouncing his knee, rubbing his arm, and rolling his shoulders up and down.

In an effort to move himself toward a calmer inner world, Emil pulled a two-liter bottle of beer from his bag, untwisted the cap, and took a long pull. Leonard, the center's administrator, warned Emil about the beer. Drinking was, after all, strictly prohibited at Stefan's Place, particularly in the early morning hours. If Emil wanted to drink, Leonard explained in a tone that struck me as matter-of-fact, he would have to go elsewhere. Emil found Leonard's basic enforcement of Stefan's Place's prohibition on alcohol, however, to be deeply patronizing. The enforcement of the center's rules on alcohol ultimately framed Emil as an irresponsible homeless man in need of moral discipline, rather than as a skilled manual laborer coping with unwanted free time in a highly competitive labor market. Feeling the affront, but not wanting to jeopardize his reservation for the evening meal, Emil obliged Leonard's request and recapped his beer. Playing with the letter of the law, Emil stood up with a half smile, and invited Eveline, his camp neighbor Nicolaie, and me to join him on the stretch of sidewalk immediately outside of the front gate. Under Leonard's disapproving stare, I followed along.[12] Standing a few feet beyond the property line of Stefan's Place's, and in clear view of Leonard and all of the other beneficiaries, Emil uncapped his beer and passed it to me. Wanting to bond with Emil without alienating Leonard, I took a half sip and tried to hand the bottle over to Eveline. "What's wrong with you! Drink like a man!" Emil blasted. I obliged by taking several long gulps before sending the bottle back into circulation. It emptied quickly. Emil let the bottle drop to the ground next to his feet before pulling a second, flask-shaped liquor bottle from his coat, which he also passed around. The contents tasted like vodka mixed with chocolate syrup. The second bottle emptied as quickly as the first, and Emil tossed that bottle to the ground too. The watching beneficiaries sitting inside Stefan's Place began to laugh at Emil's defiance. With the mood growing festive, at least for those in the drinking circle, Emil announced loudly enough for Leonard and the others to hear that he wanted to host me for lunch at his encampment (*acasă*). He waved his wallet stuffed with bills at Leonard, who looked on disapprovingly. Emil's wife, Eveline, by contrast, took to the idea. She smiled and nodded, but she insisted that we go immediately to Hypermarket—a mega–grocery store located inside an upscale shopping center—to do our provisioning. Although a few bus stops away, Hypermarket's prices were cheaper and its selection far wider than at the considerably closer minimarkets and corner stores where the homeless bought most of their food.[13] The group collected their bags before heading toward the bus stop located along the main road.

On the ride over to Hypermarket, Emil groused about Leonard being a stickler for rules, and we all chuckled lightheartedly at Emil's efforts to thumb his nose at them. Emil was even willing to concede that he might have overreacted. Leonard, after all, was only doing his job. We were all in good humor when Eveline paused the banter in preparation for our stop. The bus slowed to a halt in front of a multistory complex built of opaque glass and steel. The surface shimmered and shined in the late-morning light. "This is it," Eveline indicated. While Eveline had shopped for groceries at Hypermarket before, Emil and Nicolaie had not. They were sufficiently successful on the day labor market to get out of contributing to their encampment's efforts at domestic reproduction. The jovial atmosphere faded as we made our way across the parking lot and toward the row of glass doors marking the entranceway. The group quieted their tones, and Emil and Nicolaie straightened their demeanor. The swagger that the two men had put on display when exiting Stefan's Place had dissipated entirely. As we approached the entrance, Eveline and I gravitated toward the central pair of doors. Turned off by the steady trickle of customers who were already coming and going from those central doors, Emil instead hurried ahead and directed us toward a quiet set of doors off to the side. Emil was trying to slip into the mall discreetly. His efforts at making a quiet entrance, however, ultimately failed. The peripheral doors were locked. They rattled loudly as he tried to push, then pull, the doors open with increasing force on the off chance that they were merely stuck. With a hint of frustration, Emil looped around toward the central doors and rushed through just as another set of customers were exiting, causing a small traffic jam. Emil offered a hurried apology before pushing further forward into the lobby, where he stopped to wait for the rest of us. Eveline chortled at Emil's mildly flustered demeanor. "Good God—look at this place," Emil muttered uneasily to Nicolaie and me once we joined him inside. An entranceway made of glass and steel gave way to an interior of faux-marble floors and store windows that extended all the way up to the high ceiling. The signage of the first few retailers invited us to buy Sony laptops, diamond bracelets, and designer jeans. The mall's ecology of luxury goods contrasted sharply with Emil's day of forgone earnings. "Look at all of this expensive shit," Emil noted. An aesthetic of superfluity intended to arouse middle-class consumers and to stoke their fantasies of upward mobility had the opposite effect on Emil.[14] The mall's bombastic makeup signaled instead to down-and-out men that they were out of place, that they were where they could not afford to imagine being, much less actually be.

Our lingering just beyond the entryway slowed traffic in and out of the mall and eventually attracted the attention of the security guard pacing around the lobby. The guard met our eyes and gestured for us to step aside. At another moment, Emil would have obliged. In the spirit of acting the part, he would have nodded politely at the half-interested guard and folded himself into the steady stream of shoppers headed down the main corridor and, ultimately, found his way toward the Hypermarket. But after a morning marked by a string of indignities that started with not finding work at the black market, only to then be subjected to the petty discipline of the well-intended aid worker, Emil erupted under the security guard's half-interested gaze. "Hey!" Emil called out in a raised voice. Locking eyes with the now startled guard, Emil then made a long and rapid jerking motion that extended out from his belt and let out a loud "raspberry" sound from his mouth. Laughter bellowed out of Nicolaie and Eveline as the guard's jaw fell agape. With the attention of almost everyone in the lobby on us, Emil asked Eveline to lead us toward the Hypermarket. Eveline walked briskly down the corridor with a continued chuckle, even as she now kept Emil several paces behind her.

The group was still laughing moments later when we reached the Hypermarket at the far end of the complex. Emil split the shopping list, instructing Eveline and Nicolaie to find salami from the deli and a loaf of bread from the bakery. Emil waited for Eveline and Nicolaie to walk five aisles down the store before clarifying with a loud shout, "Get sweet bread (*cozonac*), not brown! We'll get the beer! Beeeeeeer for the parrrr-tay!" drawing out the critical words *beer* and *party*. Eveline and Nicolaie laughed at the ruckus as shoppers looked on and fidgeted uncomfortably. Their arched eyebrows and open but silent mouths provided the group with additional comedic fodder.

I followed Emil on the beer run. Along the way, Emil picked up and opened a bag of sunflower seeds. He tore open the bag, popped a handful of seeds in his mouth, and began to chew. He spit out the empty shells onto the grocery store's floor. "It's just like being in the countryside," Emil reasoned with a laugh. He offered me a handful, which I declined purely out of concern for my own technique. I had never mastered the process of separating out the meat of a sunflower seed so as to spit out only the shell. Customers looked on with wrinkled noses. Their eyes fixated on the trail of detritus left behind us. We eventually made our way down the main aisle of the store until we came across the one designated for beer. Emil turned and strolled down to peruse its offerings until he settled on a can of inexpensive Romanian beer. He tried to crack it open to drink while he finished up the shopping. The sunflower seeds were salted, and he was feeling parched. The tab, however, only partially punctured the mouth of the can before snapping off. Foam sprayed out of the top, into the air, and ultimately showered down onto me. "Yeahhhhh!!!" Emil called out at full volume. With a laugh he turned so as to face down the aisle. He continued to jerk the can back and forth, now at waist height, so that foam ejaculated out onto the floor. Emil then took a screwdriver from his coat pocket and jammed it through the top to fully open the can, spilling more beer in the process. Emil chugged what remained of his drink in one extended gulp. I laughed at the antics even as I began to look over my shoulder. I expected security to intervene at any moment. Emil, however, did not break stride. He placed the now-empty can with an ironically delicate care into his basket. Not a thief by any stretch of the imagination, Emil intended to pay for his party.

With a growing sense of unease, I encouraged Emil to hurry up and grab whatever remained on his list. Noting my anxious tone, Emil waved away my suggestion. Instead, he made his way further down the aisle, placing a couple of 2.5-liter bottles of Romanian beer into his basket. "We have an American as our guest of honor," Emil announced festively to a handful of other shoppers now gawking at us. "You drink Heineken, Bruce, right?" I shook my head no and explained that I would rather have Romanian beer, but Emil insisted on paying the leu ($0.30) upcharge per can so that I could drink imported beer. He opened one of the Heinekens and handed it to me so that we could drink together while we collected the final items on our list. I accepted the gift and took a large gulp, to Emil's satisfaction.

We set about rejoining Eveline and Nicolaie, whom we eventually found at the far end of another aisle. As we made our way toward our friends, Emil hurried ahead a few paces, only to stop abruptly behind a smartly dressed twenty-something woman standing in the middle of the aisle. The woman was too engrossed in a text message to notice Emil sneaking up behind her. Emil let out a full-throated and drawn-out climactic groan: "UUUUGHHHHH!!!," only to then circle behind me and briskly walk away. The bewildered woman slowly raised her head and reluctantly turned around to find me standing alone, utterly speechless, holding an open container, and soaked in beer. Eveline and Nicolaie doubled over in uproarious laughter as I got fingered for Emil's prank. When I eventually unfroze, I shook my head innocently and stammered out a flat-footed apology. Other shoppers eyeing the scene simply stood scandalized. Another called for security. While my companions gasped for air, I set my Heineken on the nearest shelf and made my way toward the register. I beckoned for the group to hurry up and follow suit.

Eveline, Nicolaie, and Emil emerged moments later, still laughing jovially, but now with a security guard shadowing them closely. I took out my wallet to pay for the groceries, but Emil chided me to put it away. "You're my guest," he reminded me. "You don't pay." While taken aback by the bill, Emil covered it in full, including the Heineken I had carelessly stranded on the store shelf. The guard then followed us out of the Hypermarket, back through the mall, and outside the front doors. Once we reached the parking lot the guard returned inside. We all then fell over with laughter. "Hold on for one second," Emil said as he gasped for air. Emil headed back toward the entrance of the shopping center to the very set of locked side doors that had given him so much trouble at the start of our visit. He unzipped his pants and started to urinate on them. With choked breath, Nicolaie waved Eveline and me to grab the grocery bags and make a run for it. Nicolaie waited for Emil while Eveline and I hurried as quickly as we could toward the bus stop. We were relieved to see one pulling in just as we arrived. We hopped through the crowded bus's back door, and as the bus pulled away, we watched Nicolaie and Emil taking flight. Running at full speed, they pulled confidently away from the mall security, who gave chase. Meanwhile, the others standing in the back of the bus groaned at our presence and pressed themselves forward down the middle aisle in an effort to distance themselves. Eveline and I, by contrast, struggled to compose ourselves amid the spectacle.

The group reconvened about half an hour later at the encampment. It was made up of a series of tents tucked away behind some trees on an undeveloped plot of land. The location's main selling point was its close proximity to Stefan's Place. Eveline opened fresh beers for Emil and Nicolaie upon their triumphant return. The two told tall tales of their harrowing escape from mall security. Eveline also turned on music from a battery-powered radio. The men relaxed while she set the table—an overturned milk crate with a blanket on top to provide an even surface. Eveline lit a cigarette, and unlike when she smoked at the park or at Stefan's Place, she carried an ashtray with her as she set about her work. She was, after all, at home (*acasă*)

FIGURE 6.6. Washing dishes. Photo by Bruce O'Neill.

and did not want to make a mess of it. Eveline removed the packaged meats, bread, and cheese from their cellophane wrappers and carefully laid them out before inviting us to gather around.

Emil began the meal with a friendly scolding directed my way. He ordered me not to eat like a "city boy" while parodying dainty gestures such as taking small nibbles, drinking with one's pinky finger in the air, and dabbing the corners of one's mouth repeatedly with a napkin. Emil was parodying my first visit to his camp, when I balked at using a spoon that he had, with the best of intentions, spit-cleaned for me to taste a soup that, to my nose, had already turned. Instead, Emil told me to eat as though from the country. Emil demonstrated by biting down into the loaf of bread and ripping off a large chunk with his teeth, then taking a large swig of beer. I dutifully followed suit as the others laughed and cheered encouragingly.

To be clear, Emil and Eveline were by no means ill mannered or anti-social. Over the course of my repeated trips to their encampment in the city, but also to their home in the countryside, Eveline and Emil always presented themselves as thoughtful and caring. The two generally placed a premium on conforming to a sense of working-class respectability. Emil's turn toward the carnivalesque in this instance was principled and strategic rather than ignorant. The production of carnivalesque laughter enabled this skilled construction worker with a home in the countryside to momentarily transcend the indignant scrutiny that homeless men received in the city.

Amid the carnivalesque festivities, time flew. An incidental glance at my watch indicated that it was just past three thirty, and the evening meal at Stefan's Place was to be served in less than an hour. Even though everyone had just eaten, no one was willing to pass on a free meal. We cleaned off our plates as well as our hands and faces and headed back to the parking lot where we had begun our morning. There we found the other beneficiaries we had left five hours earlier, still sitting on the curb and lying beneath the trees, with pained expressions of waiting on their faces. The laughter died out of Emil, Eveline, and Nicolaie as we resumed our earlier places on the same stretch of curb. Emil offered Leonard a half nod, and he, in turn, welcomed us back.

On Boredom and Resignation

"There is a general boredom that is now in Romania, which is a kind of resignation," the creative director responsible for the Nescafé advertisement explained. High-earning young professionals sporting designer sneakers and fitted T-shirts held a breakout session at a nearby table. The chatter of their brainstorming rumbled in the background. "Maybe you were twenty when the revolution came, and you were full of hope," the director continued, "but now you have this sense that politics disappointed a lot. Now you are pretty bitter with society because this is it. Communism was better. Now you just have to cope and wait to die."

From the distant vantage of the creative director, downwardly mobile Romanians might very well appear to be resigned. The homeless, after all, showed no sign of taking up the instruments of civil society to advocate for an alternative future, one where they might exist as something other than collateral damage. They did not picket the government building, occupy a

FIGURE 6.7. Drinking Nescafé. Photo by Bruce O'Neill.

main square, or message a general public. Instead, the homeless directed their energies toward buying into various forms of self-stimulation. At such a distance, resignation, rather than revolution, appeared to encapsulate the homeless's politics.[15]

Such an analysis, however, elided the tremendous coordinated and collective effort that the homeless invested in these acts of consumption and in the claims of belonging embedded within them. Time and again, boredom compelled the homeless into action, often in dramatic and compromising ways. The homeless timed their showers, buffed their shoes, and contributed to economies of toiletries. They sifted through trash bags filled with donated clothes, and they scrimped, scavenged, and saved their money. At stake in these occasionally epic struggles to manage their personal appearance and finances was not just the stimulating jolt that a rush of caffeine or sugar could afford. Their efforts, when successful, achieved nothing less than a sense of belonging to the mental and material spaces that global consumerism made available but that generally existed just out of their reach. Outside the shower of Stefan's Place and down the aisles of the Hypermarket, homeless men and women fought to incorporate themselves into the pleasures and possibilities that liberal reformers had long promised.

The homeless, ultimately, were not submissive but active, and their efforts should not be so quickly dismissed as apolitical. The homeless's efforts to gorge on fast food and relax on IKEA sofas opened up a space of incorporation for themselves into the city, but also into the larger imagined communities of Europe and of the global economy. Rather than being resigned, the homeless battled exclusion as much as boredom, one trip to the mall at a time. On successful occasions, these efforts left the homeless somewhere other than on the margins and feeling something other than boredom.

This is not to say that the homeless's strategy is satisfying. The effects of consumerism, even when politically invested, are thin and fleeting by design.[16] The things that sate desire and that mark incorporation in one moment fail to do so in the next. This is why the battle against boredom, when waged at the level of consumption, is always fought uphill. The homeless's lurking anxiety about their embodiment and comportment while inhabiting consumer spaces only complicated the endeavor, tilting the battlefield ever more steeply against them. Rather than advancing, the homeless's efforts at consumption inevitably led them right back where they started, albeit determined to try all the more intently to consume their way out of boredom again. Examples abounded wherever the homeless took shelter. "One night, about three years ago," Marian began to recount in his dormitory at Backwoods, where we sat sipping coffee, "I tried to drink a whole canister of Nes[café]." Marian had to shout his story to me. News headlines blasted out of his television set so that they could be heard over the techno music that streamed out of his boom box. "What else was there to do? I mean, I'm stuck in this filthy place," Marian sneered as he looked around his room. "I just wanted to feel something!" he cried out above the cacophony. "So I drank three large mugs really quickly—as fast as I could, one right after the other. I then kept drinking Nes for four more hours. By then my heart was pounding really hard. My entire body was shaking with powerful tremors (şoc puternic)." Marian shook himself to illustrate. "My wife took me to the hospital, and I got pills to help me calm down. The doctor said I might have had a mild heart attack. I'm supposed to feel lucky to be alive," he said while shaking his head. He drained the contents of his mug and instantly set about boiling some more water. Rather than being the solution, yet another mug of Nescafé should really be seen as part of the problem.

CONCLUSION

The collective bass from dozens of nightclubs reverberated through the winding streets of Lipscani, Bucharest's old-town district, while higher notes and burlesque dancers competed for the attention of the tightly packed crowd milling past. Located a ten-minute walk away from the black market, the newly gentrified Lipscani development suggested in 2014 that another kind of life entirely had finally arrived in Bucharest. The historic neighborhood's corridors were clogged with revelers. Half-clad women stood on tabletops and inside empty window frames. They shouted shot prices and, with puckered lips, forced eye contact with passersby in an effort to lure people into dance clubs bearing names like Bordello, Banker's Bar, and Sin City. Just beyond their doorways, strobe-lit dance floors flickered, showcasing an undulating mix of expats and tourists but also Romanian professionals and aspirational college students.

The effervescent affluence of this newly developed nightlife district stood in sharp contrast to Lipscani's decades of neglect. The historically stately neighborhood had been, in the time before communism, the home of artisans and craftspeople. Its baroque architecture, cobbled streets, and winding roads had contributed to Bucharest's once-proud reputation as an epicenter of art and culture. Its bourgeois aesthetic, however, had placed the neighborhood out of favor during communism. Following the earthquake of 1977, communist-era planners and bureaucrats neglected Lipscani entirely. Rather than repairing shaken walls and damaged roofs, the neighborhood's residents and businesses relocated into new construction

FIGURE CONC.1. The New "Old Town." Photo by Bruce O'Neill.

elsewhere in the city. Impoverished Roma families squatted in these otherwise abandoned buildings under conditions described by local architects
and urbanists as "unsanitary" and "unhygienic."[1] Windows lacked panes,
cracks spidered through drywall, and roofs threatened to cave in as Lipscani degenerated into blight.

The largely pre-twentieth-century building stock eventually caught the
attention of local developers interested in creating a nightlife district in
Bucharest. The hope was that new life could be breathed into the historic
neighborhood in such a way that it might attract international tourists.[2]
With the backing of the European Bank for Reconstruction and Development, as well as local investors, the gentrification of Lipscani's main corridor began in 2005.[3] Construction crews completed the majority of the renovations at about the same time as this study came to its own conclusion.

FIGURE CONC.2. Renovation. Photo by Bruce O'Neill.

Lipscani's mud roads, crumbling façades, and impoverished Roma families quickly gave way to an upscale clientele shuffling between 140 different stylized bars, clubs, and restaurants, almost all of which stayed open well into the early hours of the morning.[4]

In the international press, the Lipscani development stood as a testament that Bucharest had shed its reputation for poverty. Instead, Bucharest was emerging as an up-and-coming place to be.[5] The Romanian National Tourist Office, eager to attract young visitors with loose wallets, actively marketed Bucharest's bars and clubs, as well as Romania's Black Sea beaches, to international audiences as the new "party capital of Central Europe."[6] One particularly lucrative niche was as an inexpensive destination for British and Australian bachelor parties and so-called lads' weekends.[7] Websites such as BucharestStag.com, LastNightOfFreedom.co.uk,

FIGURE CONC.3. Another kind of life. Photo by Bruce O'Neill.

and StagDoBucharest.com assembled weekend packages that shepherded the drunk and rowdy from three-star hotels to shooting ranges, bars, and strip clubs. These efforts at rebranding Bucharest were effective. By 2013 the Lipscani neighborhood was recording thousands of visitors each weekend and generated €150 million in annual revenue, placing the development's value on par with the city's largest and most luxurious malls.[8] Lipscani's corridors rapidly emerged as a favorite destination for Bucharest's stable of expats as well as the growing number of tourists passing through town. Guides with oversized fire-engine-red umbrellas tacked back and forth between Italian and German as they hurried their tours through tight turns on newly cobblestoned streets in an effort not to completely arrest the flow of foot traffic. Inside Lipscani's gourmet cafés and gelato shops, pubs, and nightclubs, orders placed in English were as likely to be heard as those in

Romanian. For those spending their time in Lipscani with foreign currency in their pockets, Bucharest did not appear to be so much boring as a bacchanal. Cheap drinks, delicious food, and an Old World charm could be had in the newly revived Paris of the Balkans for a fraction of what it cost to visit Paris, France.

With all the revelry, it would be tempting to infer that Bucharest's time had come. After decades of economic instability—marked most recently by communist-era austerity, then the shock of transitioning toward the global economy, only to be followed by the great recession of 2008—Lipscani suggested that the Romanian economy had finally found its place in the world. Lipscani certainly captured the imagination of young and seasoned travelers who were eager to find the next Prague, and the money that now pumped through Lipscani's bars and clubs also circulated through to nearby hotels, banks, and restaurants. The nightlife development provided a glossy example of the ways in which those in Bucharest were getting incorporated into a global system of stylized production and consumption. "It's great money if you can tap into it," noted one taxi driver earning his keep shuttling tourists to nights on the town and back to their hotels. With great fanfare, overwhelming noise, and colorful flashing lights, those partying late into the night found themselves worked up in a lather.

"Yeah," Florin explained to me just down the road at the black market as the Lipscani development was taking shape, "when you come from abroad, or if you work for a foreign firm, then life in Bucharest is pretty good." Like the others at the black market, Florin occasionally pitched in on building renovations in Lipscani when the official construction crew needed an extra pair of hands. "Foreigners can afford to do whatever they want here because they get paid in euros or dollars, but then they get to spend in lei. That makes them feel really wealthy and this city becomes really cheap, and then all kinds of possibilities open up here," Florin assessed with a sense of envy.

Those stuck at the black market did not deny that there was material well-being to be found in Bucharest. For those who had money to spend, the city opened up into a wealth of stimulating possibilities. Fine dining, luxurious malls, ubiquitous drinks, and casual sex could be found in numerous neighborhoods throughout the capital. The catch, these downwardly mobile manual laborers continued to insist, was that such expanding possibilities had little to do with them. The possibilities posed by these developments did not flow evenly throughout Romania to encompass all of its inhabitants. Instead, developments such as Lipscani worked to incorporate only very particular people and locations into the action while pushing out and skipping over others.[9] This was certainly true of foreign tourists: favorable exchange rates allowed them to take taxis rather than wait for public transit and to order another round of drinks without fretting over the coming bar bill. But those stuck at the black market also associated this cosmopolitan otherness, with a sense of self-evidence, with Romania's burgeoning professional class. They too worked for foreign firms, and while salaries in the Bucharest back office did not keep pace with those of their counterparts in Paris or Rome, for example, the salaries for these positions were regularly quoted in euros, even if they were ultimately paid out in the Romanian lei. It was also common for upwardly mobile Romanians to maintain a bank account in euros to manage their savings and to facilitate major purchases such as real estate, automobiles, and international travel. From the perspective of those at the black market, the ability of Romania's professional class to navigate Bucharest in terms of euros afforded them a material well-being and capacity to consume that was associated with other places in Europe. To those unable to flourish in a competitive labor market, it came as no surprise that highly trained professionals enjoyed themselves in places like Lipscani, while they themselves could not. Whether foreign or Romanian, well-trained professionals found themselves already caught up in near-constant market-driven production and consumption. Those who were already keyed in to globalization were now enjoying in Lipscani yet another highly stylized space to get keyed up.[10]

"But it's a different story for us," Florin continued. "We have to earn in lei and spend in lei. It's really hard being Romanian in Romania. The people here can't afford to go to Lipscani." The other men waiting at the black market agreed. These men were, after all, not the targeted demographic of the new nightlife district. While its renovation provided some occasional work, these men had no reason to believe that the Lipscani development would ever incorporate them in any sustained way. Priced out of the bars as consumers, these establishments also did not provide employment opportunities once the drywalling was done and the sawdust swept away. Although bars, clubs, and restaurants are dependent on countless hours of unskilled labor to bus tables, hose down toilets, and scrub dishes, these redundant construction workers knew they did not look the part to participate in the day-to-day operations of a stylized, nighttime economy. "Those clubs want young faces doing the work. They'll get college kids to clean the tables," acknowledged another with blunt honesty. Rather than getting caught up in the smooth space of global consumerism, these men, much like the Roma families who had squatted in Lipscani when the neighborhood had fallen out of favor, remained stuck on the outside of the excitement with little else to do but look longingly inside. Opportunity, for those sitting around the black market, remained foreclosed. Rather than sweeping them up in global flows of money, media, and people, globalization left the noncompetitive laborers standing around the black market stuck in a space of boredom.

What Bucharest's homeless and unemployed men and women made clear, ultimately, is just how integral boredom is to a globalism that presents itself as a phenomenon of pure acceleration. The market pressure introduced to Romania after the fall of communism to speed up life for the affluent and well trained simultaneously had the opposite effect on those displaced by it. The global financial crisis of 2008 threw this slowing global affect into clear relief as markets crashed, jobs dissolved, and savings accounts emptied in the blink of an eye.[11] The effect of Romania's troubled efforts at global integration was, for many, to place on pause their life narratives, rather than move them forward at a greater clip.

Importantly, this viscerally embodied sense of life coming to a halt is not a symptom of an episodic crisis of globalization. Globalization's slowing down of the world is no accident. Rather, the episodic crisis provided a point of entry into the quiet affective politics of boredom and displacement that is endemic to the global economy. The smooth space of flows that efficiently shuttle some people and things, and that brightly capture global imaginaries along the way, are unthinkable without the simultaneous tying down of other people and things. Speed, after all, requires logistics.[12] As David Harvey clearly illustrates, the annihilation of space by time necessitates the production of a particular landscape that is "fixed" in space. This fixed landscape facilitates movement but itself does not move.[13] Harvey's notion of fixity points to the inert infrastructure that is as necessary for the movement of the migrant laborer and the transatlantic jet-setter as it is for the instant message and the coffee bean.[14] All are dependent on the production of stationary infrastructure such as depots, airports, roads, and cables to enable the steady flow from an over here to an over there.

But fixity is more than infrastructural. As the proliferation of boredom makes clear, fixity is also a profound mode of being imposed on those who have been displaced by globally competitive markets. Fixity as a social relationship gets internalized and interpreted by the displaced as boredom.

Shelters and day centers, squatter camps and black labor markets, are integral to globalization not because they smooth out global flows but precisely because they evoke the opposite effect. These marginal spaces make up a sticky periphery that fixes the undesirable out of the way. The poorhouse, as Paul Virilio notes, "solve[s] a problem less of enclosure or exclusion than of traffic."[15]

The boredom experienced by those fixed along globalism's sticky periphery is not only a matter of the dragging passage of time. It is also fundamentally an issue of place amid the global production of desire.[16] Boredom captures the inability to move beyond the sticky periphery in order to get caught up in globalism's smooth space of flows, which stretches, in this instance, from Lipscani's stylized bars and clubs to the better life believed to exist in Italy, Spain, and France. It is over there, in the global economy's much-talked-about fast lane, that the opportunity to live the good life hangs ever so cruelly out of reach through the perceived availability of steady work, high-value currencies, and comfortable levels of consumption. Boredom registers across the senses of discarded workers this yawning gap between globalization's promise of hypermobility and the everyday fact of being tossed away from the action.

This ethnographic observation allows for a dramatic rethinking of both boredom and alienation in the global economy. The boredom that plagues globalization does not drift back and forth over a bourgeoisie disenchanted with the immediacy of surrounding train stations, as it did in Martin Heidegger's time.[17] The global economy has largely succeeded in connecting and accelerating the lives of the people caught up in it, keeping those with money to spend steadily stimulated and always on the move. Boredom may mark sticky moments for the comfortably off, but these moments are fleeting. Internet portals proliferating on the glossy surfaces of phones, watches, and eyeglasses, for example, offer the promise, for those who can afford them, not only of staying informed and connected but also of being always able to escape. Delayed trains, for today's ticketed passengers, do not stall movement so much as change its trajectory, sending the physically inert to explore an endless web of digital spaces and mental worlds, for example, while they await their movement down the track.

Boredom, instead, grinds down on the global economy's most peripheral populations as once-viable careers dissolve, previously stable households foreclose, and a lifetime of savings evaporates. A gnawing sense of the world slowing down is as endemic to the aged and unwanted bodies aggregated along the global periphery as acceleration is to the youthful and well-trained who race through its smooth center. Not only do boredom and poverty go hand in hand amid globalization, but boredom marks globalization's politics of life and death. In a moment where mobility is life, boredom emerges as the affective expression of one's condemnation to a slow death. Boredom, here, is not a petty condition, as it has been so commonly posed since the nineteenth century. In an era of global capitalism, boredom is a biopolitical state that corrodes inner worlds and social networks just as material deprivation ravishes the body.

The emergence of boredom as an enduring and brutalizing affect of globalization, ultimately, provides a vantage from which to rethink the politics of alienation anew. Nearly a century ago, social theorists were also struck by a widely felt sense of displacement amid a rapidly changing economy. Writing at the onset of twentieth-century urban industrial expansion, Émile Durkheim sounded the alarm over what he saw as waning social solidarity. "As the market extends," Durkheim warned, "machines replace men; manufacturing replaces hand-work. The worker is regimented, separated from his family throughout the day."[18] The economic boom, as much as the bust, Durkheim concluded, eroded the moral rules that rendered the masses a coherent society. These moral rules not only restricted behaviors and imposed obligations but also constituted a durable sense of community among otherwise disparate people that grounded each and every person. These moral rules tied people down and gave each individual his or her collective bearings. Moral rules provided a framework through which people could feel out their place in the world. The great danger of alienation from the factory and from family, Durkheim concluded in his time, was the dissolution of these moral rules. As the very ties that bind erode, people become alienated, uprooted, and set adrift without a moral compass to guide them.[19]

Amid the chaotic upheaval of the city's expanding industrial economy, one that threatened to uproot and to set adrift, Durkheim called for a reinvestment in the most local of scales, to "contract our horizon" and to completely immerse oneself in one's immediacy.[20] Deeply nostalgic, Durkheim wished to combat a growing sense of alienation by tying people down, shrinking the world so that people might regain their bearings. It was a solution that looked to past social forms in order to mediate the fallout of emerging problems.

Nearly a century later, a deeply felt alienation linked to a changing economy persists. But its dynamics have inverted in critical ways. For those who are bored in Bucharest, the great danger is not that alienation leaves them aimlessly adrift. Rather, the danger of alienation is that it pins people down, preventing them from moving in the ways that global flows make possible. To be tied down, in this moment, is to be trapped by all the wrong forces. Fixed in place along the periphery, the economically vulnerable are unable to move toward a horizon that they themselves clearly identify as highly desirable. This horizon is made up of the places located beyond globalism's sticky periphery and within its smooth spaces, where the promise of a good life not only clusters but also flows. This is the life organized by market-driven production and consumption: steady work, a finished home, drinks on the town, and weekends at the mall. This is the direction in which Bucharest's homeless seek to move, if only they had the right kind of inertia to get there.

The deeply felt problem posed by boredom in this historical moment cannot be remedied by a return to a past form, as Durkheim once suggested.[21] Whereas Durkheim proposed overcoming alienation by tying people down, relief for those stuck in the space of boredom now comes through moving toward opportunity. As global capitalism expands horizons and opens up new possibilities, the challenge posed by alienation is to find new ways to uproot. Uprootedness, in this moment, allows those fixed along the global periphery to move in desired directions, advancing their own life narratives by bringing new opportunities within reach. The struggle to get caught up with globalism is being undertaken day in and day out by Bucharest's homeless and unemployed, a struggle that undoubtedly resonates within the quiet moments and idle chatter of people the world over who are also wondering how to gain their own traction in an evermore competitive global economy.

NOTES

PREFACE

1   I conducted the ethnographic fieldwork for this book in Bucharest, Romania, from June 2007 to June 2008 and from June 2010 to November 2011, with shorter research trips to Bucharest in the summers of 2009 and 2012. Throughout the book I use pseudonyms when referring to the men and women I interviewed and observed in order to protect their anonymity. In certain ethnographic vignettes, I have obscured or changed minor details that are immaterial to the analysis but that could be used to reveal a person's identity. I draw the quotations for this book from recorded and transcribed interviews and from detailed notes. With rare exception, these interviews were conducted in Romanian. I translated and edited transcripts and field notes cautiously and with great care to preserve the original meaning and emotion of the ethnographic moment. To that end, I use ellipses within quotes to punctuate the moments when voices trail off or when speakers struggle to find words, rather than to denote the omission of small phrases, repetitive information, or extraneous details.

2   Joanne Passaro, *The Unequal Homeless: Men on the Streets, Women in Their Place* (New York: Routledge, 1996).

3   For the law defining homelessness, see Romania, Parlamentul României, LEGE Nr. 292/2011, 2011.

4   Dimitrina Petrova, "The Roma: Between a Myth and the Future," *Social Research* 70, no. 1 (2003): 111–61.

5   The Chicago school of sociology characterizes homeless persons as leading adventurous lives. In the early twentieth century, working-class men looking to escape the boredom of routinized factory or farm work took to the rails to live a hobo lifestyle of travel, drunkenness, and law breaking. See Nels Anderson, *The Hobo: The Sociology of the Homeless Man* (Chicago: University of Chicago Press,

1965); and Todd DePastino, *Citizen Hobo: How a Century of Homelessness Shaped America* (Chicago: University of Chicago Press, 2003).

6   Tim Allen, "Euro Area Unemployment Rate at 10.0%," Eurostat Newsrelease 59/2010 (Luxembourg, 2010).

7   Allen, "Euro Area Unemployment Rate."

8   On U.S. unemployment levels, see Catherine Rampell, "Still Nearly Five Unemployed Workers for Every Opening," *New York Times*, February 8, 2011. Krugman's argument, ultimately, is that the economic crisis of 2008 had lasting effects on employment trends in the United States, offering the unemployed little hope of becoming economically active in the foreseeable future. See Paul Krugman, "The Wrong Worries," *New York Times*, August 4, 2011, http://www .nytimes.com/2011/08/05/opinion/the-wrong-worries.html?_r=0. The American media cast the hauntingly quiet life of unemployment as a new economic reality rather than as a blip that is necessarily followed by recovery.

9   For example, see James Ferguson, *Give a Man a Fish: Reflections on the New Politics of Distribution* (Durham, NC: Duke University Press, 2015); Craig Jeffrey, *Timepass: Youth, Class, and the Politics of Waiting in India* (Stanford, CA: Stanford University Press, 2010); and Zygmunt Bauman, *Wasted Lives: Modernity and Its Outcasts* (Cambridge: Polity, 2004).

10 Saskia Sassen, *Expulsions: Brutality and Complexity in the Global Economy* (Cambridge, MA: Harvard University Press, 2014).

11 On the forces that reproduce poverty, see, for example, Thomas Belmonte, *The Broken Fountain* (New York: Columbia University Press, 1989); Loïc Wacquant, *Urban Outcasts: A Comparative Sociology of Advanced Marginality* (Cambridge: Polity, 2008); Laurence Ralph, *Renegade Dreams: Living through Injury in Gangland Chicago* (Chicago: University of Chicago Press, 2014); and Philippe Bourgois, *In Search of Respect: Selling Crack in El Barrio*, 2nd ed. (Cambridge: Cambridge University Press, 2003). On the effects of becoming poor, see Katherine S. Newman, *Falling from Grace: Downward Mobility in the Age of Affluence* (Berkeley: University of California Press, 1988); see also Mun Young Cho, *The Specter of "the People": Urban Poverty in Northeast China* (Ithaca, NY: Cornell University Press, 2013).

12 Thorstein Veblen writes, "In order to gain and to hold the esteem of men it is not sufficient merely to possess wealth or power. The wealth or power must be put in evidence, for esteem is awarded only on evidence. And not only does the evidence of wealth serve to impress one's importance on others and to keep their sense of his importance alive and alert, but it is of scarcely less use in building up and preserving one's self-complacency." Veblen, *The Theory of the Leisure Class*, ed. M. Banta, Oxford World's Classics (Oxford: Oxford University Press, 2007) 26. Conspicuous consumption serves to demonstrate a superior class status. It is a theme taken up and developed in the writings of Jean Baudrillard on the middle class: "The middle class tends rather towards conspicuous consumption. They are, in this regard, heirs to the great capitalist dinosaurs of the nineteenth and early twentieth centuries." Baudrillard, *The*

Consumer Society: Myths and Structures (London: Sage, 1998), 91. Pierre Bourdieu adds horizontal nuance to the conversation, noting how consumer taste and style can be used to differentiate social actors within a given class strata. Pierre Bourdieu, *Distinction: A Social Critique of the Judgment of Taste* (Cambridge, MA: Harvard University Press, 1987).

13 Daphne Berdahl illustrated how citizenship and mass consumption became entangled in a reunified Germany, whereby East Germans became incorporated into a democratic nation-state through their participation in consumer practices. Berdahl, *On the Social Life of Postsocialism: Memory, Consumption, Germany*, ed. Matti Bunzl (Bloomington: Indiana University Press, 2010). Jennifer Patico's work with teachers in St. Petersburg showed that consumerism is a critical site for tracking the shift in status boundaries and one's incorporation into Russia's emerging middle class after the fall of communism. Patico, *Consumption and Social Change in a Post-Soviet Middle Class* (Stanford, CA: Stanford University Press, 2008). In her work on home renovations, Krisztina Fehérváry documents the struggle of Hungarian households to replicate a standard of living believed to be "normal" across Europe. At stake in remodeled kitchens and bathrooms is a claim to incorporation in a fully European standard of living. Fehérváry, *Politics in Color and Concrete: Socialist Materialities and the Middle Class in Hungary*, New Anthropologies of Europe (Bloomington: Indiana University Press, 2013).

14 On social death, see Michel Foucault, *The Birth of Biopolitics: Lectures at the Collège de France, 1978–79*, Michel Foucault: Lectures at the Collège de France (New York: Palgrave Macmillan, 2008).

15 Katherine Verdery, "The 'Etatization' of Time in Ceausescu's Romania," in *What Was Socialism, and What Comes Next?* (Princeton, NJ: Princeton University Press, 1996), 39–58.

16 For Eastern Europe, see, for example, Martin Demant Frederiksen, *Young Men, Time, and Boredom in the Republic of Georgia* (Philadelphia: Temple University Press, 2013); Tova Hojdestrand, *Needed by Nobody: Homelessness and Humanness in Post-socialist Russia* (Ithaca, NY: Cornell University Press, 2009); and David A. Kideckel, *Getting By in Postsocialist Romania: Labor, the Body, and Working-Class Culture* (Bloomington: Indiana University Press, 2008). For cities in the global south, see Daniel Mains, *Hope Is Cut: Youth, Unemployment, and the Future in Urban Ethiopia*, Global Youth (Philadelphia: Temple University Press, 2013); and Jeffrey, *Timepass.*

17 João Guilherme Biehl, Byron Good, and Arthur Kleinman, *Subjectivity: Ethnographic Investigations* (Berkeley: University of California Press, 2007).

INTRODUCTION

1 Unless otherwise noted, currency is given in the new Romanian *lei*, or RON, which became the currency of Romania in July 1, 2005. The prior currency is referred to as the ROL, or the old Romanian lei, which circulated between 1952 and 2005. Over the course of this research, the exchange rate of the RON varied

from 2.97 to 4.0 against the U.S. dollar. Throughout the book, I convert the value of RON into U.S. dollars according to the exchange rate at the time of the vignette as recorded in my field notes.

2   The global studies literature posits an ever-accelerating universe, one where industry and infrastructure accelerate the movement of people, objects, and ideas, whereby speed ultimately transforms the material basis of our lives; see Manuel Castells, *The Rise of the Network Society: The Information Age; Economy, Society, and Culture* (London: Wiley, 2011), xliv. Global connections, for example, work to ease "friction," so that resources may circulate rapidly to distant markets; see Anna L. Tsing, *Friction: An Ethnography of Global Connection* (Princeton, NJ: Princeton University Press, 2004). Media and objects from one country appear on the screens and on the store shelves of other countries, creating international competition for the attention of local consumers; see Arjun Appadurai, *Modernity at Large: Cultural Dimensions of Globalization* (Minneapolis: University of Minnesota Press, 1996). Labor in demand flies comfortably across oceans, moving with ease past border security; see Aihwa Ong, *Neoliberalism as Exception: Mutations in Citizenship and Sovereignty* (Durham, NC: Duke University Press, 2006). The digitization of financial markets has rendered trade instantaneous, as well as political messaging and coordination; see, respectively, Caitlin Zaloom, *Out of the Pits: Traders and Technology from Chicago to London* (Chicago: University of Chicago Press, 2006); and Jeffrey S. Juris, *Networking Futures: The Movements against Corporate Globalization*, Experimental Futures (Durham, NC: Duke University Press, 2008). Across the literature, the global is structured around a "politics of speed," one that gets internalized by the body as workers ingest an expanding array of beverages and pharmaceuticals in an effort to keep apace; see Paul Virilio, *Speed and Politics*, Foreign Agents (Los Angeles: Semiotext(e), 2006); and Jason Pine, "Economy of Speed: The New Narco-Capitalism," *Public Culture* 19, no. 2 (2007): 357–66. While individuals seek chemical solutions to the intensification of movement, the state streamlines its institutions in order to stay responsive; see Saskia Sassen, *Losing Control? Sovereignty in the Age of Globalization*, Leonard Hastings Schoff Lectures (New York: Columbia University Press, 2013).

3   David Harvey describes the condition of postmodernity as "the annihilation of space through time," or the overcoming of spatial divides through the speeding up of movement. Harvey, *The Condition of Postmodernity: An Enquiry into the Origins of Cultural Change* (London: Blackwell, 1992), 205.

4   Charles Dickens, *Bleak House*, ed. H. K. Browne (London: Bradbury and Evans, 1853).

5   See Louis-Ferdinand Céline, *Journey to the End of the Night* (New York: New Directions, 2006). More recently, in an effort to interpret the suicide of the American writer David Foster Wallace, Jonathan Franzen links boredom, despair, and solitude, writing that "it seems fair to say that David died of boredom." Franzen, "Farther Away: 'Robinson Crusoe,' David Foster Wallace, and the Island of Solitude," *New Yorker*, April 18, 2011, http://www.newyorker.com/magazine/2011/04

/18/farther-away-jonathan-franzen. Wallace, Franzen notes, positioned himself with "nothing but his own interesting self to survive on." While this ethnography foregrounds historical and political forces that isolate vulnerable populations, as opposed to individual dispositions as does Franzen, the terrain of boredom explored overlaps.

6 This book takes a phenomenological approach to affect and is situated most clearly within the approaches of Kathleen Stewart, *Ordinary Affects* (Durham, NC: Duke University Press, 2007); Lauren Berlant, *Cruel Optimism* (Durham, NC: Duke University Press, 2011); and Sara Ahmed, *The Promise of Happiness* (Durham, NC: Duke University Press, 2010), rather than the ontological line of affect theory, which begins with Gilles Deleuze in *Spinoza: Practical Philosophy* (San Francisco: City Lights, 1988). From this phenomenological perspective, affect promises a way of theorizing how individual bodies and historical processes come into contact, revealing how the body mediates between what is sensed and what is known; see Donovan Schaefer, "The Promise of Affect: The Politics of the Event in Ahmed's *The Promise of Happiness* and Berlant's *Cruel Optimism*," *Theory and Event* 16, no. 2 (2013), https://muse.jhu.edu/ (accessed July 6, 2016). As Stewart writes, "Ordinary affects are the varied, surging capacities to affect and to be affected that give everyday life the quality of a continual motion of relations, scenes, contingencies, and emergences. . . . [They] are public feelings that begin and end in broad circulation, but they're also the stuff that seemingly intimate lives are made of." Stewart, *Ordinary Affects*, 1–2. Ordinary affect is a zone of convergence between the body and politics, a social and historical sensorium that "makes itself present to us before [the present] becomes anything else." Berlant, *Cruel Optimism*, 4. This book traces how boredom, as an ordinary affect, captures the way global circulations are felt by the body and, in the spirit of Ahmed's *The Promise of Happiness*, how these feelings of boredom shape the way individuals evaluate their own lives and their relationship to society, providing a window into the historical and the political from the most intimate to the broadest of scales.

7 From Karl Marx to Antonio Gramsci to David Harvey, a major underlying assumption of nineteenth- and twentieth-century urban theory is that cities shape subjects through the material conditions of labor. See Marx, *Capital: An Abridged Edition* (New York: Oxford University Press, 2008); Gramsci, "Americanism and Fordism," in *A Gramsci Reader: Selected Writings, 1916–1935*, ed. Hannan Hever and Eric J. Hobsbawm (New York: New York University Press, 2000), 275–99; and Harvey, *Condition of Postmodernity*. It is a mode of theorizing tied to the rising prosperity found within cities throughout the so-called Western world. Even those excluded from the formal economy of cities could participate in robust shadow economies that, while exploitive, nevertheless facilitated material well-being and ambition; see Philippe Bourgois, *In Search of Respect: Selling Crack in El Barrio*, 2nd ed. (Cambridge: Cambridge University Press, 2003). However, at the dawn of the twenty-first century, and in the wake of a global financial crisis, the demand for labor in cities contracted throughout

Africa, India, and Eastern Europe; see, respectively, James Ferguson, *Give a Man a Fish: Reflections on the New Politics of Distribution* (Durham, NC: Duke University Press, 2015); Craig Jeffrey, *Timepass: Youth, Class, and the Politics of Waiting in India* (Stanford, CA: Stanford University Press, 2010); and Martin Demant Frederiksen, *Young Men, Time, and Boredom in the Republic of Georgia* (Philadelphia: Temple University Press, 2013). As surplus labor expanded, a growing number of urban residents are now shaped not in relation to production but by their irrelevance to it; see Zygmunt Bauman, *Wasted Lives: Modernity and Its Outcasts* (Cambridge: Polity, 2004).

8   Michel Foucault, *Society Must Be Defended: Lectures at the Collège de France* (New York: Picador, 2003), 256.

9   Lauren Berlant, "Slow Death (Sovereignty, Obesity, Lateral Agency)," *Critical Inquiry* 33, no. 4 (2007): 780.

10 The longest philosophical treatise addressing boredom to date is Martin Heidegger's *The Fundamental Concepts of Metaphysics*. Its guiding question asks, "Do things ultimately stand in such a way with us that a profound boredom draws back and forth like a silent fog in the abysses of Dasein?" Heidegger, *The Fundamental Concepts of Metaphysics: World, Finitude, Solitude* (Bloomington: Indiana University Press, 2001), 77. While inspired by the framing of Heidegger's question, this book does not adopt the ontological certainty of Heidegger's phenomenology. Instead, this book contextualizes boredom in historical and material relations through extended ethnographic fieldwork.

11 David Turnock, "Railways and Economic Development in Romania before 1918," *Journal of Transport Geography* 9, no. 2 (2001): 137–50.

12 Philip G. Eidelberg, *The Great Rumanian Peasant Revolt of 1907: Origins of a Modern Jacquerie*, East Central European Studies (Leiden: Brill Archive, 1974), 10.

13 Eidelberg, *Great Rumanian Peasant Revolt*, 11.

14 David Mitrany, *Marx against the Peasant: A Study in Social Dogmatism* (New York: Collier, 1961), 77. In 1905, 0.6 percent of all landowners owned 48.7 percent of the land in Romania, while the remaining 95.4 percent of landowners divided up just 40.3 percent of the land. Daniel Chirot and Charles Ragin, "The Market, Tradition and Peasant Rebellion: The Case of Romania in 1907," *American Sociological Review* 40, no. 4 (1975): 431. The imbalanced distribution of land left millions of Romanian peasants struggling to grow enough food to achieve self-sufficiency.

15 Mitrany, *Marx against the Peasant*, 53.

16 By 1906, one-third of peasant households could no longer afford large animals; the legislature also had to intervene to guarantee peasants two days a week to cultivate their own fields. Mitrany, *Marx against the Peasant*, 77.

17 Dennis Deletant, *Ceaușescu and the Securitate: Coercion and Dissent in Romania, 1965–1989* (London: M. E. Sharpe, 1995), 307.

18 Dan Petrescu, *Romania Country Brief: Europe and Central Asia Region* (Bucharest, Romania: World Bank Group, 2002).

19 Michael Vachon, "Bucharest: The House of the People," *World Policy Journal* 10, no. 4 (1993): 59–63.

20 Olivier Jean Blanchard, Kenneth A. Froot, and Jeffrey D. Sachs, *The Transition in Eastern Europe*, vol. 1 (Chicago: University of Chicago Press, 1994).

21 Nigel Harris, "Structural Adjustment and Romania," *Economic and Political Weekly* 29, no. 44 (1994): 2861.

22 Harris, "Structural Adjustment and Romania," 2862.

23 The inflation statistics are from International Monetary Fund, IMF *Approves Stand-By Credit for Romania*, press release no. 99/38 (Washington, DC: International Monetary Fund, 1999), and the unemployment and wage information is from Adrian-Nicolae Dan and Mariana Dan, "Housing Policy in Romania in Transition: Between State Withdrawal and Market Collapse," presented at the *International Conference on Globalization, Integration, and Social Development in Central and Eastern Europe*, 16 (Sibiu, Romania, September 6–8, 2003).

24 Dan and Dan, "Housing Policy in Romania."

25 Peter Gross and Vladimir Tismăneanu proclaimed the "end of postcommunism in Romania" based on the victory of pro-European democratic politicians over communist-era politicians in the elections of 2004. They also pointed to the development of a strong and active civil society in Romanian politics. Gross and Tismăneanu, "The End of Postcommunism in Romania," *Journal of Democracy* 16, no. 2 (2005): 149.

26 World Bank, *Country Partnership Strategy for Romania for the Period July 2009–June 2013*, Report No. 48665-ro, Central Europe and the Baltic Countries Country Unit (2009), 6.

27 Martin Brown and Ralph De Haas, "Foreign Banks and Foreign Currency Lending in Emerging Europe," *Economic Policy* 27, no. 69 (2012): 57–98. More than 60 percent of the outstanding loans to nonbanks in Romania were in a foreign currency. Pınar Yesin, "Foreign Currency Loans and Systemic Risk in Europe" (St. Louis, 2013), 220. Extensive borrowing on foreign currencies, mainly the euro, exposed Romanian households to a high risk of default owing to currency fluctuations.

28 Lars Svennebye, "GDP per Capita, Consumption per Capita and Comparative Price Levels in Europe," *Eurostat* (Luxembourg, 2008), 3.

29 D. L. Constantin, Zizi Goschin, and A. R. Danciu, "The Romanian Economy from Transition to Crisis: Retrospects and Prospects," *World Journal of Social Sciences* 1, no. 3 (2011): 155–71.

30 World Bank, *Country Partnership Strategy for Romania*.

31 J. Blazek and P. Netrdova, "Regional Unemployment Impacts of the Global Financial Crisis in the New Member States of the EU in Central and Eastern Europe," *European Urban and Regional Studies* 19, no. 1 (2012): 42–61, 53–54.

32 International Monetary Fund, *Romania—Fifth Review under the Stand-By Arrangement*, IMF Country Report (Washington, DC: International Monetary Fund, 2010), 11.

33 BBC *News*, "Romania Plans Big VAT Rise to Secure Bail-Out Fund," June 26, 2010, http://www.bbc.co.uk/news/10424900.

34 World Bank, *Partnership Strategy for Romania*, 11. Given how rarely the World Bank chastises low-income states for an inefficient social service system, it is worth quoting the World Bank report at length: "Social protection schemes do not address poverty well. Romania's social protection expenditure per capita is the lowest in the EU, and spending on poverty-targeted programs is low in proportion to GDP and to needs; it has actually declined in recent years. Only a few safety net programs perform well. . . . Leakages and inequity in social assistance programs are high: only 17 percent of the social assistance benefits reach the poorest quintile, 29 percent of the poor are excluded from the system, and half of the funds spill to the wealthier quintiles."

35 David Turnock, "Housing Policy in Romania," in *Housing Policies in Eastern Europe and the Soviet Union*, ed. J. A. A. Sillince, 134–69 (New York: Routledge, 1990).

36 Turnock, "Housing Policy in Romania."

37 United Nations Economic Commission For Europe, *Romania Country Profile on the Housing Sector* (Geneva: UNECE, 2001).

38 Homelessness in the United States and the United Kingdom is a social scientific and bureaucratic category that developed over the course of the twentieth century. See Nels Anderson, *The Hobo: The Sociology of the Homeless Man* (Chicago: University of Chicago Press, 1965); Christopher Jencks, *The Homeless* (Cambridge, MA: Harvard University Press, 1995); and William Julius Wilson, *The Truly Disadvantaged: The Inner City, the Underclass, and Public Policy* (Chicago: University of Chicago Press, 1990). Early twentieth-century investigations of homelessness focused on the so-called hobohemia or skid row, where socially dislocated men aggregated in single-room-occupancy hotels, boardinghouses, and day labor agencies. Anne Shlay and Peter Rossi, "Social Science Research and Contemporary Studies of Homelessness," *Annual Review of Sociology* 18, no. 1 (1992): 130–31. While these men had roofs over their heads, they lacked the familial and employment relationships needed to constitute a normative sense of home. Following processes of urban renewal in the 1980s and 1990s, the term *homelessness* evolved to denote a housing hardship linked to extreme poverty. Barrett A. Lee, Kimberly A. Tyler, and James D. Wright, "The New Homelessness Revisited," *Annual Review of Sociology* 36 (2010): 501–21. In this sense, "homelessness," both as a social category and as an analytical concept, was "invented." Ian Hacking, "Making Up People," in *Reconstructing Individualism: Autonomy, Individuality, and the Self in Western Thought*, ed. T. C. Heller and C. Brooke-Rose (Stanford, CA: Stanford University Press, 1986), 222–36.

39 Food and housing insecurity continues to be interpreted and addressed through a wide range of institutions. Medical doctors in Romania, for example, diagnose the poor as "social cases" so that they may reside in sanatoriums and

hospitals to receive basic food and shelter during the bitter cold of the winter months. Jack R. Friedman, "The 'Social Case,'" *Medical Anthropology Quarterly* 23, no. 4 (2009): 375–96.

40 This is true across socialist Eastern Europe. Take the figure of the *bomzh* in the Soviet Union. The term *bomzh* typically referred to un- or underemployed workers who did not have a registered address for their internal passport. Given universal housing policies, bomzh did not exist in the Soviet Union as an official bureaucratic category, even as it circulated as a social category referring to "bums." Douglas Rogers, "Moonshine, Money, and the Politics of Liquidity in Rural Russia," *American Ethnologist* 32, no. 1 (2005): 63–81, doi:10.1525/ae.2005.32.1.63. While they experienced housing insecurity, bomzh were not subjected to government enumeration, analysis, and intervention during communism as were the "homeless" found in liberal democracies.

41 Zoltán Kovács, "Cities from State-Socialism to Global Capitalism: An Introduction," *GeoJournal* 49, no. 1 (1999): 1–6.

42 Edet Belzberg, dir., *Children Underground* (Belzberg Films, 2001).

43 FEANTSA (European Federation of National Organizations Working with the Homeless), *Romania:* FEANTSA *Country Fiche* (Brussels: FEANTSA, 2012).

44 Romania, Parlamentul României, LEGE Nr. 292/2011, 2011.

45 FEANTSA, *Romania*.

46 Mary Douglas, *Purity and Danger: An Analysis of Concepts of Pollution and Taboo* (London: Taylor, 2002).

47 On occasion, I left expensive camera equipment, audio recording equipment, and winter clothes with my informants while I went to the bathroom or ran over to a grocery store to pick up snacks. While my informants could easily have stolen these items for their own use or for sale on the black market, the items were always presented back to me undisturbed.

48 Elizabeth Goodstein, *Experience without Qualities: Boredom and Modernity* (Stanford, CA: Stanford University Press, 2004).

49 See Dickens, *Bleak House*; David Foster Wallace, *The Pale King* (New York: Little, Brown, 2011); Friedrich Nietzsche, *Human, All Too Human: A Book for Free Spirits* (Cambridge: Cambridge University Press, 1996); and Heidegger, *Fundamental Concepts of Metaphysics*. On boredom in literature, see Patricia Meyer Spacks, *Boredom: The Literary History of a State of Mind* (Chicago: University of Chicago Press, 1996).

50 See Anton Chekhov, *The Duel* (Brooklyn: Melville House, 2011). Boredom frames much of Chekhov's writing. Chekhov associates boredom with the repetitive life of the countryside and juxtaposes it against the bustle of the city. Carol A. Flath, "Art and Idleness: Chekhov's 'The House with a Mezzanine,'" *Russian Review* 58, no. 3 (1999): 456–66. Chekhov develops boredom as a contemptible disposition, one closely intertwined with banality, senselessness, a stunted intellect, and moral emptiness. George Z. Patrick, "Chekhov's Attitude towards Life," *Slavonic and East European Review* 10, no. 30 (1932):

658. Chekhov's struggle with tuberculosis produced a spiritual ennui, a kind of separation from life that Chekhov found very frightening. Boredom emerged for Chekhov as a dark adversary to be conquered or ignored. Irene Oppenheim, "Chekhov's TB," *Threepenny Review* 29 (1987): 10–11.

51 "A relation of cruel optimism exists," Lauren Berlant writes, "when something you desire is actually an obstacle to your flourishing. . . . They become cruel only when the object that draws your attachment actively impedes the aim that brought you to it initially." Berlant, *Cruel Optimism*, 1–2. Consumer capitalism is a case in point, in that the production of new wants and needs outpaces the ability of consumers to achieve fulfillment. Rather than sating people, hyperconsumption ultimately leaves people unfulfilled and desiring more and different.

52 Consider this passage from the opening pages of Heidegger's *Fundamental Concepts of Metaphysics*: "Boredom is not simply an inner spiritual experience, rather something about it, namely *that which bores* and which lets being bored arise, comes toward us precisely *from out of things themselves*. It is much rather the case that boredom is outside, seated in what is boring, and creeps into us from the outside." Heidegger, *Fundamental Concepts of Metaphysics*, 83. For Heidegger, boredom is a property that belongs to objects in their temporal relationship to subjects. Using the example of a stranded traveler, Heidegger argues that train stations become boring when trains get delayed. This is because the temporal relationship of the train, the station, and the traveler has fallen out of place, instilling in the traveler a sense of being held in limbo and of being left empty (86). For Heidegger, boredom is an ontological state linked to a particular set of temporal relationships.

53 Similar to Ahmed's work on "happy objects," I approach boredom as occurring in proximity to boring places, or the places where boredom is expected to be found. See Ahmed, *Promise of Happiness*, 21. At the same time, I am also interested in the way individuals use boredom to evaluate or judge a location, such as a neighborhood or institution.

54 Akhil Gupta and James Ferguson, "Discipline and Practice: 'The Field' as Site, Method and Location in Anthropology," in *Anthropological Locations: Boundaries and Grounds of a Field Science*, ed. Akhil Gupta and James Ferguson, (Berkeley: University of California Press, 1997), 1–46.

55 Again taking inspiration from Ahmed's work on "happy objects," I think about boredom as occurring in proximity to undesirable places or at a distance from desired ones. See Ahmed, *Promise of Happiness*, 21.

56 João Guilherme Biehl, Byron Good, and Arthur Kleinman, *Subjectivity: Ethnographic Investigations* (Berkeley: University of California Press, 2007).

57 Edward W. Soja, *Postmetropolis: Critical Studies of Cities and Regions* (London: Wiley-Blackwell, 2000).

58 Part of the cruelty of cruel optimism is, as Berlant writes, that the ordinary "becomes a landfill for overwhelming and impending crises of life-building

expectations whose sheer volume so threatens what it has meant to 'have a life.'"
Berlant, *Cruel Optimism*, 3.

1 · SPACE-TIME EXPANSION

1   Romania, Marea Adunare Națională, Law 119 for the Nationalization of Indus-
    trial Enterprises, Banking, Insurance, Mining and Transport, 1948.

2   Liviu Chelcea, "Ancestors, Domestic Groups, and the Socialist State: Housing
    Nationalization and Restitution in Romania," *Comparative Studies in Society and
    History* 45, no. 4 (2003): 714–40. As Chelcea summarizes, "The declared inten-
    tion of the [People's Republic of Romania] was to eliminate housing inequality
    and the private rental sector in urban areas. In 1950, the state appropriated both
    leased and family homes that were considered to have too much domestic space.
    The inhabitants of confiscated houses became tenants instead of owners. Ten-
    ants were made to live with the former owners in such expropriated domestic
    space" (714).

3   Jeffrey Sachs, *Poland's Jump to the Market Economy* (Cambridge, MA: MIT
    Press, 1994). Rhetorically, the communist state justified Law 119 as a measure
    to bring Romania's economy under the working class's control. The Romanian
    Communist Party instituted Law 119 as a way to resolve the contradiction of the
    working class having ascended to political power and yet not having control
    of the economy. In practice, however, Law 119 facilitated a remarkable central-
    ization of power. Heavy industries such as the steel, electrical machinery, and
    chemical industries came under the control of the state and were developed to
    enhance the power of the state. This move toward heavy industrialization meant
    the restructuring of Romania's once agrarian economy. Vladimir Tismăneanu,
    Stalinism for All Seasons: A Political History of Romanian Communism (Berkeley:
    University of California Press, 2003), 107–8.

4   Dennis Deletant, *Ceaușescu and the Securitate: Coercion and Dissent in Romania,
    1965–1989* (London: M. E. Sharpe, 1995).

5   David A. Kideckel, "The Undead: Nicolae Ceaușescu and Paternalist Politics in
    Romanian Society and Culture," in *Death of the Father: An Anthropology of the
    End in Political Authority*, ed. John Borneman, New Directions in Anthropology
    (New York: Berghahn Books, 2004), 123–47.

6   Steven D. Roper, *Romania: The Unfinished Revolution* (New York: Routledge,
    2000) 52.

7   Duncan Light and David Phinnemore, *Post-communist Romania: Coming to
    Terms with Transition* (New York: Palgrave Macmillan, 2001). Between 1965 and
    1975, communist Romania created its own version of a national hotel industry.
    The state undertook massive investments in hotel building along with road
    construction and other public works. Every urban settlement of any industrial,
    administrative, or political significance was given at least one hotel complex of
    150 beds or more as a demonstration of the town's status. Planners also concen-
    trated hotel complexes in recreational destinations—such as the Black Sea coast,

the Prahova Valley, and the Carpathian Mountains—to facilitate controlled mass domestic tourism. Light and Phinnemore, *Post-communist Romania*, 208–9.

8   David Turnock, *Aspects of Independent Romania's Economic History with Particular Reference to Transition for EU Accession* (London: Ashgate, 2007). "Legitimacy was secured," Turnock writes, "during the 'golden years' of the late 1960s with genuine solidarity during the 1968–69 time of potential Soviet invasion of Czechoslovakia. Ceaușescu saw Romania as 'independent within the Warsaw Pact': a developing socialist state linked with Africa and Asia and a bridge between East and West built out of opportunism during the Sino-Soviet dispute" (33).

9   *Shortage economy* is a term associated with the Hungarian dissident Janos Kornai, who observed that socialist economies kept "encountering shortage phenomena not only as consumers but also as producers." Kornai, *Contradictions and Dilemmas: Studies on the Socialist Economy and Society* (Cambridge, MA: MIT Press, 1986), 6. Kornai argued that these shortages were not "temporary, provisional, occasional events" but a complex of phenomena that constantly reproduced itself within a planned economy (7).

10   Imbalance plagued four critical stages of production and consumption. First, central planners determined the allocation of economic resources rather than allowing liberal market processes to strike a balance among producers, capital, and customer demand. Miscalculations by central planners meant certain firms failed to receive the necessary inputs to meet their output quotas. Second, the state's commitment to universal employment moved planners to protect nationalized industry from free-market penalties for overstaffed production lines. As a result, factories commonly had an excess of labor and high production costs. Third, government planners overinvested in heavy industry, particularly in the production of petrochemicals for export, at the expense of domestic consumable goods like automobiles or washing machines. Fourth, stalled production resulted in shortages for consumers and the proliferation of lines for everyday goods. See Katherine Verdery, "The 'Etatization' of Time in Ceausescu's Romania," in *What Was Socialism, and What Comes Next?* (Princeton, NJ: Princeton University Press, 1996), 39–58. See also Stephen Crowley, *Hot Coal, Cold Steel: Russian and Ukrainian Workers from the End of the Soviet Union to the Post-communist Transformations* (Ann Arbor: University of Michigan Press, 1997).

11   The term *shortage economy* frames production across socialist Eastern Europe through the language of failure, noting the inability of its industry to produce sufficiently. This trope, scholars note, fails to account for the dynamic material worlds that socialist industry did support and that comes to be thought of as inadequate only when compared to the tremendous waste found in capitalism. See Krisztina Fehérváry, *Politics in Color and Concrete: Socialist Materialities and the Middle Class in Hungary*, New Anthropologies of Europe (Blooming-

ton: Indiana University Press, 2013). Rather than a "shortage economy," socialism could be said to have produced an "economy of *storage*," or a historically specific constellation of material objects, infrastructure, and values that produced unrecognized or underappreciated abundances in socialist society. See Serguei Alex Oushakine, "'Against the Cult of Things': On Soviet Productivism, Storage Economy, and Commodities with No Destination," *Russian Review* 73, no. 2 (2014): 198–236. While Romanian industry no doubt produced the kind of material abundance that could fill up a storage facility, the politics of distribution in communist Romania prevented the people from directly benefiting from that surplus in their everyday lives.

12   "Consumption per capita stagnated throughout the decade but, more importantly perhaps, the shortages of basic consumer goods in the latter part of the decade meant that welfare probably fell by more than indicated by the consumption per capita statistics. Particularly harsh restrictions were placed on the consumption of energy by households: in most parts of the country, only a few hours of electricity and heating were allowed per day, even during winter, in order not to disrupt the supply of energy to industry. At the same time, most social indicators took a turn for the worse: the average caloric intake of the population and the access to doctors and hospital beds declined in the period 1980–89, as did the life expectancy for men." Dimitri Demekas and Mohsin S. Khan, *The Romanian Economic Reform Program*, International Monetary Fund Occasional Paper (Washington, DC: International Monetary Fund, 1991), 14–15.

13   Tismăneanu, *Stalinism for All Seasons.*

14   Dragoș Voicu, *Coada* (Bucharest: Cartea Românească, 2009). Although not a classic, the book was released at the time of this fieldwork and serves as a relevant point of reference for how Romanians remembered the cultural form of the breadline at that time. The book received the 2008 award for debut fiction organized by Editura Cartea Romaneasca and was heralded in Romanian literary blogs as an "x-ray of the psycho-social form" (*radiografie psihosocială*) of the breadline in Ceaușescu's Romania. Marius Miheț, "Comunismul, Ce Poveste . . . ," *FAMILIA: Revistă de Cultură* (2009): 30.

15   The series claimed (despite its evocative title) to offer a balanced set of perspectives about life under communism. Each episode is about three minutes in length and combines testimonials from workers in a variety of different industries with black-and-white still photographs and propaganda reels from the communist era. The production is smooth and uses stylized cartoon graphics to introduce and conclude each episode. Music is used to heighten moments of sadness and irony, prompting the viewer to feel empathy or to laugh aloud following a given testimony. Realitatea TV marketed the serial as "revolutionary," documenting memories of everyday life under communism offered by both communists and "enemies of the people," by workers and technicians as well as intellectual elites. Realitatea TV, "La Coadă," *Comunism pe Burta Goală*, 2009.

Realitatea TV models itself after English-language cable news channels such as the BBC or CNN and predominantly features news and analysis programming.

16 Verdery, "'Etatization' of Time in Ceausescu's Romania."

17 Paul Cernat, *Cozi și Oameni de Rând în Anii '80*, ed. Adrian Neculau, *Viața Cotidiană în Comunism* (Iași, Romania: Polirom, 2004), 191. The translation is my own. Cernat continues, "Families with many children could buy additional portions of goods, motivating those without kids to (for a small fee) 'borrow' their neighbor's children to stand with them so as to receive additional packets of butter or meat. That is, of course, if they were lucky" (191).

18 Karl Marx, *Grundrisse*, Penguin Classics (London: Penguin Adult, 1993), 231. On the overabundance of labor, see Zygmunt Bauman, *Wasted Lives: Modernity and Its Outcasts* (Cambridge: Polity, 2004); and Hannah Arendt, *The Origins of Totalitarianism* (Cleveland, OH: World Publishing, 1966). On the overabundance of consumer pleasures, see Jean Baudrillard, *The Consumer Society: Myths and Structures* (London: Sage, 1998); and Fernand Braudel, *Civilization and Capitalism, 15th–18th Century*, vol. 1, *The Structure of Everyday Life* (Berkeley: University of California Press, 1992). More recently, *superfluity* has come to refer to the dialectics of indispensability and expendability of both people and things. See Achille Mbembe, "Aesthetics of Superfluity," *Public Culture* 16, no. 3 (2004): 374.

19 David A. Kideckel, "The Unmaking of an East-Central European Working Class," in *Postsocialism: Ideals, Ideologies and Practices in Eurasia*, ed. Christopher M. Hann (London: Routledge, 2003), 118.

20 Cristina Vatulescu, *Police Aesthetics: Literature, Film, and the Secret Police in Soviet Times* (Stanford, CA: Stanford University Press, 2010).

21 Gail Kligman, *The Politics of Duplicity: Controlling Reproduction in Ceausescu's Romania* (Berkeley: University of California Press, 1998).

22 Sachs, *Poland's Jump to the Market Economy*, 6. While the contents of the lecture draw on specific examples from Poland, Sachs understands Poland's transition as a replicable model for other postcommunist Eastern European countries. Sachs does offer the caveat that Romania and Bulgaria would experience additional difficulties and a longer "transition" due to the extent of the two countries' poverty and the communist-era isolation of their industry (6–7).

23 Lavinia Stan, "Romanian Privatization: Assessment of the First Five Years," *Communist and Post-communist Studies* 28, no. 4 (1995): 428.

24 Sachs, *Poland's Jump to the Market Economy*, 2–3. Sachs has been widely critiqued for failing to take into account cultural and historical specificities across Eastern Europe in his analysis. Sachs, and other Western consultants, operated with little to no historical awareness; most aid was given in the form of loans rather than grants, leaving recipient countries with obligations; and Western aid workers, in their effort to avoid ongoing corruption in government, used nongovernmental organizations to circumvent government decision-making processes or regulations. This, however, only allowed corruption to take new forms as consultants pocketed hundreds of millions of dollars for their "help."

See Janine R. Wedel, *Collision and Collusion: The Strange Case of Western Aid to Eastern Europe, 1989–1998* (London: St. Martin's, 1998).

25 Stan, "Romanian Privatization."

26 Stan, "Romanian Privatization," 429–30.

27 Demekas and Khan, *Romanian Economic Reform Program.*

28 With liberal reforms, work ceased to be an entitlement in Romania, bringing to an end the idleness of communist production. As payrolls grew ever more efficient, workers came to understand idle time at work in a new way. Standing around with nothing to do came to imply that one was not necessary. Idleness could lead to unemployment. A heightened sense of personal accountability prompted individual workers to become more active (if not entirely engaged) throughout the day to justify their employment. This division received considerable attention in episode 7 of *Comunism pe Burta Goală*. See Realitatea TV, "Episode 7: Munca la Stat," *Comunism pe Burta Goală*, 2009.

29 Cristian Ghinea and Alina Mungiu-Pippidi, *Media Policies and Regulatory Practices in a Selected Set of European Countries, the EU and the Council of Europe: The Case of Romania* (Athens, Greece: mediadem, 2010). Around 2009 there were still approximately twenty Bucharest-based daily newspapers, fourteen of them with reliable circulation figures. Larger cities in Romania had three to four local daily newspapers, although few were able to function as market-oriented outlets. Most were essentially public relations operations for local politicians and business circles. Ghinea and Mungiu-Pippidi, *Media Policies*, 10.

30 David Berry, *The Romanian Mass Media and Cultural Development* (Burlington, VT: Ashgate, 2004).

31 Conversations with Bucharest's contemporary, college-educated middle class refer to the Bucharest Mall's opening as a seminal moment when Western shopping standards became accessible in Romania.

32 Social and cultural anthropologists such as Aihwa Ong and James Holston and Arjun Appadurai have noted a need to update notions of citizenship to take into account its increasingly "graduated" quality. See Ong, "Graduated Sovereignty in South-East Asia," *Theory, Culture and Society* 17, no. 4 (2000): 55–75; and Holston and Appadurai, "Introduction: Cities and Citizenship," in *Cities and Citizenship (a Public Culture Book)*, ed. James Holston (Durham, NC: Duke University Press, 1998), 1–20. At the crux of this argument is the observation that market elites enjoy greater substantive rights than do migrant laborers. These extended rights include greater mobility across borders as well as a greater capacity for consumption, allowing professional elites to inhabit transnational and multilingual spaces structured more along the needs of markets than along state boundaries. See Néstor García Canclini, *Consumers and Citizens: Globalization and Multicultural Conflicts* (Minneapolis: University of Minnesota Press, 2001). Migrant laborers, by contrast, not only lack access to these more substantive rights but, as these authors show, are also subject to greater forms of policing.

33 Fehérváry, *Politics in Color.*

34 Gilles Deleuze and Félix Guattari stress the prolific nature of desire as free-floating, autonomous, and abundant. It is reconfigured as productive and generative, rather than lacking and limited: "It is at work everywhere, functioning smoothly at times, at other times in fits and starts. It breathes, it heats, it eats. It shits and fucks." Deleuze and Guattari, *Anti-Oedipus: Capitalism and Schizophrenia* (New York: Continuum, 2004), 1.

35 Early department stores arose in Paris, New York, and Chicago and are credited with the production of mass consumption. Indeed, the growing necessity of sales planning, marketing, distribution of work, accurate price calculation, expansion strategies, and so on transformed the entire business process within the department stores into a factory-like affair. In a word, they changed consumption into an industry. Much of the production of consumption hinged on the situation of commodities within fantastic displays, suggesting that the department store brought the exotic world of Paris or the Orient to the consumer, wherever he or she might be. See Rosalind H. Williams, *Dream Worlds: Mass Consumption in Late Nineteenth-Century France* (Berkeley: University of California Press, 1991).

36 Roughly ten years after the fall of communism, global media accounts depicted Berlin, Moscow, and Krakow as the centers of robust, emerging economies in line with, if not surpassing, the strength of Western Europe. See Alan Riding, "The New Berlin—Building on the Rubble of History; A Capital Reinstated and Remodeled," *New York Times*, April 11, 1999; Chris Stephen, "Moscow 'World's Most Costly City,'" *Irish Times*, June 6, 2007; and *The Economist*, "Central Europe: Converging Hopes," February 11, 1999, http://www.economist.com/node /186307. These cities evidenced the success of postcommunist Eastern Europe's economic transition in cultivating consumer citizens in ways that resonate with William Mazzarella's development of the term in postcolonial India, where "the civil franchise of the *right to choose* triumphs serenely over the arduous, contradictory, and messy procedures of representative democracy. . . . [It] is the story of liberalization: how the consuming energies of the people had been liberated from the paternalist grip of the state." Mazzarella, *Shoveling Smoke: Advertising and Globalization in Contemporary India* (Durham, NC: Duke University Press, 2003), 70.

37 Juan José Linz and Alfred C. Stepan, *Problems of Democratic Transition and Consolidation: Southern Europe, South America, and Post-communist Europe* (Baltimore: Johns Hopkins University Press, 1996), 344.

38 Steven Erlanger, "Romania Seeks to Stay on the Track to Europe," *New York Times*, February 11, 2001; and Ian Fisher, "Romania, Wooed by U.S., Looks to a Big NATO Role," *New York Times*, October 23, 2002.

39 G. Parker, "Romania Denies EU Entry Will Spark a Wave of Emigration," *Financial Times*, September 24, 2006.

40 Will Woodward, "Romanians and Bulgarians Face Immigration Curbs: EU Entry Will Not Mean Open Door, Minister Says Restrictions on Workers Opposed by Foreign Office," *Guardian*, August 21, 2006.

41 Most notable was the tension that developed in Italy following the apparent homicide of an Italian citizen at the hands of a Romanian immigrant. The incident prompted Italian officials to publicly warn Italian citizens against xenophobic attacks on Romanian immigrants, while simultaneously pursuing the emergency deportation of some Romanian workers. See Daniel McLaughlin, "Romanian Leaders Urge Italy to Prevent Attacks on Immigrants," *Irish Times*, November 11, 2007.

42 The three descriptions come from Bauman, *Wasted Lives*, 5; Mbembe, "Aesthetics of Superfluity" 381; and Arendt, *Origins of Totalitarianism*, 150.

43 The Antena 1 campaign was conceived by the Leo Burnett advertising agency in 2003 in an effort to rebrand the station as a provider of positive, humor-oriented programming. See *BizCity.ro*, "Campanie Antiplictiseală de La Leo Burnett Pentru Antena 1," October 3, 2003, http://www.bizcity.ro/stiri /campanie-antiplictiseala-de-la-leo-burnett-pentru-antena-1.html?id=10326. The three related television spots parodied a wave of social campaigns that aired in Romania, encouraging Romanians to prepare for EU accession by, for example, drinking less and curbing domestic violence. Later, in 2010, the Nescafé brand took up the theme of boredom in its "Defeat Boredom!" (Învinge Plictiseala!) campaign for its three-in-one instant coffee packets (see chapter 6 of this book).

44 Corneliu Porumboiu, dir. *Polițist, Adjectiv* [Police, adjective] (București, România: 42 Km Film, 2009), 115 min.; Cristian Nemescu, dir. *California Dreamin'* (București, România: Media Pro Pictures, 2007), 155 min.; and Cristi Puiu, dir. *Moartea Domnului Lăzărescu* [*The Death of Mr. Lazarescu*] (București, România: Mandragora, 2005), 153 min.

45 Guess Who, "3.7.2006." *Probe Audio.* București, Romania: Okapi Sound, Cat Music, 2009.

46 This is a methodological approach exemplified by João Guilherme Biehl, *Vita: Life in a Zone of Social Abandonment.* (Berkeley: University of California Press, 2005); Clara Han, *Life in Debt: Times of Care and Violence in Neoliberal Chile* (Berkeley: University of California Press, 2012); and Kevin L. O'Neill, *Secure the Soul: Christian Piety and Gang Prevention in Guatemala* (Berkeley: University of California Press, 2015).

47 The Romanian verb *a face* means "to do or to make." It is worth noting that in the absence of Mircea's ability to participate in production, he felt as though there was nothing for him to do.

48 St. Ignatius Loyola is a nongovernmental organization administered by the Catholic Church. Situated on the outskirts of Bucharest, near the Backwoods Shelter, St. Ignatius Loyola targeted street orphans and younger homeless adults. From the outside, St. Ignatius Loyola looked like an elementary school: a three-story building with a playground and blacktop basketball courts in the back. The facility also had a separate building that housed an indoor soccer court, a weight-room facility, and a recreation room for playing table tennis or watching television. The main building featured a café, a restaurant, a medi-

cal cabinet, a clothes depot, and a dormitory that accommodated a hundred people. St. Ignatius Loyola's wide array of offerings made it a popular place for homeless youth to visit.

49   As will be explained in chapter 2, homeless shelters in Bucharest expect beneficiaries to subsidize the cost of services by providing a rent or payment.

50   See David Harvey, *The Condition of Postmodernity: An Enquiry into the Origins of Cultural Change* (London: Blackwell, 1992).

51   See Luiza Chiroiu, "Salariul Minim Pe Economie: România vs. Europa," *Gândul.info*, February 26, 2015, http://www.gandul.info/financiar/salariul -minim-pe-economie-romania-vs-europa-13897442.

52   See *Ziuaveche.Ro*, "David: În Afara Granițelor Trăiesc între Șase și Opt Milioane de Români," December 13, 2013. EU officials estimate that approximately three million Romanians work in Western Europe, with the remaining migrants working in Russia and Eastern Europe but also in North America and East Asia. Laszlo Andor, "End of Restrictions on Free Movement of Workers from Bulgaria and Romania," European Commission Memo 14/1, Brussels, January 1, 2014.

53   Homi K. Bhabha, "Double Visions," *Artforum* 30, no. 5 (1992): 88.

2 · BLEAK HOUSE

1   Marc Augé coined the term *nonplaces* to refer to the generic and highly functional spaces typical of a modern landscape. These are places people regularly pass through but without establishing significant social or historical relations. Augé, *Non-places: An Introduction to Supermodernity* (London: Verso, 2009). I use the term here to refer to bureaucratically administered spaces, like a homeless shelter, which people occupy without formulating positive attachments. I also include the back alleys, stairwells, and out-of-the-way corners of public parks where the street homeless spend large portions of their days.

2   Justin Keay, "A Live-Wire Mayor for a Tired Old City," *BusinessWeek*, December 16, 2001.

3   Keay, "Live-Wire Mayor." Keay's representation of Bucharest as dirty and overrun with urban blight is emblematic of similar accounts from this time in the *Washington Post*, the *Boston Globe*, and the *Economist*. See Peter Finn, "In Bucharest, a Dogfight over Strays; Crusading Mayor Hailed, Scorned for Planned Roundup of Proliferating Canines," *Washington Post*, February 18, 2001; Susan Milligan, "Revival Moves Slowly in Eastern Europe," *Boston Globe*, May 10, 1998; and *The Economist*, "Romania's Capital Mayor," London, September 7, 2000, http://www.economist.com/node/360036. These representations contributed to what many understood as a national embarrassment that potentially hindered foreign investment, tourism, and accession to the European Union.

4   Neil Smith, *The New Urban Frontier: Gentrification and the Revanchist City* (London: Routledge, 1996). This logic motivated similar processes to displace the homeless from key public spaces at roughly the same moment in cities throughout Europe and the Americas. See Tova Hojdestrand, *Needed*

by Nobody: Homelessness and Humanness in Post-socialist Russia (Ithaca, NY: Cornell University Press, 2009); Joe Doherty, Volker Busch-Geertsema, Vita Karpuskiene, Jukka Korhonen, Eoin O'Sullivan, Ingrid Sahlin, Antonio Tosi, Agostino Petrillo, and Julia Wygnańska, "Homelessness and Exclusion: Regulating Public Space in European Cities," *Surveillance and Inequality* 5, no. 3 (2008): 290–314; Teresa P. R. Caldeira, *City of Walls: Crime, Segregation, and Citizenship in São Paulo* (Berkeley: University of California Press, 2001); and Setha Low, "The Edge and the Center: Gated Communities and the Discourse of Urban Fear," in *Anthropology of Space and Place: Locating Culture*, ed. Setha Low and Denise Lawrence-Zúñiga (Malden, MA: Blackwell, 2003), 387–407.

5 The municipal government's destruction of vendor stalls resulted in the stalls' owners and employees losing their property and employment. Most vendors operated informally, meaning that those who lost their jobs would not be eligible for benefits of any kind. While Mayor Băsescu framed the eviction of street vendors as an attack against corruption and "mafia-type groups" that operated through the kiosks, the mayor's attempts at urban renewal also functioned as an attack on the working class. Lucian Branea, "Bulldozing Bucharest: After Squatting Kiosk Owners Refused to Clear Out, a Hard-Hitting New Mayor Moved In—with Bulldozers," *Transitions Online* (Prague), September 11, 2000.

6 Andrew's surprise at receiving a valuable building without bribery reflects a kind of cultural hangover from the workings of the communist-era bureaucracy in Romania. Under communism, the completion of even the most mundane requests required the bribing of functionaries. See Dennis Deletant, *Ceaușescu and the Securitate: Coercion and Dissent in Romania, 1965–1989* (London: M. E. Sharpe, 1995); and Katherine Verdery, *What Was Socialism, and What Comes Next?* (Princeton, NJ: Princeton University Press, 1996). While anticorruption reforms worked to curb bribery practices, bribery remained common at the time Second Chances was founded.

7 By *central Bucharest*, I do not mean a geometric or demographic center of the city. Instead, I make use of a discursive practice among residents of Bucharest that identifies the city center as the region inscribed by the Metro's circle line (M1). Residents of Bucharest typically locate themselves within the city center by referencing a series of squares serviced by the Metro's central line, namely, Victoriei Square, Romană Square, Universității Square, and Unirii Square.

8 "The right to the city," wrote Henri Lefebvre, "manifests itself as a superior form of rights: right to freedom, to individualization in socialization, to habitat and to inhabit." Lefebvre, *Writings on Cities* (London: Wiley-Blackwell, 1996), 174. As envisioned by Lefebvre and developed by others, the right to the city is "the right to live in a society in which all persons are similarly free to fulfill their own desires and in which all are supported in doing so." Peter Marcuse, "Rights in Cities and the Right to the City?," in *Cities for All: Proposals and Experiences towards the Right to the City*, ed. Ana Sugranyes and Charlotte Mathivet (Santiago: Habitat International Coalition, 2010), 87–98, 88. Rather than discarding urban

residents to the urban periphery for being something other than affluent, the right to the city fosters different kinds of people by advocating for different kinds of flourishing.

9   Vladimir Tismăneanu, for example, writes, "The new European democracies have avoided the rise to power of staunchly illiberal forces and, in spite of widespread cynicism and corruption, there is a growing consensus regarding the desirability of markets, free media and pluralist institutions. . . . The magnetism of united Europe (or perhaps the political myth of unified Europe) has thus played a decisive role in preventing anti-democratic forces taking the lead and subverting the democratic institutions." Tismăneanu, "Discomforts of Victory: Democracy, Liberal Values and Nationalism in Post-communist Europe," *West European Politics* 25, no. 2 (2002): 81–82.

10   Michel Foucault, *Discipline and Punish: The Birth of the Prison* (London: Penguin, 1977). At stake in Foucault's notion of unintended consequences is a divide between discursive regularities and causal principles, whereby certain phenomena come into being in the absence of a liberal subject intending to bring those phenomena about. Actions seem to lack subjects, which bring events into being that no one intended. See Hubert L. Dreyfus and Paul Rabinow, *Michel Foucault: Beyond Structuralism and Hermeneutics* (Chicago: University of Chicago Press, 1983).

11   R. Antony French and F. E. Ian Hamilton, *The Socialist City: Spatial Structure and Urban Policy* (New York: Wiley, 1979), 9.

12   David Harvey, *Rebel Cities: From the Right to the City to the Urban Revolution* (London: Verso, 2012).

13   Ethnographies of shelters in the United States describe shelters as places that provide homeless people with beds but that also seek to reshape the homeless into another kind of subject—one capable of regular work and life in the private sector—through intensive counseling, disciplinary practices, and, at times, formal education and instruction. See Robert R. Desjarlais, *Shelter Blues: Sanity and Selfhood among the Homeless* (Philadelphia: University of Pennsylvania Press, 1997); Kim Hopper, *Reckoning with Homelessness*, The Anthropology of Contemporary Issues (Ithaca, NY: Cornell University Press, 2003); and Vincent Lyon-Callo, *Inequality, Poverty, and Neoliberal Governance: Activist Ethnography in the Homeless Sheltering Industry* (Toronto: University of Toronto Press, 2008).

14   When I first started visiting the shelter, the administration placed no term limits on beneficiaries. Some had resided at the shelter for over five years. By the end of this research project, the shelter had shifted to a "medium-term" stay facility that beneficiaries could use for a maximum of six months out of the year. The shift in policy caught its residents by surprise, pressuring shelter residents long removed from the workings of the private housing market to search out a viable place to live and to sign a housing contract. Once shelter residents signed a contract, the local government guaranteed the landlord one year's

rent. Confusion abounded among shelter beneficiaries over basic questions such as where to find listings for available housing and how government payments would be made to their new landlords. At the same time, landlords were skeptical of shelter beneficiaries and reluctant to rent properties to persons dependent on state aid.

15 Dragos is referring to the privatization of housing after communism (see the introduction of this book). State social service providers are suspicious of those who sold such an important asset and did not save the money for future rent. Dragos assumes these homeless persons are liberal subjects empowered to make financial decisions unconstrained by other obligations.

16 Second Chances takes a "third-sector approach" to social welfare that is common in Central and Eastern European countries: as much as 30 percent of the operating costs are generated through fees passed on to the beneficiaries themselves. See Ilja Hradecky, "Building Capacity of Homeless Services in the Czech Republic," *European Journal of Homelessness* (2008): 177–90. Shelter residents in Bucharest, as in many other postsocialist states, are held personally responsible for financing their placement inside shelters through work obligations linked to shelter beds.

17 Tony Judt, *Postwar: A History of Europe since 1945* (New York: Penguin, 2006); and Mălina Voicu and Bogdan Voicu, "Volunteering in Romania: A Rara Avis," in *The Values of Volunteering: Cross-Cultural Perspectives*, ed. P. Dekker and L. Halman, 143–60, Nonprofit and Civil Society Studies (New York: Kluwer Academic/Plenum, 2003)

18 See Desjarlais, *Shelter Blues*; João Guilherme Biehl, *Vita: Life in a Zone of Social Abandonment* (Berkeley: University of California Press, 2005); and Philippe Bourgois and Jeffrey Schonberg, *Righteous Dopefiend* (Berkeley: University of California Press, 2009).

19 Homeless persons' invocations of "another lifestyle" or "another kind of life" resonate with Lauren Berlant's notion of "the good life." "The good life" is a kind of fantasy through which "people hoard idealizing theories and tableaux about how they and the world 'add up to something.'" Berlant, *Cruel Optimism* (Durham, NC: Duke University Press, 2011), 2. A sense of that "other kind of life," as Sorin describes it, provides a set of images and fantasies about what it means to have a life. The distance between that fantasy and Sorin's day-to-day existence is marked by the dreary sense that nothing (meaningful) is happening; and boredom abounds.

20 On boredom and factory labor, see Melvin Seeman, "On the Meaning of Alienation," *American Sociological Review* 24, no. 6 (1959): 783–91; on boredom in the office, see David Foster Wallace, *The Pale King* (New York: Little, Brown, 2011).

21 See Foucault, *Discipline and Punish*.

22 From a Marxist perspective, the politics of leisure has long been seen as central to the reproduction of labor. Antonio Gramsci, for example, described Prohibi-

tion and the nuclear family as ways of shaping leisure that maximized workers' output during their shifts. Gramsci, "Americanism and Fordism," in *A Gramsci Reader: Selected Writings, 1916–1935*, ed. Hannan Hever and Eric J. Hobsbawm (New York: New York University Press, 2000), 275–99. Henri Lefebvre similarly identifies leisure as a critical space within modernity to address the human needs that alienated labor cannot satisfy, while Guy Standing identifies the inability to partake in leisure as a central dilemma of the growing class of the "precariat." Lefebvre, *Critique of Everyday Life*. vol. 1, *Introduction*, ed. J. Moore and M. Trebitsch (London: Verso, 2008); and Standing, "Tertiary Time: The Precariat's Dilemma," *Public Culture* 25, no. 1 (2013): 5–23.

3 · THE GRAY YEARS

1 Generally speaking, Tudor refers to Backwoods as a nursing home when he wants to narrate his present life with a sense of dignity, and he refers to Backwoods as a shelter when he wants to foreground a sense of disinvestment by the state and by his family.

2 Elaine Fultz, *The Gender Dimensions of Social Security Reform: Case Studies of Romania and Slovenia* (Budapest, Hungary: International Labour Office, 2006). Romania's communist-era legacies shaped the country's provision of pensions after communism. These legacies included (1) the requirement that everyone work, which produced high national employment rates for both men and women; (2) a relatively flat wage structure, which contributed to homogeneous pension payments based on the number of years worked under communism; and (3) a preferential retirement age for women, which was five years earlier than that for men. These factors create heavy financial obligations in the present. Fultz, *Gender Dimensions*, 59–60. The value of a pension is based on the sum of the contributions paid by a worker during his or her career, relative to those paid by other workers. Two main elements influence this sum: the number of years worked and the value of that person's earnings relative to those of other workers for each work year. Fultz, *Gender Dimensions*, 65.

3 Katherine Verdery, *What Was Socialism, and What Comes Next?* (Princeton, NJ: Princeton University Press, 1996), 65; and Gail Kligman, *The Politics of Duplicity: Controlling Reproduction in Ceausescu's Romania* (Berkeley: University of California Press, 1998), 84.

4 Laura Olson, *The Not-So-Golden Years: Caregiving, the Frail Elderly, and the Long-Term Care Establishment* (New York: Rowman and Littlefield, 2003). The Social Security Act of 1935 enabled the development of retirement centers in the United States. Olson, *Not-So-Golden Years*, 158. The government-backed production of these institutions moved care for the elderly out of American homes and into bureaucratic settings, outsourcing the burden of parent care for working-age adults.

5 Dimitri A. Sotiropoulos, Ileana Neamtu, and Maya Stoyanova, "The Trajectory of Post-communist Welfare State Development: The Cases of Bulgaria and Romania," *Social Policy and Administration* 37, no. 6 (2003): 667.

6 Georges de Menil and Eytan Sheshinski, "Romania's Pension System from Crisis to Reform," in *Social Security Pension Reform in Europe*, ed. Martin Feldstein and Horst Siebert, National Bureau of Economic Research Conference Report (Chicago: University of Chicago Press, 2009), 401–38. Approximately one million former contributors became unemployed and thus were exempt from making social security contributions. Menil and Sheshinski, "Romania's Pension System," 405.

7 Fultz, *Gender Dimensions*.

8 European Commission, *Strategic National Report Regarding Social Protection and Social Inclusion 2008–2010*. European Commission: Employment, Social Affairs, and Inclusion (Bucharest, Romania, 2008), 39.

9 Romania's pension reform is based on the World Bank's multipillar model. It is composed of a first pillar of pension support provided by the government. A second pillar is a private pension system that is required for all employees below the age of thirty-five and is voluntary for employees aged thirty-five to forty-five. The third pillar of pension reform is a voluntary private pension system. Participation is open to anyone earning income. This pillar functions similarly to an investment. See Cristiana Tudor, "A Quantitative Assessment of the Outcome of Pension Reforms in Transition Economies: The Case of Romania," *International Research Journal of Finance and Economics*, no. 56 (2010): 152–53. The reform agenda moved to both address the sudden deterioration of the pension system brought by the economic crisis in 2008 and manage longer-term sustainability and equity concerns. See International Monetary Fund, *Romania—Fifth Review under the Stand-By Arrangement*, IMF Country Report (Washington, DC: International Monetary Fund, 2010), 11. For additional commentary on pension restructuring, see World Bank, *Romania Public Expenditure and Institutional Review* (2010), 1:13–16.

10 The Romanian government passed legislation for second-pillar private pension schemes in 2006, with enrollment finishing in early 2008. Voluntary third-pillar private pensions initially failed to gain popularity as hoped. Low wages provided little additional savings, in addition to a business climate that private providers deemed "uncertain." Fultz, *Gender Dimensions*, 60. As of 2010, almost 3.5 million workers were participating in the second-pillar program through fourteen pension fund management companies, mostly belonging to banking or insurance groups. See International Monetary Fund, *Romania: Financial Sector Stability Assessment* (Washington, DC: International Monetary Fund, 2010), 24.

11 A strategic national report summarizes this as follows: "Considering the statistical data that indicate the rate of dependent employees/retirees, Romania needs to develop a system for promoting active aging by means of the introduction of specific measures for the stimulation of the participation of elderly people on the labor market, but also of other vulnerable groups that are currently experiencing low participation rates." European Commission, *Strategic National Report*, 10. Pension reforms reenvisioned retirement: from a

model that viewed it as a period of state provision and care to a model in which pensioners are increasingly responsible for themselves. This vision of active retirement assumes pensioners have had a work history that allowed for additional voluntary contributions to a private pension scheme. It also assumes that pensioners will retain the physical ability to continue working and that private employers will find them to be attractive laborers.

12 Liviu Chelcea, "Marginal Groups in Central Places: Gentrification, Property Rights and Post-socialist Primitive Accumulation," in *Social Changes and Social Sustainability in Historical Urban Centers: The Case of Central Europe*, ed. Gyorgy Enyrdi and Zoltan Kovacs (Pécs, Hungary: Centre for Regional Studies of the Hungarian Academy of Sciences, 2006), 142.

13 F. R. Ghitescu and M. Banciu, "Economic Crime in Romania," *Journal of Social, Political, and Economic Studies* 26, no. 4 (2001): 643–69.

14 Filippo M. Zerilli, "Sentiments and/as Property Rights: Restitution and Conflict in Postsocialist Romania," in *Postsocialism: Politics and Emotions in Central and Eastern Europe*, ed. Maruška Svašek (London: Berghahn Books, 2008), 74–94.

15 Katherine Verdery, "Fuzzy Property: Rights, Power, and Identity in Transylvania's Decollectivization," in *Uncertain Transition: Ethnographies of Change in the Postsocialist World*, ed. Michael Burawoy and Katherine Verdery (Oxford: Rowman and Littlefield, 1999), 53–82.

16 Over the course of extended interviews, Tudor alluded to the possibility that he had been targeted by the Securitate. As evidence, Tudor cited the comprehensive knowledge of his property and finances exhibited by the creditors. He also alleged receiving blackmail and death threats after he initially refused to pay his creditors. This connection is not entirely implausible given that Romanians widely believed the communist-era secret police to be involved in the organized crime and racketeering pervading Romania in the 1990s. See Oana Mateescu, "The Dark Side of the State: 'Mafia' and 'National Interest' in Postsocialist Romania," *Romanian Journal of Society and Politics* 2, no. 1 (2002): 5–29.

17 Paul Manning, "Rose-Colored Glasses? Color Revolutions and Cartoon Chaos in Postsocialist Georgia," *Cultural Anthropology* 22, no. 2 (2005): 171–213.

18 Sixty percent of a full pension (approximately 850 lei, or $270) is a common rate for a bed in a government-administered nursing home (*azil de bătrâni*). The cost of a bed at a private nursing home, by contrast, can exceed 1,500 lei (or $475). See Elisa Bouleanu and Cristina Ciulei, "Avem Azile, Căutăm Bătrâni," *Adevărul*, 2011. Importantly, Tudor paid the same fee for his bed at Backwoods that he would for a bed in a retirement center. Tudor would at times point to this fact when arguing for better service at Backwoods.

19 Elizabeth Dunn's ethnography of a baby-food plant in Poland corroborates Ana's assertion that Western firms preferred younger workers. Dunn details the skepticism private Western firms had about those trained in the communist era. Managers viewed the middle-aged and elderly "as people who could not

understand the changes in the economy and therefore in business practice."
Dunn, *Privatizing Poland: Baby Food, Big Business, and the Remaking of Labor*
(Ithaca, NY: Cornell University Press, 2004), 79–80. This assumption limited the job opportunities of older workers based on their perceived inability
to think.

20   While *gypsy* is an ethnic slur that refers to the Roma, homeless Romanians I
spoke with often used the term to identify a particular person as a "thief" or as
"dishonest," regardless of their ethnic affiliation. During my fieldwork, I routinely heard, for example, dark Roma and "white" Romanians alike call drunk,
loud, or notoriously dishonest "white" Romanians "gypsies." In this sense, the
term functions as a moral category as well as an ethnic slur. In Ana's case, the
"gypsies" who "took" her house could very well have been part of organized
crime, but also a bank or property manager whose terms and processes she did
not understand. When pressed for clarification, Ana only reiterated her claim
that she was cheated of her home by "thieving gypsies."

21   Ana, like many of the shelter's older beneficiaries, quoted me prices in Romania's previous currency, the Romanian leu (ROL). In 2005 Romania switched to
the Romanian new leu (RON). The banknotes and coins looked the same, except for the removal of four zeroes from each denomination. A 1,000,000 ROL
banknote, for example, became a 100 RON note. The switch was designed to
curb the effects of inflation and to render the prices of everyday purchases into
more manageable numbers. Adding to the confusion between the old and new
currencies was the tendency for Romanians to drop the last three zeroes on
the old notes. For example, a homeless mother might ask to borrow a "100" for
groceries. This could mean either 100,000 ROL (approximately $3) or 100 RON
(approximately $30). Guessing the wrong banknote often led to embarrass-
ment, as conveyed in statements like "Jesus, Bruce, I could never pay you back
that much (100 RON). I just wanted a bag of potatoes to fry," or, alternatively,
"But Bruce, I have three kids. 100 (RON) is nothing to you, but it means my
kids will eat for a week."

22   *Ziuaveche.Ro*, "David: În Afara Granițelor Trăiesc între șase și Opt Milioane
de Români," 2013. European Union officials estimate that approximately three
million Romanians are working in Western Europe. Laszlo Andor, "End of
Restrictions on Free Movement of Workers from Bulgaria and Romania," European Commission Memo 14/1, Brussels, January 1, 2014.

23   José de Sousa and Laetitia Duval, "Geographic Distance and Remittances
in Romania: Out of Sight, Out of Mind?," *International Economics* 121, no. 1
(2010): 84.

24   According to the World Bank, remittance inflows to Romania for 2007 were
estimated to be $9 billion, 27 percent higher than the amount received in
2006. At such rates, remittances become thinkable as "transnational welfare."
Flavia Piperno, "From Care Drain to Care Gain: Migration in Romania and
Ukraine and the Rise of Transnational Welfare," *Development* 50, no. 4 (2007):
63–68.

25 It is worth noting that, given Victoria's failing health, I regularly characterized her slow and arduous trek from Stefan's Place to the bus stop, and from the bus stop to the monastery, as inhumane.

26 For Romanians to qualify for a B-2 tourist visa for the United States, they must complete an interview at the U.S. embassy, where they must demonstrate evidence of funds to cover their expenses while in the United States. They must also demonstrate binding social or economic ties in Romania that will ensure their return. The visa itself carries a fee of $160. See U.S. Embassy, "Embassy of the United States: Bucharest, Romania," *Tourist and Business Visas*, 2014, http://romania.usembassy.gov/visas/tourist.html. While anthropologists elsewhere have demonstrated that the U.S. visa process can be manipulated, such applicants still require significantly more money than Victoria could ever produce on a bank statement to satisfy the visa officer. On such manipulations, see Charles Piot, *Nostalgia for the Future: West Africa after the Cold War* (Chicago: University of Chicago Press, 2010).

27 In 2011 the Romanian government spent 230 million lei (approximately $73 million) to develop an additional seventy-one nursing homes to serve an additional 2,500 to 4,800 people. This expansion targeted hospitals deemed "small" and "inefficient" by the Ministry of Health, which were to be repurposed as bed space for elderly pensioners. See Cristina Sbîrn, "Căminele Pentru Bătrâni, Create Cu Bani de La Buget, Nu de La Autoritățile Locale," *Adevărul*, 2011; and Marian Stoica, "Spitalele Care Au Fost Închise în Județul Brașov Nu Vor Fi Transformate în Azile de Bătrâni," *Adevărul*, 2011.

4 · BORED TO DEATH

1 As Martin Demant Frederiksen notes, marginalization is a temporal as well as a social and spatial phenomenon. Working with underemployed men in Georgia, Frederiksen shows marginalization to be an experience of being disconnected from a past that is no more, dislocated in the present, and excluded from the imaginings of a future that has not yet come into being. Frederiksen refers to this impasse as "temporal marginality." Frederiksen, *Young Men, Time, and Boredom in the Republic of Georgia* (Philadelphia: Temple University Press, 2013).

2 Lauren Berlant, *Cruel Optimism* (Durham, NC: Duke University Press, 2011), 96–97. This chapter uses Berlant's concept of "slow death" as a framework for exploring the intersection of boredom and homelessness biopolitically. For those incorporated into global capitalism, life is defined by acceleration. Hartmut Rosa identifies the acceleration of life along three lines: technological acceleration, evident in transport and communication; acceleration of social change, as evident in institutions and relationships; and acceleration of the pace of life itself. Rosa, *Social Acceleration: A New Theory of Modernity*, New Directions in Critical Theory (New York: Columbia University Press, 2013). The acceleration of life, others have argued, is further embodied through the ingestion of caffeine and other pharmaceuticals that speed up the body. See

Jason Pine, "Economy of Speed: The New Narco-Capitalism," *Public Culture* 19, no. 2 (2007): 357–66.

3 According to the World Health Organization, the number of suicides per 100,000 people decreased in Romania by 5.2 percent between 2000 and 2012, to a rate of 18.4 persons per 100,000. While this number decreased, it still exceeds the European Union average of 12 for low- and middle-income countries. Of critical interest to this chapter is what others have described as the "will to live" that encourages people to endure in the face of life's wearing out. See João Guilherme Biehl, *Will to Live: AIDS Therapies and the Politics of Survival* (Princeton, NJ: Princeton University Press, 2007).

4 Michel Foucault, *Society Must Be Defended: Lectures at the Collège de France* (New York: Picador, 2003).

5 Michel Foucault, *Discipline and Punish: The Birth of the Prison* (London: Penguin, 1977). With the rise of biopolitics, Foucault observes the hiding away of death. Foucault writes, "Power has no control over death, but it can control mortality. . . . In the right of sovereignty, death was the moment of the most obvious and most spectacular manifestation of the absolute power of the sovereign; death now becomes, in contrast, the moment when the individual escapes all power, falls back on himself and retreats, so to speak, into his own privacy. Power no longer recognizes death. Power literally ignores death." Foucault, *Society Must Be Defended*, 248.

6 Tania Murray Li, "To Make Live or Let Die? Rural Dispossession and the Protection of Surplus Populations," *Antipode* 41, no. 1 (2010): 66–93.

7 Angela Garcia notes that as governments scale back social protections, the responsibility for care gets displaced from the state onto family members. This displacement prompts families to ask who is to provide care, what kind of care, and how much. These questions raise painful decisions about abandonment and the refusal of care. Garcia, "Reading 'Righteous Dopefiend' with My Mother," *Anthropology Now* 2, no. 3 (2010): 31–36.

8 Berlant, *Cruel Optimism*, 95.

9 In context, the quotation reads: "The social world gives what is rarest, recognition, consideration, in other words, quite simply, reasons for being. It is capable of giving meaning to life, and to death itself, by consecrating it as the supreme sacrifice." Pierre Bourdieu, *Pascalian Meditations* (Stanford, CA: Stanford University Press, 2000), 240. Bourdieu continues, "One of the most unequal of all distributions, and probably, in any case, the most cruel, is the distribution of symbolic capital, that is, of social importance and of reasons for living. . . . Conversely, there is no worse dispossession, no worse privation, perhaps, than that of the losers in the symbolic struggle for recognition, for access to a socially recognized social being, in a word, to humanity. . . . [S]ymbolic power, charm, seduction, charisma, appear as endowed with an objective reality" (241).

10 Shame, Jack R. Friedman shows, impresses itself on interpersonal relations in postcommunist Romania, where an unstable economy has left unemployed workers with "a desire to disappear, to melt away in the face of the recognition

that the self is profoundly out-of-sorts with a set of expected cultural norms." Friedman, "Shame and the Experience of Ambivalence on the Margins of the Global: Pathologizing the Past and Present in Romania's Industrial Waste-lands," *Ethos* 35, no. 2 (2007): 239. Shame compels many of these Romanians to let relationships dissolve entirely rather than reimagine them.

11 Zygmunt Bauman, *Wasted Lives: Modernity and Its Outcasts* (Cambridge: Polity, 2004), 11.

12 Anthropologists across the global south have identified pools of labor, composed of permanently unemployed men and women, that are unlikely to ever be incorporated into formal production. As Partha Chatterjee writes, "the technological conditions of early industrialization which created the demand for a substantial mass of industrial labor have long passed. Capitalist growth today is far more capital-intensive and technology-dependent than it was even some decades ago. Large sections of peasants who are today the victims of the primitive accumulation of capital are completely unlikely to be absorbed into the new capitalist sectors of growth." Chatterjee, "Democracy and Economic Transformation in India," *Economic and Political Weekly* 43, no. 16 (2008): 55.

13 In another context, Svetlana Stephenson interprets postsocialist homelessness in Russia as "waste" that is a result of displacement. Stephenson's focus on displacement seeks to contextualize changes in individual social positions within a wider network of relations rather than defining them simply as direct access to collective goods. Homelessness becomes, from her perspective, a temporal process of displacement from settled society and a loss of the previous resources and identities that flowed through these networks. Stephenson, *Crossing the Line: Vagrancy, Homelessness and Social Displacement in Russia* (London: Ashgate, 2006), 5. Similarly, Tova Hojdestrand also understands postsocialist homeless persons as a form of "waste" in two senses. In the first, homeless persons are objectified as things that are "needed by no one"; in the second, homeless persons are forced to live on waste: the food, spaces, things, and relations that have been discarded by the rest of society. Hojdestrand, *Needed by Nobody: Homelessness and Humanness in Post-socialist Russia* (Ithaca, NY: Cornell University Press, 2009). This chapter contributes to this line of analysis by highlighting the subjective and affective dimension of being coded as waste.

14 Tania Li notes that the permanently unemployed are not deficient physically or intellectually but are people who are capable of labor but are nevertheless surplus to the needs of capital. As Li writes, "The key to [the dispossessed's] predicament is that their labor is surplus *in relation to* its utility for capital. . . . I see their perilous condition, rather, as a sign of their very limited relevance to capital at any scale. If the population rendered surplus to capital's requirements is to live decently, it will be because of the activation of a biopolitics that places the intrinsic value of life—rather than the value of people as workers or consumers—at its core." Li, "Make Live or Let Die?," 67–68.

15 Here I refer to a Marxist tradition that examines the efforts of capital to produce dependable workers. These efforts range from restrictions on work-

ers' lifestyles by directly and indirectly regulating the sexuality and alcohol consumption of labor to, more perniciously, the contraction of welfare and other social benefits to pressure workers to perform dangerous and undesirable tasks. See Antonio Gramsci, "Americanism and Fordism," in *A Gramsci Reader: Selected Writings, 1916–1935*, ed. Hannan Hever and Eric J. Hobsbawm (New York: New York University Press, 2000), 275–99; and Francis Fox Piven and Richard A. Cloward, *Regulating the Poor: The Functions of Public Welfare* (New York: Vintage, 1956). Building on this line of inquiry, Loïc Wacquant reveals the role of the prison in disciplining low-skilled workers who are resisting the exploitation of capital. Wacquant, *Punishing the Poor: The Neoliberal Government of Social Insecurity*, Politics, History, and Culture (Durham, NC: Duke University Press, 2009).

16 Bauman, *Wasted Lives*, 16.

17 Captured most succinctly in the writings of Charles Baudelaire and later by Benjamin, the flâneur is an uprooted person who is at home neither in his class nor in his birthplace. See David Frisby, *Cityscapes of Modernity: Critical Explorations* (New York: John Wiley and Sons, 2002). Typically male, this figure is well educated with a bourgeois upbringing; his education and his discomfort with his social placement afford the flâneur a critical space. Rather than accepting the city as intended, the flâneur can resist the city's planned experience—in his looking, observing, and reading of the city, the flâneur develops his own unique experience. Walter Benjamin, *The Arcades Project* (Cambridge, MA: Belknap Press of Harvard University Press, 2002), 37–38, 48. In *The Arcades Project*, Benjamin notes how the development of the arcades tamed this rogue figure (31). The arcade slowly replaced the city as the flâneur's source of inspiration—the excitement of faintly lit city streets was replaced by the phantasmagoria of the arcade. As a fantasy world of its own, the arcade invoked the imaginative qualities of the city without its deleterious attributes. Ultimately, it served as an ideal cityscape that was explicitly scripted to invoke fantasy and wonder around the commodities that it housed.

   With regard to "passing the time," Heidegger defines it as indicative of "*our entire comportment and behavior.*" Heidegger, *The Fundamental Concepts of Metaphysics: World, Finitude, Solitude* (Bloomington: Indiana University Press, 2001), 112. By this, Heidegger means embodied practices or emplaced movements that bring the inner self into relationship with its external environment, such as the self's engagement with the environment through discourse and practice.

18 Elizabeth Dunn's work with internally displaced people in Georgia notes that senses of having, doing, and being "nothing" are social productions. Sometimes nothingness results from events that disrupt one's sense of normal. In other moments, a sense of nothingness is derived from acts of care and humanitarian aid, whose presence highlights the absences in one's life. Dunn, "Humanitarianism, Displacement, and the Politics of Nothing in Postwar Georgia," *Slavic Review* 73, no. 2 (2014): 287–306. This is a helpful way of thinking about boredom

in a state of social death, where present relationships serve only to highlight a sense of the normative, which has been lost amid an ever-faltering economy.

19   Walter Benjamin, *Illuminations* (New York: Houghton Mifflin Harcourt, 1968), 227. The snapshot in its ethnographic form, others have argued, is not so different; like snapping a photo, the ethnographic engagement is all about capturing inversions of one's own reality. Christopher Pinney, "The Quick and the Dead: Images, Time and Truth," *Society for Visual Anthropology Review* 6, no. 2 (1990): 53.

20   The ethnographic negative, continuing in the spirit of Benjamin, does not try to index the world so much as provide an essence from which a presentiment can be extracted. Benjamin, *Illuminations*, 227.

21   Despite Costel's concern, Bear worked the weekend, received payment, and was back at the black market the following week.

22   This point is inspired by Michael T. Taussig's own thoughts about boredom in the context of village life in Columbia. Taussig, in *My Cocaine Museum* (Chicago: University of Chicago Press, 2004), writes,

> In a well-intentioned effort to combat racist stereotyping, anthropologists are often moved to evoke equally stereotyped tropes of the cultural "dynamism" and cultural "richness" of the coast, yet I find it hard to know what is meant here. . . . For what is elided by such tropes is the existential soul strength that monotony demands. Here ethnography fares poorly because this formative experience, namely, this sticky vacuum of heat and boredom, seems pretty well unconveyable and, worse still, all manner of narrative, paradox, and so-called data are then desperately shaped by the observer so as to jolt the emptiness with meaning. (59)

In the same vein, this book resists the temptation to jolt the emptiness that Bucharest's homeless experienced with a sense of meaning and productivity that they did not share but, instead, aims to make sense of how emptiness comes into being and to what ends.

23   This boredom results, to draw on Berlant's words, from maintaining an attachment to a significantly problematic object: in this case, it refers to a quality of life that was once attainable but now no longer is. This is distinct from melancholia, which is enacted to temporize an experience of the loss of an object in which one's ego is invested. Berlant, *Cruel Optimism*, 24.

24   To be sure, Romania was a hotbed for structural violence in many ways: two decades of tumultuous postcommunist transition followed by a global economic crisis and a government whose social spending was curbed by austerity measures imposed by the International Monetary Fund. Faced with a stagnant economy and a torn safety net, homeless men lamented time and again that there was no work to be found in Bucharest. Although work could in fact be found in Bucharest, it was for the multilingual with professional degrees. None of these opportunities, however, concerned those hanging around homeless shelters, squatter camps, and transit stations.

25 See Paul Farmer, "An Anthropology of Structural Violence," *Current Anthropology* 45, no. 3 (2004): 305–25; and Arthur Kleinman, Veena Das, and Margaret Lock, "Introduction," in *Social Suffering* (Berkeley: University of California Press, 1997), ix–xxvii. Kleinman, Das, and Lock write that social suffering "brings into a single space an assemblage of human problems that have their origins and consequences in the devastating injuries that social forces can inflict on human experience. Social suffering results from what political, economic and institutional power does to people and, reciprocally, from how these forms of power themselves influence responses to social problems. . . . [I]t points to the often close linkage of personal problems with societal problems. It reveals the interpersonal grounds of suffering: in other words, that suffering is a social experience" (ix).

26 Nancy Scheper-Hughes and Philippe Bourgois, *Violence in War and Peace*, Blackwell Readers in Anthropology (New York: Blackwell, 2004).

27 Jonathan Stillo, "The Romanian Tuberculosis Epidemic as a Symbol of Public Health," in *Romania under Basescu: Aspirations, Achievements, and Frustrations during His First Presidential Term*, ed. R. King and P. Sum (New York: Rowman and Littlefield, 2011), 273–92.

28 Importantly, slow death is distinct from Giorgio Agamben's notion of bare life. See Agamben, *Homo Sacer: Sovereign Power and Bare Life* (Stanford, CA: Stanford University Press, 1998). While bare life is extrajuridical and situated outside the regular workings of society (*Homo Sacer*, 71), slow death is endemic to society; it is a crisis that unfolds within the ordinary. As Berlant writes, slow death "is neither a state of exception nor the opposite, mere banality, but a domain of revelation where an upsetting scene of living that has been muffled in ordinary consciousness is revealed to be interwoven with ordinary life after all, like ants revealed scurrying under a thoughtlessly lifted rock." Berlant, "Slow Death (Sovereignty, Obesity, Lateral Agency)," *Critical Inquiry* 33, no. 4 (2007): 761.

5 · BORED STIFF

1 Constantin's utterance, "dă-le în pula mea de curve," is more directly translated as an expression of attitude, as in "I go to the Gara de Nord, and I'm like fuck these bitches!" Extensive follow-up interviews and observations with Constantin, however, confirmed that this statement of swagger coincided with actually having sex with male prostitutes at the train station.

2 *Downtime* is my own term for the long periods of waiting that punctuated employment in Romania's informal economy.

3 Boredom, Saikat Majumdar argues, is a central experience of the periphery. Administrators working in the colonial periphery evoked boredom to describe their frustration and estrangement from the central metropolis. Instead of being immersed in its consumerist culture, those at the colonial periphery struggled with their immediate surroundings, insisting that their political, economic, and cultural center was located elsewhere. See Majumdar, *Prose of the*

World: Modernism and the Banality of Empire (New York: Columbia University Press, 2013).

4 Following the end of communism, international news agencies scrutinized the poor conditions inside Romanian orphanages. While many of those in orphanages had lost both of their parents, there were also a large number of "social orphans" from families whose parents were alive but unable to support them, suggesting that the state had become the default custodian of a startlingly large number of the population's children. Toby Volkman, *Cultures of Transnational Adoption* (Durham, NC: Duke University Press, 2005), 186. As Gail Kligman details, the high number of orphaned children was linked to the draconian reproductive policies of communist Romania. Kligman, *The Politics of Duplicity: Controlling Reproduction in Ceausescu's Romania* (Berkeley: University of California Press, 1998).

5 The most widely circulated example is a string of news reports by the news program *20/20*. See Tom Jarriel and Janice Tomlin, "Nobody's Children: The Shame of a Nation," *20/20* (New York: ABC News, 1990). The footage includes a panorama of a state orphanage filled with skeletally thin children, most of whom are naked. The lens focuses on one child covered with flies but too tired to wave them away, only to then show another naked child seated on a plastic bucket, moving his bowels as he is simultaneously served lunch. The report raised a swell of outrage among American audiences at large but also specifically aroused the interest of middle-class households who were eager to adopt white babies. See also John Upton, "Take Me to America," *20/20* (New York: ABC News, 1993).

6 *Survival sex* refers, in the public health and medical anthropology literatures, "to the selling of sex to meet subsistence needs. It includes the exchange of sex for shelter, food, drugs or money." Jody M. Greene, Susan T. Ennett, and Christopher L. Ringwalt, "Prevalence and Correlates of Survival Sex among Runaway and Homeless Youth," *American Journal of Public Health* 89, no. 9 (1999): 1406. The terms *prostitution, sex work*, and *survival sex* tend to be used interchangeably in the academic literature to mean transactional sex. Survival sex links into the anthropological literature on structural violence, showing political and economic factors as shaping sexual experience and practice. See Richard Parker, "Sexuality, Culture, and Power in HIV/AIDS Research," *Annual Review of Anthropology* 30 (January 2001): 168–69. As the discussion of sexual exchange shifts—from the moral overtones of *prostitution* to recognition of material conditions and structural violence—anthropologists have emphasized that culturally specific notions of gender mediate one's relationship to economic structures. See Suzanne Leclerc-Madlala, "Transactional Sex and the Pursuit of Modernity," *Social Dynamics* 29, no. 2 (2003): 213–33; and Holly Wardlow, "Anger, Economy, and Female Agency: Problematizing 'Prostitution' and 'Sex Work' among the Huli of Papua New Guinea," *Signs* 29, no. 4 (2004): 1017–40.

7 This confirms observations made by anthropologists working in Latin America, who similarly found that sex work enabled upward mobility or, at the very

least, did not exacerbate one's exclusion: "For the young *jotas* who have left
school and not had the opportunity to enter the labor market, starting to sell
sexual services does not represent further exclusion, does not mean that the
distance from straight society increases." Annick Prieur, *Mema's House, Mexico
City: On Transvestites, Queens, and Machos*, Worlds of Desire: The Chicago
Series on Sexuality, Gender, and Culture (Chicago: University of Chicago Press,
1998), 72.

8   See Pierre Bourdieu, "Men and Machines," in *Advances in Social Theory and
Methodology: Toward an Integration of Micro- and Macro-Sociologies*, ed. Karin
Knorr-Cetina and Aaron Victor Cicourel (London: Routledge and Kegan Paul,
1981).

9   In another time and place, Joanne Passaro found that women gained preferential access to homeless and housing programs in the United States over and
above men owing to cultural associations that place women in the home and
men at work. The gendered place of men and women helps to constitute a
welfare regime that systematically treats men as deserving of their poverty. See
Passaro, *The Unequal Homeless: Men on the Streets, Women in Their Place* (New
York: Routledge, 1996). It is a cultural logic that holds in Romania.

10 Kerwin Kaye, "Male Prostitution in the Twentieth Century," *Journal of Homosexuality* 46, nos. 1–2 (2004): 1–77.

11 Manele is a pop music genre prominent in Romania and across the Balkans.
Manele mixes Roma folk sounds with electronic dance beats. For a wider
discussion, see Ioana Szeman, "'Gypsy Music' and Deejays: Orientalism,
Balkanism, and Romani Musicians," *TDR: The Drama Review* 53, no. 3 (2009):
98–116.

12 On September 6, 2001, Romania abrogated article 200 of its penal code, which
had criminalized same-sex relations between consenting adults with prison
terms of up to five years. The repeal came after significant external pressures
from the Council of Europe, which Romania joined in 1993, and the European
Union, during Romania's accession negotiations beginning in 2000. Romanians resisted such pressures, citing the country's "cultural specificity" and
claiming that homosexuality was alien to Romania. See Voichita Nachescu,
"Hierarchies of Difference: National Identity, Gay and Lesbian Rights, and the
Church in Postcommunist Romania," in *Sexuality and Gender in Postcommunist Eastern Europe and Russia*, ed. A. Štulhofer and T. Sandfort (New York:
Routledge, 2005), 58. An opinion poll conducted in 1993 showed that four out
of five Romanians believed that homosexual acts were never justified and that
the complete eradication of homosexuality would serve a legitimate national
interest. Eight years later, another poll found that 86 percent of Romanians
would not want a gay or lesbian person as their neighbor. Lucian Turcescu and
Lavinia Stan, "Religion, Politics and Sexuality in Romania," *Europe-Asia Studies*
57, no. 2 (2005): 292–93.

13 Havelock Ellis, *Studies in the Psychology of Sex*, vol. 2 (Philadelphia: F. A. Davis,
1906), 13. By "lower classes," Ellis means both the working class of industrial

societies such as Europe and the "primitive cultures" in the classical anthropological sense, found in Zanzibar and New Guinea, for example. Ellis writes that "on the whole, the evidence shows that among lower races homosexual practices are regarded with considerable indifference" (22). In this account, homosexuality is understood not as "unnatural" but as reflective of a certain lack of cultivation.

14 Steven Maynard, "'Horrible Temptations': Sex, Men, and Working-Class Male Youth in Urban Ontario, 1890–1935," *Canadian Historical Review* 78, no. 2 (1997): 191–235.

15 As Steven Maynard writes, "In view of the dangers and meager remuneration of the workplace, it is perhaps not so hard to understand why some boys chose the streets and sex with men, in which a few minutes up a laneway or in a theatre might earn them as much as or more than a long day at a mill or factory." Maynard, "'Horrible Temptations,'" 231. With the factory foreclosed to them, young men at the station pointed to the absence of viable alternatives to justify sex work.

16 While tramp communities were overwhelmingly male, women and prostitutes were nevertheless present. Nels Anderson explains that male tramps have sex with other men even when female prostitutes are present along a similar market logic. Anderson concludes that the available prostitutes are insufficiently attractive: "The professional prostitutes who do cater to the small purse of the tramp are generally women who have not been able to compete in better-paying circles. They are women who have seen their best days and are not even attractive to the average tramp." Anderson's argument speaks to the way gender is mediated by economic pressures, but it also denies the possibility of a male preference for other men. Anderson, "The Juvenile and the Tramp," *Journal of the American Institute of Criminal Law and Criminology* 14, no. 2 (1923): 290–312.

17 Anderson, "Juvenile and the Tramp," 305.

18 Foucault observes:

> As defined by the ancient civil or canonical codes, sodomy was a category of forbidden acts; their perpetrator was nothing more than the judicial subject of them. The nineteenth-century homosexual became a personage, a past, a case history, and a childhood, in addition to being a type of life, a life form, and a morphology, with an indiscreet anatomy and possibly a mysterious physiology. . . . Homosexuality appeared as one of the forms of sexuality when it was transposed from the practice of sodomy onto a kind of interior androgen, a hermaphrodism of the soul. The sodomite had been a temporary aberration; the homosexual was now a species.

Michel Foucault, *The History of Sexuality*, vol. 1 (New York: Penguin, 1984), 43. Foucault's larger argument is that sexual practices and subjectivities are neither stable nor natural but historically contingent, social, and connected to discourses of power. Men having sex with men does not indicate homosexuality until an apparatus of cultural categories and assumptions enables the idea of homosexuality to become thinkable. For this reason, Foucault argues elsewhere that while it was common in ancient Greece for men to have sex with men, the ancient Greeks were not gay in any social or cultural sense. Foucault, "Erotics," *October* 33 (July 1985): 4.

19 As Todd DePastino argues, "Hobo sexual practices . . . must be understood in terms of the general assumptions about sex and gender that pervaded working-class culture in the late nineteenth and early twentieth centuries. For workers, masculinity or 'manliness' derived not so much from sex, or the sex of sexual partners, but rather from gender status: that is, the bundles of attributes, values and behaviors believed to be desirable or normal in men." DePastino, *Citizen Hobo: How a Century of Homelessness Shaped America* (Chicago: University of Chicago Press, 2003), 89. This represents a shift from the middle class's tendency to base a heteronormative masculine identity on having a female partner.

20 In the 2000s Philippe Bourgois and Jeffrey Schonberg documented that "lumpen and poor working-class men might, under certain conditions, have sex and fall in love with one another without altering their masculine self-conception. They could even remain aggressively homophobic. . . . Although [men having sex with men] is frequently described, this form of masculine sexuality remains under-theorized, and it is not generally analyzed as a class-based phenomenon. It is often presented as an ambiguous cultural phenomenon that is framed as the domination of one participant by the other." Bourgois and Schonberg, *Righteous Dopefiend* (Berkeley: University of California Press, 2009), 198.

Mark Padilla found in Santo Domingo that male sex workers "tend to conceptualize their sexuality very differently than do gay-identified men. For example, while the latter are generally more effeminate in their gender performance and stereotypically . . . participate in *pasivo* (passive, or receptive) sex with their male partners, many [sex workers] attempt to assimilate to normative constructions of masculinity, are often married, typically request payment for sex, and almost universally claim to participate exclusively in *activo* (active, or insertive) anal sex with their male partners. These men frequent many of the spaces where gay-identified men congregate, often develop close friendships and long-term relationships with gays. Yet . . . the boundaries established by cultural constructions of gender and sexuality create palpable divisions between gays and [sex workers]." Padilla, *Caribbean Pleasure Industry: Tourism, Sexuality, and AIDS in the Dominican Republic*, Worlds of Desire: The Chicago Series on Sexuality, Gender, and Culture (Chicago: University of Chicago Press, 2007), 11. For a comprehensive literature review on male prostitution, from which this chapter section has benefited immensely, see Kaye, "Male Prostitution."

21 Denise Roman writes that the LGBT community "encounters widespread reactions of conservatism and denial in contemporary post-communist Romania.

Sinners from an ethico-religious viewpoint, and outcasts in the juridico-political discourse of the state apparatuses, queers are either considered pariah in present Romanian society, or they are victims through omission." Roman, *Fragmented Identities: Popular Culture, Sex, and Everyday Life in Postcommunist Romania* (Plymouth, UK: Lexington, 2007), 127. The repeal of article 200 did not change the social status or public perception of sexual minorities in Romania. Human rights organizations reported that job losses, police harassment, physical attacks, and verbal abuse remained common in Romania. Victims were reluctant to report such incidents out of fear of media coverage and public disclosure of their sexual activities. Deviations from masculine roles as husband and father brought about shame within families and communities. See Kim Longfield, Hibist Astatke, Reid Smith, Georgia Mcpeak, and Jim Ayers, "Men Who Have Sex with Men in Southeastern Europe: Underground and at Increased Risk for HIV/STIs," *Culture, Health and Sexuality* 9, no. 5 (2007): 474.

22 As Harry Oosterhuis writes, in reference to Victorian England,

> bourgeois respectability with all its sexual and moral constraints also posed a problem, which in part explains why some preferably looked for their sexual contacts among the lower classes in particular. As a possible escape from the restraints of bourgeois respectability, the looseness of lower-class sexuality, though generally considered dangerous, still seemed enticing. . . . In fact, many middle- and upper-class urnings indicated that they preferred sex with lower-class men; some of them stated they were not sexually aroused by men of their own class. . . . Apparently, some social distance made it easier for these men to discard any psychological inhibitions they might have.

Harry Oosterhuis, *Stepchildren of Nature: Krafft-Ebing, Psychiatry, and the Making of Sexual Identity* (Chicago: University of Chicago Press, 2000), 201–2. See also Henry L. Minton, *Departing from Deviance: A History of Homosexual Rights and Emancipatory Science in America* (Chicago: University of Chicago Press, 2002), 217.

23 Matti Bunzl studied Austrian gay male sex tourists visiting Prague. Bunzl notes Austrian men's excitement over the prevalence of Prague men who made themselves sexually available in exchange for small gifts. Bunzl writes that "the tropes of availability, passion, and pan-sexuality ultimately congeal into a topography of embodied Otherness. Constructed on the neocolonial terms of a Western gay male subject seeking adventure in an exoticised East, they delineate a socio-sexual field structured by an economy of Eastern supplies for Western demands." Bunzl, "The Prague Experience: Gay Male Sex Tourism and the Neocolonial Invention of an Embodied Border," in *Altering States: Ethnographies of Transition in Eastern Europe and the Former Soviet Union*, ed. Daphne Berdahl, Matti Bunzl, and Martha Lampland (Ann Arbor: University of Michigan Press, 2000), 86.

24 See João Guilherme Biehl, *Vita: Life in a Zone of Social Abandonment* (Berkeley: University of California Press, 2005); and Pierre Bourdieu, *Pascalian Meditations* (Stanford, CA: Stanford University Press, 2000).

25 "At the very moment when the iron law of ennui and mechanization was being imposed, when there would soon be the law of the division of labor, Tarde sings the praises of idleness, of the chatter of the idle classes.... 'There is no manager more powerful than consumption, nor, as a result, any factor more powerful—albeit indirect—in production than the chatter of individuals in their idle hours.'" Bruno Latour and Vincent Antonin Lepinay, *The Science of Passionate Interests: An Introduction to Gabriel Tarde's Economic Anthropology* (Chicago: Prickly Paradigm, 2010), 48–49. For Tarde, consumption *flows* under the force of idle chatter. By *flow*, Gilles Deleuze and Félix Guattari explain, Tarde means belief and desire: "Beliefs and desires are the basis of every society, because they are flows and as such are 'quantifiable'; they are veritable social Quantities.... For in the end, the difference [for Tarde] is not at all between the social and the individual (or inter-individual), but between the molar [or stable] realm of representations, individual and collective, and the molecular [or shifting] realm of beliefs and desires in which the distinction between the social and the individual loses all meaning since flows are neither attributable to individuals nor over-codable by collective signifiers." Deleuze and Guattari, *A Thousand Plateaus: Capitalism and Schizophrenia* (Minneapolis: University of Minnesota Press, 1987), 218–19. Boredom is a central flow, among others, constitutive of the social relations of Romania's homeless.

26 Jean Genet's *The Thief's Journal* explores the intimate relationship between the sacred and the profane. Genet, *The Thief's Journal* (New York: Grove/Atlantic, 1994). A predominant theme in this work is an inversion of ideals, whereby sacred values get pursued through ostensibly profane acts of crime and homosexuality. Michael T. Taussig uses Genet's work to develop a sense of *maleficium*, the sacred power of impurity, and to open up a discussion about the relation between misfortune and social process. Taussig, "Maleficium: State Fetishism," in *Fetishism as Cultural Discourse*, ed. Emily S. Apter and William Pietz (Ithaca, NY: Cornell University Press, 1993), 237.

27 Jean Baudrillard, *The Consumer Society: Myths and Structures* (London: Sage, 1998), 43.

28 Others have noted the complex social networks that emerge through sex markets, pointing to the emergence of important relationships in urban communities that take shape across race and class and that are mediated by peep shows, public restrooms, and parks. Samuel R. Delany, *Times Square Red, Times Square Blue*, Sexual Cultures (New York: New York University Press, 1999).

29 See Foucault, "On the Genealogy of Ethics: An Overview of Work in Progress," in *Ethics: Subjectivity and Truth*, ed. Paul Rabinow (New York: New Press, 1997), 1:256. Foucault writes, "My point is not that everything is bad, but that everything is dangerous, which is not exactly the same as bad. If everything is dangerous, then we always have something to do" (256). Foucault is comment-

ing on the open-endedness of activity, in which the full consequences of any act cannot be known in advance. Rather than nihilism, Foucault responds to ever-present danger with a call for constant vigilance and reform.

30 Philippe Bourgois, *In Search of Respect: Selling Crack in El Barrio*, 2nd ed. (Cambridge: Cambridge University Press, 2003).

31 Padilla, *Caribbean Pleasure Industry*.

6 · DEFEAT BOREDOM!

1 PR Romania, "Peste 1,7 Milioane de Intrări La Promoția 'NESCAFÉ 3în1 și NESCAFÉ Frappé înving Plictiseala,'" Pr-Romania.Ro, July 9, 2010, http://www .pr-romania.ro/comunicate-de-presa/728-peste-17-milioane-de-intrari-la -promotia-nescafe-3in1-si-nescafe-frappe-inving-plictiseala.html.

2 By the rhythm of everyday life, I refer to the tension, described by Henri Lefebvre, between the cyclical repetition of nature and the linear repetition of production and consumption. Henri Lefebvre, "The Everyday and Everyday-ness," *Yale French Studies*, no. 73 (January 1987): 10. In the modern era, Lefebvre notes, the linear time of the economy comes to mask the cyclical repetition of nature, turning production and "the imposition of consumption" into the organizing mechanisms of society (10). The rhythm of everyday life structured by the commodity turns time into an endless series of "nows" to be crammed with more activities and distractions, but this is also experienced as endless and empty repetition. Michael E. Gardiner, "Henri Lefebvre and the 'Sociology of Boredom,'" *Theory, Culture and Society* 29, no. 2 (2012): 44, 46.

3 Public space is becoming increasingly privatized, with the public square giving way to the shopping mall just as parks and sidewalks are reappropriated as ter-race bars and cafés. One consequence of the increasingly commercial character of public spaces is that these places are no longer freely accessible to all mem-bers of the public in the broadest sense. Instead, semipublic places are actively policed to restrict unwanted populations, such as the homeless. See Lynn A. Staeheli and Don Mitchell, *The People's Property? Power, Politics, and the Public* (New York: Routledge, 2007); see also Néstor García Canclini, *Consumers and Citizens: Globalization and Multicultural Conflicts* (Minneapolis: University of Minnesota Press, 2001).

4 Through the careful production of space, from its material design to its lighting, sound, and scent, merchants work to project a sense of luxury and taste onto goods that are otherwise indistinguishable. The retail space of the department store is one where the commodity is intended to entertain, if not excite, customers; it is a stage on which the commodity undergoes a theatrical change, becoming something more than what it was. See Rosalind H. Wil-liams, *Dream Worlds: Mass Consumption in Late Nineteenth-Century France* (Berkeley: University of California Press, 1991), 67; and Rudi Laermans, "Learn-ing to Consume: Early Department Stores and the Shaping of the Modern Consumer Culture (1860–1914)," *Theory, Culture and Society* 10, no. 4 (1993): 92–93.

5   See Liviu Chelcea, "The Culture of Shortage during State-Socialism: Consump-
    tion Practices in a Romanian Village in the 1980s," *Cultural Studies* 16, no. 1
    (2002): 16–43.

6   In referring to a "capitalist elsewhere," I draw on the work of Lauren Berlant,
    who writes of a tendency in this present moment for capitalism to generate opti-
    mistic attachments to a good life, or idealized fantasies about how a person and
    the world "add up to something." Berlant, *Cruel Optimism* (Durham, NC: Duke
    University Press, 2011), 2. As Berlant argues, these fantasies are cruel in that they
    are unattainable: they always seem to fall out of reach or are located elsewhere.

7   This is a consumer-based claim to social belonging that is well documented in
    the so-called capitalist West but that also resonates among those who came of
    age during Eastern European socialism, where notions of respectability and
    cosmopolitanism were tethered to hygiene, fashion, and home decoration. See
    Pierre Bourdieu, *Distinction: A Social Critique of the Judgment of Taste* (Cam-
    bridge, MA: Harvard University Press, 1987); and Susan Emily Reid and David
    Crowley, eds., *Style and Socialism: Modernity and Material Culture in Post-war
    Eastern Europe* (London: Berg, 2000). Victor Buchli notes that the development
    of socialist housing and furniture was part of a concerted effort by the state to
    materially structure domestic relations. Buchli, *An Archaeology of Socialism*,
    Materializing Culture (London: Berg, 2000). The globally competitive econ-
    omy, ultimately, did not introduce the relationship between consumption and
    social belonging to Romania so much as heighten it by redefining well-being in
    a materially richer way. See Krisztina Fehérváry, *Politics in Color and Concrete:
    Socialist Materialities and the Middle Class in Hungary*, New Anthropologies of
    Europe (Bloomington: Indiana University Press, 2013). In this spirit, Bucharest's
    homeless turn to the varied spaces of mass consumerism in search of inclusion
    as much as stimulation.

8   Thorstein Veblen argues that capitalist accumulation is oriented toward narrow-
    ing the gap between one's own pecuniary strength and that of one's neighbors,
    if not surpassing one's community in wealth. Veblen links this comparative gap
    with emotive well-being, writing, "So long as the comparison is distinctly unfa-
    vorable to himself, the normal, average individual lives in chronic dissatisfaction
    with his present lot; and when he has reached what may be called the normal
    pecuniary standard of the community . . . this chronic dissatisfaction will give
    place to a restless straining to place a wider and ever-widening pecuniary inter-
    val between himself and this average standard." Veblen, *The Theory of the Leisure
    Class*, ed. M. Banta (Oxford: Oxford University Press, 2007), 23. This wealth,
    Veblen goes on to write, must be put in evidence through dress, bodily com-
    portment, and modes of leisure, for example (26). Community, in this instance,
    is increasingly transnational, with homeless men comparing their pecuniary
    strength not only within the city and the nation but also against their imagined
    counterparts across Europe.

9   Cultural competency, Mary Douglas and Baron Isherwood noted, is a question
    not just of knowledge but also of embodiment. Douglas and Isherwood write,

"The cultured person has made of what he knows a synthesis so complete that his behavior implies a natural mastery. . . . [C]ulture should fit, not like a glove, but like a skin. The fake could be bought, but true culture [is] a synthesis that had to grow naturally." Douglas and Isherwood, *The World of Goods: Towards an Anthropology of Consumption* (New York: Routledge, 1979), 52. When one is at home in the world, Douglas observes, cultural competency fits seamlessly like a skin. The ease with which cultural competency is embodied quickly dissolves as one moves out of place so that the comfort of living in one's own skin gives ways to the clumsiness of even the best tailored glove.

10   See Mikhail M. Bakhtin, *Rabelais and His World* (Bloomington: Indiana University Press, 1984), 19. Carnivalesque laughter plays on an absolute and topographical meaning of *upward* and *downward*. Upward refers to heaven but also the face or head, while downward refers to the earth and the lower parts of the body: belly, genitals, and buttocks. These absolute topographical coordinates are played on in order to turn the inside out, invert the top to bottom, and turn the front to rear to produce numerous parodies and travesties, humiliations, profanations, and comic crownings and uncrownings. The carnivalesque turns the world inside out (11). This turning of the world inside out, Bakhtin explained, centers on a festive laughter, one that takes as its object the droll quality of society in order to upend it triumphantly and mockingly, but always temporarily (11–12). The carnivalesque disrupts social norms, unsettling for the briefest of moments otherwise given horizontal distinctions and hierarchical relations.

11   James C. Scott develops the term "weapons of the weak" to refer to the silent and nonviolent techniques that vulnerable populations mobilize in their struggle against authority, such as foot-dragging, false compliance, stealing, feigned ignorance, and sabotage. Scott, *Weapons of the Weak: Everyday Forms of Peasant Resistance* (New Haven, CT: Yale University Press, 1985).

12   Over the course of this research, I had to constantly clarify to homeless men and women my position within Backwoods and Stefan's Place as an independent researcher rather than an extension of the administrative staff. To that end, I often participated in mundane rule breaking. In addition to building rapport with those participating, such as Emil and Eveline, these moments also assured to the homeless beneficiaries who were watching that they did not need to conceal their own rule breaking from me. Methodologically, these acts allowed me greater insight into the lives of homeless men and women, even if they did tax my relationships with the social service providers granting me access.

13   Low-income neighborhoods, a thickening literature notes, have become "food deserts"; that is, the residents of impoverished urban neighborhoods lack access to the generally less expensive and healthier food options found in full-service supermarkets. See Neil Wrigley, "'Food Deserts' in British Cities: Policy Context and Research Priorities," *Urban Studies* 39, no. 11 (2002): 2029–40. Not only did Bucharest's homeless reside within marginal spaces that fit the de-

scription of food deserts, but their efforts at accessing supermarkets were often frustrated by private security guards. As a result, the homeless did most of their provisioning at grab-and-go corner stores, where prices were higher and fresh food options fewer.

14 The aesthetics of superfluity does not refer only to the aesthetics of surfaces and quantities, writes Achille Mbembe, but also "to how such an aesthetics is premised on the capacity of things to hypnotize, overexcite, or paralyze the senses." Mbembe, "Aesthetics of Superfluity," *Public Culture* 16, no. 3 (2004): 374. To that end, in metropolitan modernity, luxury, pleasure, consumption, and other stimuli affect the sensory foundations of mental life and play a central role in the process of subject formation in general. This luxury inspires the upwardly mobile administrator just as it works to discourage the downwardly mobile manual laborer.

15 Through an analysis of tobacco companies and mining corporations, Peter Benson and Stuart Kirsch demonstrate how corporations contribute to a "politics of resignation," a general feeling of disempowerment that characterizes contemporary political life and that benefits corporations financially. Benson and Kirsch, "Capitalism and the Politics of Resignation," *Current Anthropology* 51, no. 4 (2010): 460. Here I make a similar kind of claim by demonstrating that the practices of global scale making that displace people from work and home become framed as the solution to the affective consequences of that very displacement. The turn toward consumerism that follows among the displaced stifles more substantive political criticism.

16 Under capitalism, commodities organize desires and provoke fantasies, writes Mbembe in "Aesthetics of Superfluity" (401). While fantasies proliferate amid capitalist production, this sense of desire is never sated. As Berlant writes, "consumption promises satisfaction in substitution and then denies it because all objects are rest stops amid the process of remaining unsatisfied that counts for being alive under capitalism." Berlant, *Cruel Optimism*, 42. It is the commodity's production of insatiable desire that drives capitalism. Just as this dynamic has the potential to excite, it always eventually disappoints.

CONCLUSION

1 *Igloo.ro*, "Reabilitarea Centrului Istoric Al Bucureştiului," May 2005.

2 *Igloo.ro*, "Reabilitarea Centrului Istoric."

3 A €9.5 million investment from the European Bank for Reconstruction and Development and an additional €1.5 million from local investors funded the development of Lipscani's main corridor as a so-called pilot project. See *Igloo.ro*, "Reabilitarea Centrului Istoric." The pilot project's success drew an additional €80–€100 million in private investment. See Radu Racu, "Cât Costă Să Faci Din Centrul Bucureştiului Un Al Doilea Sibiu," *Ziarul Financiar*, May 25, 2011, http://da.zf.ro/business-construct/cat-costa-sa-faci-din-centrul-bucurestiului-un-al-doilea-sibiu-8281928

4   Corina Vârlan, "Gândul Vă Prezintă Harta Nouă a Centrului Vechi Al Capita-
    lei," *Gândul.info*, August 28, 2011. Business and government leaders heralded
    the redevelopment as an overwhelming success. The nightlife district reported
    attracting thousands of visitors each night. As businesses flourished, early
    investors celebrated the district's rising real estate values.

5   Mark Baker, "Bucharest's New Old City," *BBC Travel*, July 16, 2013, http://www
    .bbc.com/travel/story/20130712-bucharests-new-old-city.

6   Personal correspondence with the Romanian National Tourist Office for North
    America. The National Tourist Office's strategy, the office reports, is working:
    in 2014 the office recorded an 11.5 percent growth in foreign tourists visiting
    Romania.

7   Holly Ellyatt, "Can Dracula, Communism and Bachelors Help Emerging
    Europe?," *CNBC.com*, January 29, 2014, http://www.cnbc.com/2014/01/29/can
    -dracula-communism-and-bachelors-help-emerging-europe.html.

8   Racu, "Cât Costă Să Faci."

9   As other anthropologists have already documented, globalization is an uneven
    process, one that incorporates some while leaving out others. See Arjun Appa-
    durai, *Modernity at Large: Cultural Dimensions of Globalization* (Minneapolis:
    University of Minnesota Press, 1996); and Homi K. Bhabha, "Double Visions,"
    Artforum 30, no. 5 (1992): 85–89. This is because the wealth and opportunity
    that globalism makes possible do not coat the globe but rather jump from point
    to point in order to connect discrete points on it. See James Ferguson, *Global
    Shadows: Africa in the Neoliberal World Order* (Durham, NC: Duke University
    Press, 2006), 37–38. For this reason, the National Tourist Office's efforts to
    position Lipscani within a global tourism market have more to do with interna-
    tional travelers than with manual laborers waiting at the black market for work
    just a few miles away.

10 Teresa P. R. Caldeira identifies a similar phenomenon in the hypersegregated
    city of São Paulo, where professional classes living in gated communities and
    consuming media and commodities are more akin to professionals in other
    elite cities than to the city residents living just beyond their walls. Caldeira, *City
    of Walls: Crime, Segregation, and Citizenship in São Paulo* (Berkeley: University
    of California Press, 2001).

11 In his opening commentary on *Speed and Politics*, Benjamin Bratton explains
    that, for Paul Virilio, "the invention or adoption of a new technology is always
    also the invention and adoption of a new accident." Bratton, "Introduction: Logis-
    tics of Habitable Circulation," in Virilio, *Speed and Politics* (Los Angeles: Semio-
    text(e), 2006), 20. Techniques that serve to speed the world up also bring about
    a dramatic slowing down when technologies falter or practices fall out of step.

12 Logistics, for Virilio, refers to the infrastructure that makes mobility pos-
    sible, in particular as it pertains to warfare. It implies the transformation of
    a landscape into a planned and strategic space. Virilio, *Speed and Politics*,
    73–74.

13 Harvey uses the word *fix* to focus on the problem of "fixity" versus the motion
   and mobility of capital. Harvey notes that capitalism has to fix space in order
   to overcome space. Harvey, "Globalization and the Spatial Fix," *Geographische
   Revue* 2, no. 3 (2001): 25. The mobility of some people, objects, and ideas
   requires a rooted landscape for its own functioning. In a parallel way, I argue,
   the heightened mobility of some is achieved through the stasis of those deemed
   superfluous as producers and consumers. These redundant workers are fixed
   to the unwanted spaces of the city, where they experience boredom and stasis
   rather than accelerated mobility.

14 A rich anthropological literature documents the material logistics of global
   flows, not only of physical commodities, but also of the so-called wireless tech-
   nologies that make up cloud computing as well as facilitate the digitization of
   stock trading. See Anna L. Tsing, *Friction: An Ethnography of Global Connection* (Princeton, NJ: Princeton University Press, 2004); Nicole Starosielski, *The
   Undersea Network*, Sign, Storage, Transmission (Durham, NC: Duke University
   Press, 2015); and Caitlin Zaloom, *Out of the Pits: Traders and Technology from
   Chicago to London* (Chicago: University of Chicago Press, 2006). Globalism,
   this work shows, does not dematerialize social relations but rather shifts the
   materiality through which connections are made and sustained.

15 Virilio, *Speed and Politics*, 33.

16 "The integration of that market," noted Michel-Rolph Trouillot, "help[s] to
   project the same image of the good life all over the world. In that sense, we
   are truly witnessing for the first time, especially among the youth, the global
   production of desire." Trouillot, "The Anthropology of the State in the Age of
   Globalization: Close Encounters of the Deceptive Kind," *Current Anthropology*
   42, no. 1 (2001): 129.

17 Martin Heidegger, *The Fundamental Concepts of Metaphysics: World, Finitude,
   Solitude* (Bloomington: Indiana University Press, 2001), 83.

18 Émile Durkheim, *The Division of Labor in Society* (New York: Free Press,
   1933), 370.

19 As Liisa Malkki notes, anthropological notions of culture and identity are
   regularly grounded in botanical metaphors of "rootedness." These botanical
   metaphors quickly conflate culture and people, nation and nature, in ways that
   are simultaneously incarcerating and romantic. Malkki, "National Geographic:
   The Rooting of Peoples and the Territorialization of National Identity among
   Scholars and Refugees," *Cultural Anthropology* 7, no. 1 (1992): 29. Malkki notes
   that in a world ordered by nations, uprootedness is pathologized. My argument
   here is that in an economy organized by global circulation, uprootedness is a
   state of incorporation and belonging.

20 In *The Division of Labor in Society,* Durkheim argues that law and morality
   make up the totality of the ties that bind society together (399). Given the
   corrosive effects of industrialization, Durkheim continues, "our duty is not to
   spread our activity over a large surface, but to concentrate and specialize it. We

must contract our horizon, choose a definite task and immerse ourselves in it completely" (401).

21   To quote Michel Foucault, "You can't find the solution of a problem in the solution of another problem raised at another moment by other people." Foucault, "On the Genealogy of Ethics: An Overview of Work in Progress," in *Ethics: Subjectivity and Truth*, ed. Paul Rabinow (New York: New Press, 1997), 1:256. Foucault's interest is in linking progressive politics with forward thinking rather than the review of classic texts. Rather than trying to return to a moment that has passed, Foucault's challenge is to turn society into "a vast experimental field, in such a way as to decide which taps need turning, which bolts need to be loosened here or there, to get the desired change." Foucault, *Politics, Philosophy, Culture: Interviews and Other Writings, 1977–1984*, ed. Lawrence Kritzman (New York: Taylor and Francis, 2013), 165.

BIBLIOGRAPHY

Agamben, Giorgio. *Homo Sacer: Sovereign Power and Bare Life*. Stanford, CA: Stanford University Press, 1998.

Ahmed, Sara. *The Promise of Happiness*. Durham, NC: Duke University Press, 2010.

Allen, Tim. "Euro Area Unemployment Rate at 10.0%." Eurostat Newsrelease 59/2010 Luxembourg, April 30, 2010.

Anderson, Nels. *The Hobo: The Sociology of the Homeless Man*. Chicago: University of Chicago Press, 1965.

———. "The Juvenile and the Tramp." *Journal of the American Institute of Criminal Law and Criminology* 14, no. 2 (1923): 290–312.

Andor, Laszlo. "End of Restrictions on Free Movement of Workers from Bulgaria and Romania." European Commission Memo 14/1. Brussels, January 1, 2014.

Appadurai, Arjun. *Modernity at Large: Cultural Dimensions of Globalization*. Public Worlds 1. Minneapolis: University of Minnesota Press, 1996.

Arendt, Hannah. *The Origins of Totalitarianism*. Cleveland, OH: World Publishing, 1966.

Augé, Marc. *Non-places: An Introduction to Supermodernity*. London: Verso, 2009.

Baker, Mark. "Bucharest's New Old City." *BBC Travel*, July 16, 2013. http://www.bbc.com/travel/story/20130712-bucharests-new-old-city.

Bakhtin, Mikhail M. *Rabelais and His World*. Bloomington: Indiana University Press, 1984.

Baudrillard, Jean. *The Consumer Society: Myths and Structures*. London: Sage, 1998.

Bauman, Zygmunt. *Wasted Lives: Modernity and Its Outcasts*. Cambridge: Polity, 2004.

BBC News. "Romania Plans Big VAT Rise to Secure Bail-Out Fund." June 26, 2010. http://www.bbc.co.uk/news/10424900.

Belmonte, Thomas. *The Broken Fountain*. New York: Columbia University Press, 1989.

Benjamin, Walter. *The Arcades Project*. Cambridge, MA: Belknap Press of Harvard University Press, 2002.

———. *Illuminations*. New York: Houghton Mifflin Harcourt, 1968.

Benson, Peter, and Stuart Kirsch. "Capitalism and the Politics of Resignation." *Current Anthropology* 51, no. 4 (2010): 459–86.

Berdahl, Daphne. *On the Social Life of Postsocialism: Memory, Consumption, Germany*. Edited by Matti Bunzl. Bloomington: Indiana University Press, 2010.

Berlant, Lauren. *Cruel Optimism*. Durham, NC: Duke University Press, 2011.

———. "Slow Death (Sovereignty, Obesity, Lateral Agency)." *Critical Inquiry* 33, no. 4 (2007): 754–80.

Berry, David. *The Romanian Mass Media and Cultural Development*. Burlington, VT: Ashgate, 2004.

Bhabha, Homi K. "Double Visions." *Artforum* 30, no. 5 (1992): 85–89.

Biehl, João Guilherme. *Vita: Life in a Zone of Social Abandonment*. Berkeley: University of California Press, 2005.

———. *Will to Live: AIDS Therapies and the Politics of Survival*. In-Formation Series. Princeton, NJ: Princeton University Press, 2007.

Biehl, João Guilherme, Byron Good, and Arthur Kleinman. *Subjectivity: Ethnographic Investigations*. Berkeley: University of California Press, 2007.

BizCity.ro. "Campanie Antiplictiseală de La Leo Burnett Pentru Antena 1." October 3, 2003. http://www.bizcity.ro/stiri/campanie-antiplictiseala-de-la-leo-burnett-pentru-antena-1.html?id=10326.

Blanchard, Olivier Jean, Kenneth A. Froot, and Jeffrey D. Sachs. *The Transition in Eastern Europe*. Vol. 1. Chicago: University of Chicago Press, 1994.

Blazek, J., and P. Netrdova. "Regional Unemployment Impacts of the Global Financial Crisis in the New Member States of the EU in Central and Eastern Europe." *European Urban and Regional Studies* 19, no. 1 (2012): 42–61.

Bouleanu, Elisa, and Cristina Ciulei. "Avem Azile, Căutăm Bătrâni." *Adevărul*, September 1, 2011. http://adevarul.ro/locale/alexandria/avem-azile-cautam-batrani-1_50aca84e7c42d5a66387c2ef/index.html.

Bourdieu, Pierre. *Distinction: A Social Critique of the Judgment of Taste*. Cambridge, MA: Harvard University Press, 1987.

———. "Men and Machines." In *Advances in Social Theory and Methodology: Toward an Integration of Micro- and Macro-Sociologies*, edited by Karin Knorr-Cetina and Aaron Victor Cicourel, 304–18. London: Routledge and Kegan Paul, 1981.

———. *Pascalian Meditations*. Stanford, CA: Stanford University Press, 2000.

Bourgois, Philippe. *In Search of Respect: Selling Crack in El Barrio*. 2nd ed. Cambridge: Cambridge University Press, 2003.

Bourgois, Philippe, and Jeffrey Schonberg. *Righteous Dopefiend*. Berkeley: University of California Press, 2009.

Branea, Lucian. "Bulldozing Bucharest: After Squatting Kiosk Owners Refused to Clear Out, a Hard-Hitting New Mayor Moved In—with Bulldozers." *Transitions Online* (Prague), September 11, 2000. http://www.tol.org/client/article/252-bulldozing-bucharest.html.

Bratton, Benjamin H. "Introduction: Logistics of Habitable Circulation." In *Speed and Politics*, by Paul Virilio, 1–20. Lost Angeles, CA: Semiotext(e), 2006.

Braudel, Fernand. *Civilization and Capitalism, 15th–18th Century*. Vol. 1, *The Structure of Everyday Life*. Berkeley: University of California Press, 1992.

Brown, Martin, and Ralph De Haas. "Foreign Banks and Foreign Currency Lending in Emerging Europe." *Economic Policy* 27, no. 69 (2012): 57–98.

Buchli, Victor. *An Archaeology of Socialism*. Materializing Culture. London: Berg, 2000.

București Mall. "București Mall—Primul centru comercial modern deschis în România." Accessed July 6, 2016. http://bucurestimall.com.ro/despre-noi.

Bunzl, Matti. "The Prague Experience: Gay Male Sex Tourism and the Neocolonial Invention of an Embodied Border." In *Altering States: Ethnographies of Transition in Eastern Europe and the Former Soviet Union*, edited by Daphne Berdahl, Matti Bunzl, and Martha Lampland, 70–95. Ann Arbor: University of Michigan Press, 2000.

Caldeira, Teresa P. R. *City of Walls: Crime, Segregation, and Citizenship in São Paulo*. Berkeley: University of California Press, 2001.

Canclini, Néstor García. *Consumers and Citizens: Globalization and Multicultural Conflicts*. Minneapolis: University of Minnesota Press, 2001.

Castells, Manuel. *The Rise of the Network Society: The Information Age; Economy, Society, and Culture*. Information Age. London: Wiley, 2011.

Céline, Louis-Ferdinand. *Journey to the End of the Night*. New York: New Directions, 2006.

Cernat, Paul. *Cozi și Oameni de Rând în Anii '80*. Edited by Adrian Neculau. *Viața Cotidiană în Comunism*. Iași, România: Polirom, 2004.

Chatterjee, Partha. "Democracy and Economic Transformation in India." *Economic and Political Weekly* 43, no. 16 (2008): 53–62.

Chekhov, Anton. *The Duel*. The Art of the Novella. Brooklyn: Melville House, 2011.

Chelcea, Liviu. "Ancestors, Domestic Groups, and the Socialist State: Housing Nationalization and Restitution in Romania." *Comparative Studies in Society and History* 45, no. 4 (2003): 714–40.

——. "The Culture of Shortage during State-Socialism: Consumption Practices in a Romanian Village in the 1980s." *Cultural Studies* 16, no. 1 (2002): 16–43.

——. "Marginal Groups in Central Places: Gentrification, Property Rights and Post-socialist Primitive Accumulation." In *Social Changes and Social Sustainability in Historical Urban Centers: The Case of Central Europe*, edited by Gyorgy Enyrdi and Zoltan Kovacs, 127–46. Pécs, Hungary: Centre for Regional Studies of the Hungarian Academy of Sciences, 2006.

Chiroiu, Luiza. "Salariul Minim Pe Economie: România vs. Europa." *Gândul .info*, February 26, 2015. http://www.gandul.info/financiar/salariul-minim-pe -economie-romania-vs-europa-13897442

Chirot, Daniel, and Charles Ragin. "The Market, Tradition and Peasant Rebellion: The Case of Romania in 1907." *American Sociological Review* 40, no. 4 (1975): 428–44.

Cho, Mun Young. *The Specter of "the People": Urban Poverty in Northeast China.*
Ithaca, NY: Cornell University Press, 2013.

Constantin, D. L., Zizi Goschin, and A. R. Danciu. "The Romanian Economy from
Transition to Crisis: Retrospects and Prospects." *World Journal of Social Sciences* 1,
no. 3 (2011): 155–71.

Crowley, Stephen. *Hot Coal, Cold Steel: Russian and Ukrainian Workers from the End
of the Soviet Union to the Post-communist Transformations.* Ann Arbor: University
of Michigan Press, 1997.

Dan, Adrian-Nicolae, and Mariana Dan. "Housing Policy in Romania in Transition:
Between State Withdrawal and Market Collapse." Paper presented at the *International Conference on Globalization, Integration, and Social Development in Central
and Eastern Europe*, 16. Sibiu, Romania. September 6–8, 2003.

Delany, Samuel R. *Times Square Red, Times Square Blue.* Sexual Cultures. New York:
New York University Press, 1999.

Deletant, Dennis. *Ceaușescu and the Securitate: Coercion and Dissent in Romania,
1965–1989.* London: M. E. Sharpe, 1995.

Deleuze, Gilles. *Spinoza: Practical Philosophy.* San Francisco: City Lights, 1988.

Deleuze, Gilles, and Félix Guattari. *Anti-Oedipus: Capitalism and Schizophrenia.*
New York: Continuum, 2004.

———. *A Thousand Plateaus: Capitalism and Schizophrenia.* Minneapolis: University
of Minnesota Press, 1987.

Demekas, Dimitri, and Mohsin S. Khan. *The Romanian Economic Reform Program.*
International Monetary Fund Occasional Paper. Washington, DC: International
Monetary Fund, 1991.

DePastino, Todd. *Citizen Hobo: How a Century of Homelessness Shaped America.*
Chicago: University of Chicago Press, 2003.

Desjarlais, Robert R. *Shelter Blues: Sanity and Selfhood among the Homeless.* Philadelphia: University of Pennsylvania Press, 1997.

de Sousa, José, and Laetitia Duval. "Geographic Distance and Remittances in Romania: Out of Sight, Out of Mind?" *International Economics* 121, no. 1 (2010): 81–98.

Dickens, Charles. *Bleak House.* Edited by H. K. Browne. London: Bradbury and
Evans, 1853.

Doherty, Joe, Volker Busch-Geertsema, Vita Karpuskiene, Jukka Korhonen, Eoin
O'Sullivan, Ingrid Sahlin, Antonio Tosi, Agostino Petrillo, and Julia Wygnańska.
"Homelessness and Exclusion: Regulating Public Space in European Cities." *Surveillance and Inequality* 5, no. 3 (2008): 290–314.

Douglas, Mary. *Purity and Danger: An Analysis of Concepts of Pollution and Taboo.*
London: Taylor, 2002.

Douglas, Mary, and Baron Isherwood. *The World of Goods: Towards an Anthropology
of Consumption.* New York: Routledge, 1979.

Dreyfus, Hubert L., and Paul Rabinow. *Michel Foucault: Beyond Structuralism and
Hermeneutics.* Chicago: University of Chicago Press, 1983.

Dunn, Elizabeth Cullen. "Humanitarianism, Displacement, and the Politics of Nothing in Postwar Georgia." *Slavic Review* 73, no. 2 (2014): 287–306.

————. *Privatizing Poland: Baby Food, Big Business, and the Remaking of Labor.* Ithaca, NY: Cornell University Press, 2004.

Durkheim, Émile. *The Division of Labor in Society.* New York: Free Press, 1933.

The Economist. "Central Europe: Converging Hopes." February 11, 1999. http://www.economist.com/node/186307

————. "Romania's Capital Mayor." September 7, 2000. http://www.economist.com/node/360036.

Eidelberg, Philip G. *The Great Rumanian Peasant Revolt of 1907: Origins of a Modern Jacquerie.* East Central European Studies. Leiden: Brill Archive, 1974.

Ellis, Havelock. *Studies in the Psychology of Sex.* Vol. 2. Philadelphia: F. A. Davis, 1906.

Ellyatt, Holly. "Can Dracula, Communism and Bachelors Help Emerging Europe?" *CNBC.com,* January 29, 2014. http://www.cnbc.com/2014/01/29/can-dracula-communism-and-bachelors-help-emerging-europe.html.

Erlanger, Steven. "Romania Seeks to Stay on the Track to Europe." *New York Times,* February 11, 2001. http://www.nytimes.com/2001/02/11/world/romania-seeks-to-stay-on-the-track-to-europe.html.

European Commission. *Strategic National Report Regarding Social Protection and Social Inclusion 2008–2010.* Bucharest, Romania. Brussels: European Commission, 2008.

Farmer, Paul. "An Anthropology of Structural Violence." *Current Anthropology* 45, no. 3 (2004): 305–25.

FEANTSA (European Federation of European Organisations Working with the Homeless). *Romania: FEANTSA Country Fiche.* Brussels: FEANTSA, 2012.

Fehérváry, Krisztina. *Politics in Color and Concrete: Socialist Materialities and the Middle Class in Hungary.* New Anthropologies of Europe. Bloomington: Indiana University Press, 2013.

Ferguson, James. "Declarations of Dependence: Labour, Personhood, and Welfare in Southern Africa." *Journal of the Royal Anthropological Institute* 19, no. 2 (2013): 223–42.

————. *Expectations of Modernity: Myths and Meanings of Urban Life on the Zambian Copperbelt.* Berkeley: University of California Press, 1999.

————. *Give a Man a Fish: Reflections on the New Politics of Distribution.* Durham, NC: Duke University Press, 2015.

————. *Global Shadows: Africa in the Neoliberal World Order.* Durham, NC: Duke University Press, 2006.

Finn, Peter. "In Bucharest, a Dogfight over Strays; Crusading Mayor Hailed, Scorned for Planned Roundup of Proliferating Canines." *Washington Post,* February 18, 2001.

Fisher, Ian. "Romania, Wooed by U.S., Looks to a Big NATO Role." *New York Times,* October 23, 2002.

Flath, Carol A. "Art and Idleness: Chekhov's 'The House with a Mezzanine.'" *Russian Review* 58, no. 3 (1999): 456–66.

Foucault, Michel. *The Birth of Biopolitics: Lectures at the Collège de France, 1978–79.*

Michel Foucault: Lectures at the Collège de France. New York: Palgrave Macmillan, 2008.

———. Discipline and Punish: The Birth of the Prison. London: Penguin, 1977.

———. "Erotics." October 33 (July 1985): 3–30.

———. The History of Sexuality. Vol. 1. New York: Penguin, 1984.

———. "On the Genealogy of Ethics: An Overview of Work in Progress." In Ethics: Subjectivity and Truth, edited by Paul Rabinow, 1:253–80. New York: New Press, 1997.

———. Politics, Philosophy, Culture: Interviews and Other Writings, 1977–1984. Edited by Lawrence Kritzman. New York: Taylor and Francis, 2013.

———. Society Must Be Defended: Lectures at the Collège de France. New York: Picador, 2003.

Franzen, Jonathan. "Farther Away: 'Robinson Crusoe,' David Foster Wallace, and the Island of Solitude." New Yorker, April 18, 2011. http://www.newyorker.com/magazine/2011/04/18/farther-away-jonathan-franzen.

Frederiksen, Martin Demant. Young Men, Time, and Boredom in the Republic of Georgia. Philadelphia: Temple University Press, 2013.

French, R. Antony, and F. E. Ian Hamilton. The Socialist City: Spatial Structure and Urban Policy. New York: Wiley, 1979.

Friedman, Jack R. "Shame and the Experience of Ambivalence on the Margins of the Global: Pathologizing the Past and Present in Romania's Industrial Wastelands." Ethos 35, no. 2 (2007): 235–64.

———. "The 'Social Case.'" Medical Anthropology Quarterly 23, no. 4 (2009): 375–96.

Frisby, David. Cityscapes of Modernity: Critical Explorations. New York: John Wiley and Sons, 2002.

Fultz, Elaine. The Gender Dimensions of Social Security Reform: Case Studies of Romania and Slovenia. Budapest, Hungary: International Labour Office, 2006.

Garcia, Angela. "Reading 'Righteous Dopefiend' with My Mother." Anthropology Now 2, no. 3 (2010): 31–36.

Gardiner, Michael E. "Henri Lefebvre and the 'Sociology of Boredom.'" Theory, Culture and Society 29, no. 2 (2012): 37–62.

Genet, Jean. The Thief's Journal. New York: Grove/Atlantic, 1994.

Ghinea, Cristian, and Alina Mungiu-Pippidi. Media Policies and Regulatory Practices in a Selected Set of European Countries, the EU and the Council of Europe: The Case of Romania. Athens, Greece: mediadem, 2010.

Ghitescu, F. R., and M. Banciu. "Economic Crime in Romania." Journal of Social, Political, and Economic Studies 26, no. 4 (2001): 643–69.

Goodstein, Elizabeth. Experience without Qualities: Boredom and Modernity. Stanford, CA: Stanford University Press, 2004.

Gramsci, Antonio. "Americanism and Fordism." In A Gramsci Reader: Selected Writings, 1916–1935, edited by Hannan Hever and Eric J. Hobsbawm, 275–99. New York: New York University Press, 2000.

Greene, Jody M., Susan T. Ennett, and Christopher L. Ringwalt. "Prevalence and Correlates of Survival Sex among Runaway and Homeless Youth." American Journal of Public Health 89, no. 9 (1999): 1406–9.

Gross, Peter, and Vladimir Tismăneanu. "The End of Postcommunism in Romania." *Journal of Democracy* 16, no. 2 (2005): 146–62.

Guess Who. "3.7.2006." *Probe Audio.* București, România: Okapi Sound, Cat Music, 2009.

Gupta, Akhil, and James Ferguson. "Discipline and Practice: 'The Field' as Site, Method and Location in Anthropology." In *Anthropological Locations: Boundaries and Grounds of a Field Science,* edited by Akhil Gupta and James Ferguson, 1–46. Berkeley: University of California Press, 1997.

Hacking, Ian. "Making Up People." In *Reconstructing Individualism: Autonomy, Individuality, and the Self in Western Thought,* edited by T. C. Heller and C. Brooke-Rose, 222–36. History, Literature, Philosophy. Stanford, CA: Stanford University Press, 1986.

Han, Clara. *Life in Debt: Times of Care and Violence in Neoliberal Chile.* Berkeley: University of California Press, 2012.

Harris, Nigel. "Structural Adjustment and Romania." *Economic and Political Weekly* 29, no. 44 (1994): 2861–64.

Harvey, David. *The Condition of Postmodernity: An Enquiry into the Origins of Cultural Change.* London: Blackwell, 1992.

———. "Globalization and the Spatial Fix." *Geographische Revue* 2, no. 3 (2001): 23–31.

———. *Rebel Cities: From the Right to the City to the Urban Revolution.* London: Verso, 2012.

Heidegger, Martin. *The Fundamental Concepts of Metaphysics: World, Finitude, Solitude.* Bloomington: Indiana University Press, 2001.

Hojdestrand, Tova. *Needed by Nobody: Homelessness and Humanness in Post-socialist Russia.* Ithaca, NY: Cornell University Press, 2009.

Holston, James, and Arjun Appadurai. "Introduction: Cities and Citizenship." In *Cities and Citizenship,* edited by James Holston, 1–20. Durham, NC: Duke University Press, 1998.

Hopper, Kim. *Reckoning with Homelessness.* The Anthropology of Contemporary Issues. Ithaca, NY: Cornell University Press, 2003.

Hradecky, Ilja. "Building Capacity of Homeless Services in the Czech Republic." *European Journal of Homelessness* 2 (2008): 177–90.

Igloo.ro. "Reabilitarea Centrului Istoric Al Bucureștiului." May 2005. https://www.igloo.ro/articole/reabiltarea-centrului-istoric-al-bucurestiului.

International Monetary Fund. *IMF Approves Stand-By Credit for Romania.* Press release no. 99/38. Washington, DC: International Monetary Fund, 1999.

———. *Romania—Fifth Review under the Stand-By Arrangement.* IMF Country Report. Washington, DC: International Monetary Fund, 2010.

———. *Romania: Financial Sector Stability Assessment.* Washington, DC: International Monetary Fund, 2010.

Jeffrey, Craig. *Timepass: Youth, Class, and the Politics of Waiting in India.* Stanford, CA: Stanford University Press, 2010.

Jencks, Christopher. *The Homeless.* Cambridge, MA: Harvard University Press, 1995.

Judt, Tony. *Postwar: A History of Europe since 1945.* New York: Penguin, 2006.

Juris, Jeffrey S. *Networking Futures: The Movements against Corporate Globalization.* Experimental Futures. Durham, NC: Duke University Press, 2008.

Kaye, Kerwin. "Male Prostitution in the Twentieth Century." *Journal of Homosexuality* 46, nos. 1–2 (2004): 1–77.

Keay, Justin. "A Live-Wire Mayor for a Tired Old City." *BusinessWeek*, December 16, 2001. http://www.bloomberg.com/news/articles/2001-12-16/a-live-wire-mayor-for-a-tired-old-city.

Kideckel, David A. *Getting By in Postsocialist Romania: Labor, the Body, and Working-Class Culture.* Bloomington: Indiana University Press, 2008.

———. "The Undead: Nicolae Ceaușescu and Paternalist Politics in Romanian Society and Culture." In *Death of the Father: An Anthropology of the End in Political Authority*, edited by John Borneman, 123–47. New Directions in Anthropology. New York: Berghahn Books, 2004.

———. "The Unmaking of an East-Central European Working Class." In *Postsocialism: Ideals, Ideologies and Practices in Eurasia*, edited by Christopher M. Hann, 114–32. London: Routledge, 2003.

Kleinman, Arthur, Veena Das, and Margaret Lock. *Social Suffering.* Berkeley: University of California Press, 1997.

Kligman, Gail. *The Politics of Duplicity: Controlling Reproduction in Ceausescu's Romania.* Berkeley: University of California Press, 1998.

Kornai, Janos. *Contradictions and Dilemmas: Studies on the Socialist Economy and Society.* Cambridge, MA: MIT Press, 1986.

Kovács, Zoltán. "Cities from State-Socialism to Global Capitalism: An Introduction." *GeoJournal* 49, no. 1 (1999): 1–6.

Krugman, Paul. "The Wrong Worries." *New York Times*, August 4, 2011.

Laermans, Rudi. "Learning to Consume: Early Department Stores and the Shaping of the Modern Consumer Culture (1860–1914)." *Theory, Culture and Society* 10, no. 4 (1993): 79–102.

Latour, Bruno, and Vincent Antonin Lepinay. *The Science of Passionate Interests: An Introduction to Gabriel Tarde's Economic Anthropology.* Chicago: Prickly Paradigm, 2010.

Leclerc-Madlala, Suzanne. "Transactional Sex and the Pursuit of Modernity." *Social Dynamics* 29, no. 2 (2003): 213–33.

Lee, Barrett A., Kimberly A. Tyler, and James D. Wright. "The New Homelessness Revisited." *Annual Review of Sociology* 36 (2010): 501–21.

Lefebvre, Henri. *Critique of Everyday Life.* Vol. 1, *Introduction.* Edited by J. Moore and M. Trebitsch. London: Verso, 2008.

———. "The Everyday and Everydayness." *Yale French Studies*, no. 73 (January 1987): 7–11.

———. *Writings on Cities.* London: Wiley-Blackwell, 1996.

Li, Tania Murray. "To Make Live or Let Die? Rural Dispossession and the Protection of Surplus Populations." *Antipode* 41, no. 1 (2010): 66–93.

Light, Duncan, and David Phinnemore. *Post-communist Romania: Coming to Terms with Transition.* New York: Palgrave Macmillan, 2001.

Linz, Juan José, and Alfred C. Stepan. *Problems of Democratic Transition and Consolidation: Southern Europe, South America, and Post-communist Europe*. Baltimore: Johns Hopkins University Press, 1996.

Longfield, Kim, Hibist Astatke, Reid Smith, Georgia Mcpeak, and Jim Ayers. "Men Who Have Sex with Men in Southeastern Europe: Underground and at Increased Risk for HIV/STIs." *Culture, Health and Sexuality* 9, no. 5 (2007): 473–87.

Low, Setha. "The Edge and the Center: Gated Communities and the Discourse of Urban Fear." In *Anthropology of Space and Place: Locating Culture*, edited by Setha Low and Denise Lawrence-Zúñiga, 387–407. Malden, MA: Blackwell, 2003.

Lyon-Callo, Vincent. *Inequality, Poverty, and Neoliberal Governance: Activist Ethnography in the Homeless Sheltering Industry*. Toronto: University of Toronto Press, 2008.

Mains, Daniel. *Hope Is Cut: Youth, Unemployment, and the Future in Urban Ethiopia*. Global Youth. Philadelphia: Temple University Press, 2013.

Majumdar, Saikat. *Prose of the World: Modernism and the Banality of Empire*. New York: Columbia University Press, 2013.

Malkki, Liisa. "National Geographic: The Rooting of Peoples and the Territorialization of National Identity among Scholars and Refugees." *Cultural Anthropology* 7, no. 1 (1992): 24–44.

Manning, Paul. "Rose-Colored Glasses? Color Revolutions and Cartoon Chaos in Postsocialist Georgia." *Cultural Anthropology* 22, no. 2 (2005): 171–213.

Marcuse, Peter. "Rights in Cities and the Right to the City?" In *Cities for All: Proposals and Experiences towards the Right to the City*, edited by Ana Sugranyes and Charlotte Mathivet, 87–98. Santiago: Habitat International Coalition, HIC, 2010.

Marx, Karl. *Capital: An Abridged Edition*. New York: Oxford University Press, 2008.

———. *Grundrisse*. London: Penguin Adult, 1993.

Mateescu, Oana. "The Dark Side of the State: 'Mafia' and 'National Interest' in Postsocialist Romania." *Romanian Journal of Society and Politics* 2, no. 1 (2002): 5–29.

Maynard, Steven. "'Horrible Temptations': Sex, Men, and Working-Class Male Youth in Urban Ontario, 1890–1935." *Canadian Historical Review* 78, no. 2 (1997): 191–235.

Mazzarella, William. *Shoveling Smoke: Advertising and Globalization in Contemporary India*. Durham, NC: Duke University Press, 2003.

Mbembe, Achille. "Aesthetics of Superfluity." *Public Culture* 16, no. 3 (2004): 373–405.

McLaughlin, Daniel. "Romanian Leaders Urge Italy to Prevent Attacks on Immigrants." *Irish Times*, November 11, 2007.

Menil, Georges de, and Eytan Sheshinski. "Romania's Pension System from Crisis to Reform." In *Social Security Pension Reform in Europe*, edited by Martin Feldstein and Horst Siebert, 401–38. National Bureau of Economic Research Conference Report. Chicago: University of Chicago Press, 2009.

Miheț, Marius. "Comunismul, Ce Poveste . . ." *FAMILIA: Revistă de Cultură* 7–8 (July–August 2009): 30–32.

Milligan, Susan. "Revival Moves Slowly in Eastern Europe." *Boston Globe*, May 10, 1998.

Minton, Henry L. *Departing from Deviance: A History of Homosexual Rights and Emancipatory Science in America*. Chicago: University of Chicago Press, 2002.

Mitrany, David. *Marx against the Peasant: A Study in Social Dogmatism*. New York: Collier, 1961.

Nachescu, Voichita. "Hierarchies of Difference: National Identity, Gay and Lesbian Rights, and the Church in Postcommunist Romania." In *Sexuality and Gender in Postcommunist Eastern Europe and Russia*, edited by A. Štulhofer and T. Sandfort, 54–78. New York: Routledge, 2005.

Nemescu, Cristian, dir. *California Dreamin' (Nesfarsit)*. Bucuresti, Romania: Media Pro Pictures, 2007. 155 min.

Newman, Katherine S. *Falling from Grace: Downward Mobility in the Age of Affluence*. Berkeley: University of California Press, 1988.

Nietzsche, Friedrich. *Human, All Too Human: A Book for Free Spirits*. Cambridge: Cambridge University Press, 1996.

Olson, Laura. *The Not-So-Golden Years: Caregiving, the Frail Elderly, and the Long-Term Care Establishment*. New York: Rowman and Littlefield, 2003.

O'Neill, Kevin L. *Secure the Soul: Christian Piety and Gang Prevention in Guatemala*. Berkeley: University of California Press, 2015.

Ong, Aihwa. "Graduated Sovereignty in South-East Asia." *Theory, Culture and Society* 17, no. 4 (2000): 55–75.

———. *Neoliberalism as Exception: Mutations in Citizenship and Sovereignty*. Durham, NC: Duke University Press, 2006.

Oosterhuis, Harry. *Stepchildren of Nature: Krafft-Ebing, Psychiatry, and the Making of Sexual Identity*. Chicago: University of Chicago Press, 2000.

Oppenheim, Irene. "Chekhov's TB." *Threepenny Review* 29 (1987): 10–11.

Oushakine, Serguei Alex. "'Against the Cult of Things': On Soviet Productivism, Storage Economy, and Commodities with No Destination." *Russian Review* 73, no. 2 (2014): 198–236.

Padilla, Mark. *Caribbean Pleasure Industry: Tourism, Sexuality, and AIDS in the Dominican Republic*. Chicago: University of Chicago Press, 2007.

Parker, G. "Romania Denies EU Entry Will Spark a Wave of Emigration." *Financial Times*, September 24, 2006.

Parker, Richard. "Sexuality, Culture, and Power in HIV/AIDS Research." *Annual Review of Anthropology* 30 (January 2001): 163–79.

Passaro, Joanne. *The Unequal Homeless: Men on the Streets, Women in Their Place*. New York: Routledge, 1996.

Patico, Jennifer. *Consumption and Social Change in a Post-Soviet Middle Class*. Stanford, CA: Stanford University Press, 2008.

Patrick, George Z. "Chekhov's Attitude towards Life." *Slavonic and East European Review* 10, no. 30 (1932): 658–68.

Petrescu, Dan. *Romania Country Brief: Europe and Central Asia Region*. Bucharest, Romania: World Bank Group, 2002. http://lnweb90.worldbank.org/eca/eca.nsf/0/c4cfb7b8c4d1658185256c240050a6a4/$FILE/Romania%20Country%20Brief.pdf.

Petrova, Dimitrina. "The Roma: Between a Myth and the Future." *Social Research* 70, no. 1 (2003): 111–61.

Pine, Jason. "Economy of Speed: The New Narco-Capitalism." *Public Culture* 19, no. 2 (2007): 357–66.

Pinney, Christopher. "The Quick and the Dead: Images, Time and Truth." *Society for Visual Anthropology Review* 6, no. 2 (1990): 42–54.

Piot, Charles. *Nostalgia for the Future: West Africa after the Cold War*. Chicago: University of Chicago Press, 2010.

Piperno, Flavia. "From Care Drain to Care Gain: Migration in Romania and Ukraine and the Rise of Transnational Welfare." *Development* 50, no. 4 (2007): 63–68.

Piven, Francis Fox, and Richard A. Cloward. *Regulating the Poor: The Functions of Public Welfare*. New York: Vintage Books, 1956.

Porumboiu, Corneliu, dir. *Polițist, Adjectiv*. (Police, Adjective). București, România: 42 Km Film, 2009. 113 min.

Prieur, Annick. *Mema's House, Mexico City: On Transvestites, Queens, and Machos*. Worlds of Desire: The Chicago Series on Sexuality, Gender, and Culture. Chicago: University of Chicago Press, 1998.

PR Romania. "Peste 1,7 Milioane de Intrări La Promoția 'NESCAFÉ 3în1 și NESCAFÉ Frappé Înving Plictiseala.'" Pr-Romania.Ro, July 9, 2010. http://www.pr-romania .ro/comunicate-de-presa/728-peste-17-milioane-de-intrari-la-promotia-nescafe -3in1-si-nescafe-frappe-inving-plictiseala.html.

Puiu, Cristi, dir. *Moartea Domnului Lăzărescu*. [*The Death of Mr. Lazarescu*]. București, România: Mandragora, 2005. 153 min.

Racu, Radu. "Cât Costă Să Faci Din Centrul Bucureștiului Un Al Doilea Sibiu." *Ziarul Financiar*, May 25, 2011. http://da.zf.ro/business-construct/cat-costa-sa -faci-din-centrul-bucurestiului-un-al-doilea-sibiu-8281928.

Ralph, Laurence. *Renegade Dreams: Living through Injury in Gangland Chicago*. Chicago: University of Chicago Press, 2014.

Rampell, Catherine. "Still Nearly Five Unemployed Workers for Every Opening." *New York Times*, February 8, 2011. http://economix.blogs.nytimes.com/2011/02 /08/still-nearly-5-unemployed-workers-for-every-opening/?_r=0.

Realitatea TV. "Episode 1: La Coadă." *Comunism pe Burta Goală*, 2009.

———."Episode 7: Munca la Stat." *Comunism pe Burta Goală*, 2009.

Reid, Susan Emily, and David Crowley, eds. *Style and Socialism: Modernity and Material Culture in Post-war Eastern Europe*. London: Berg, 2000.

Riding, Alan. "The New Berlin—Building on the Rubble of History; A Capital Re-instated and Remodeled." *New York Times*, April 11, 1999.

Rogers, Douglas. "Moonshine, Money, and the Politics of Liquidity in Rural Russia." *American Ethnologist* 32, no. 1 (2005): 63–81.

Roman, Denise. *Fragmented Identities: Popular Culture, Sex, and Everyday Life in Postcommunist Romania*. Plymouth, UK: Lexington, 2007.

Roper, Steven D. *Romania: The Unfinished Revolution*. New York: Routledge, 2000.

Rosa, Hartmut. *Social Acceleration: A New Theory of Modernity*. New Directions in Critical Theory. New York: Columbia University Press, 2013.

Sachs, Jeffrey. *Poland's Jump to the Market Economy*. Cambridge, MA: MIT Press, 1994.

Sassen, Saskia. *Expulsions: Brutality and Complexity in the Global Economy*. Cambridge, MA: Harvard University Press, 2014.

———. *Losing Control? Sovereignty in the Age of Globalization*. Leonard Hastings Schoff Lectures. New York: Columbia University Press, 2013.

Sbîrn, Cristina. "Căminele Pentru Bătrâni, Create Cu Bani de La Buget, Nu de La Autoritățile Locale." *Adevărul*, February 2, 2011. http://adevarul.ro /news/societate/caminele-batrani-create-bani-buget-nu-autoritatile-locale -1_50abb8697c42d5a6637f36d2/index.html.

Schaefer, Donovan. "The Promise of Affect: The Politics of the Event in Ahmed's *The Promise of Happiness* and Berlant's *Cruel Optimism*." *Theory and Event* 16, no. 2 (2013). https://muse.jhu.edu/ (accessed July 6, 2016).

Scheper-Hughes, Nancy, and Philippe Bourgois. *Violence in War and Peace*. Blackwell Readers in Anthropology. New York: Blackwell, 2004.

Scott, James C. *Weapons of the Weak: Everyday Forms of Peasant Resistance*. New Haven, CT: Yale University Press, 1985.

Seeman, Melvin. "On the Meaning of Alienation." *American Sociological Review* 24, no. 6 (1959): 783–91.

Shlay, Anne, and Peter Rossi. "Social Science Research and Contemporary Studies of Homelessness." *Annual Review of Sociology* 18, no. 1 (1992): 129–60.

Smith, Neil. *The New Urban Frontier: Gentrification and the Revanchist City*. London: Routledge, 1996.

Soja, Edward W. *Postmetropolis: Critical Studies of Cities and Regions*. London: Wiley-Blackwell, 2000.

Sotiropoulos, Dimitri A., Ileana Neamtu, and Maya Stoyanova. "The Trajectory of Post-communist Welfare State Development: The Cases of Bulgaria and Romania." *Social Policy and Administration* 37, no. 6 (2003): 656–73.

Spacks, Patricia Meyer. *Boredom: The Literary History of a State of Mind*. Chicago: University of Chicago Press, 1996.

Staeheli, Lynn A., and Don Mitchell. *The People's Property? Power, Politics, and the Public*. New York: Routledge, 2007.

Stan, Lavinia. "Romanian Privatization: Assessment of the First Five Years." *Communist and Post-communist Studies* 28, no. 4 (1995): 427–35.

Standing, Guy. "Tertiary Time: The Precariat's Dilemma." *Public Culture* 25, no. 1 (2013): 5–23.

Starosielski, Nicole. *The Undersea Network*. Sign, Storage, Transmission. Durham, NC: Duke University Press, 2015.

Stephen, Chris. "Moscow 'World's Most Costly City.'" *Irish Times*, June 6, 2007.

Stephenson, Svetlana. *Crossing the Line: Vagrancy, Homelessness and Social Displacement in Russia*. London: Ashgate, 2006.

Stewart, Kathleen. *Ordinary Affects*. Durham, NC: Duke University Press, 2007.

Stillo, Jonathan. "The Romanian Tuberculosis Epidemic as a Symbol of Public Health." In *Romania under Basescu: Aspirations, Achievements, and Frustrations during His First Presidential Term*, edited by R. King and P. Sum, 273–92. New York: Rowman and Littlefield, 2011.

Stoica, Marian. "Spitalele Care Au Fost Închise în Județul Brașov Nu Vor Fi Transformate în Azile de Bătrâni." *Adevărul*, May 2, 2011. http://adevarul.ro/locale /brasov/spitalele-fost-inchise-judetul-brasov-nu-vor-transformate-azile-batrani -1_50ad80477c42d5a6639652c5/index.html.

Svennebye, Lars. "GDP per Capita, Consumption per Capita and Comparative Price Levels in Europe." *Eurostat: Statistics in Focus*. Luxembourg, 2008. http:// ec.europa.eu/eurostat/documents/3433488/5584112/KS-SF-08-112-EN.PDF /1525ad79-fd56-4e13-99fd-07d75cf2f832.

Szeman, Ioana. "'Gypsy Music' and Deejays: Orientalism, Balkanism, and Romani Musicians." *TDR: The Drama Review* 53, no. 3 (2009): 98–116.

Taussig, Michael T. "Maleficium: State Fetishism." In *Fetishism as Cultural Discourse*, edited by Emily S. Apter and William Pietz, 217–47. Ithaca, NY: Cornell University Press, 1993.

———. *My Cocaine Museum*. Chicago: University of Chicago Press, 2004.

Tismăneanu, Vladimir. "Discomforts of Victory: Democracy, Liberal Values and Nationalism in Post-communist Europe." *West European Politics* 25, no. 2 (2002): 81–100.

———. *Stalinism for All Seasons: A Political History of Romanian Communism*. Berkeley: University of California Press, 2003.

Trouillot, Michel-Rolph. "The Anthropology of the State in the Age of Globalization: Close Encounters of the Deceptive Kind." *Current Anthropology* 42, no. 1 (2001): 125–38.

Tsing, Anna L. *Friction: An Ethnography of Global Connection*. Princeton, NJ: Princeton University Press, 2004.

Tudor, Cristiana. "A Quantitative Assessment of the Outcome of Pension Reforms in Transition Economies: The Case of Romania." *International Research Journal of Finance and Economics*, no. 56 (2010): 151–66.

Turcescu, Lucian, and Lavinia Stan. "Religion, Politics and Sexuality in Romania." *Europe-Asia Studies* 57, no. 2 (2005): 291–310.

Turnock, David. *Aspects of Independent Romania's Economic History with Particular Reference to Transition for EU Accession*. London: Ashgate, 2007.

———. "Housing Policy in Romania." In *Housing Policies in Eastern Europe and the Soviet Union*, edited by J. A. A. Sillince, 134–69. New York: Routledge, 1990.

———. "Railways and Economic Development in Romania before 1918." *Journal of Transport Geography* 9, no. 2 (2001): 137–50.

United Nations Economic Commission for Europe. *Romania Country Profile on the Housing Sector*. Geneva: UNECE, 2001.

U.S. Embassy. "Embassy of the United States: Bucharest, Romania." *Tourist and Business Visas*, 2014. http://romania.usembassy.gov/visas/tourist.html.

Vachon, Michael. "Bucharest: The House of the People." *World Policy Journal* 10, no. 4 (1993): 59–63.

Vârlan, Corina. "Gândul Vă Prezintă Harta Nouă a Centrului Vechi Al Capitalei."

Gândul.info, August 28, 2011. http://campanii.gandul.info/financiar/gandul
-va-prezinta-harta-noua-a-centrului-vechi-al-capitalei-peste-140-de-restaurante
-baruri-si-locuri-de-distractie-din-cel-mai-nou-pol-de-atractie-al-bucurestilor
-8649189.

Vatulescu, Cristina. *Police Aesthetics: Literature, Film, and the Secret Police in Soviet Times*. Stanford, CA: Stanford University Press, 2010.

Veblen, Thorstein. *The Theory of the Leisure Class*. Edited by M. Banta. Oxford: Oxford University Press, 2007.

Verdery, Katherine. "Fuzzy Property: Rights, Power, and Identity in Transylvania's Decollectivization." In *Uncertain Transition: Ethnographies of Change in the Postsocialist World*, edited by Michael Burawoy and Katherine Verdery, 53–82. Oxford: Rowman and Littlefield, 1999.

——. *What Was Socialism, and What Comes Next?* Princeton, NJ: Princeton University Press, 1996.

Virilio, Paul. *Speed and Politics*. Foreign Agents. Los Angeles: Semiotext(e), 2006.

Voicu, Dragoș. *Coada*. București: Cartea Românească, 2009.

Voicu, Mălina, and Bogdan Voicu. "Volunteering in Romania: A Rara Avis." In *The Values of Volunteering: Cross-Cultural Perspectives*, edited by P. Dekker and L. Halman, 143–60. Nonprofit and Civil Society Studies. New York: Kluwer Academic/Plenum, 2003.

Volkman, Toby. *Cultures of Transnational Adoption*. Durham, NC: Duke University Press, 2005.

Wacquant, Loïc. *Punishing the Poor: The Neoliberal Government of Social Insecurity*. Politics, History, and Culture. Durham, NC: Duke University Press, 2009.

——. *Urban Outcasts: A Comparative Sociology of Advanced Marginality*. Cambridge: Polity, 2008.

Wallace, David Foster. *The Pale King*. New York: Little, Brown, 2011.

Wardlow, Holly. "Anger, Economy, and Female Agency: Problematizing 'Prostitution' and 'Sex Work' among the Huli of Papua New Guinea." *Signs* 29, no. 4 (2004): 1017–40.

Weber, Max. *The Protestant Ethic and the Spirit of Capitalism: And Other Writings*. New York: Penguin, 2002.

Wedel, Janine R. *Collision and Collusion: The Strange Case of Western Aid to Eastern Europe, 1989–1998*. London: St. Martin's, 1998.

Williams, Rosalind H. *Dream Worlds: Mass Consumption in Late Nineteenth-Century France*. Berkeley: University of California Press, 1991.

Wilson, William Julius. *The Truly Disadvantaged: The Inner City, the Underclass, and Public Policy*. Chicago: University of Chicago Press, 1990.

Woodward, Will. "Romanians and Bulgarians Face Immigration Curbs: EU Entry Will Not Mean Open Door, Minister Says Restrictions on Workers Opposed by Foreign Office." *Guardian* (Manchester, UK), August 21, 2006. http://www.theguardian.com/politics/2006/aug/21/uk.workandcareers.

World Bank. *Country Partnership Strategy for Romania for the Period July 2009–June 2013*. Report No. 48665-RO. Central Europe and the Baltic Countries Country

Unit. June 12, 2009. http://www-wds.worldbank.org/external/default/WDS
ContentServer/WDSP/IB/2009/07/20/000333038_20090720233846/Rendered
/PDF/486650CAS0P1161C0Disclosed071171091.pdf.

———. *Romania Public Expenditure and Institutional Review.* 2 vols. Report No.
51191-RO. Washington DC: World Bank, Poverty Reduction and Economic Management Unit, 2010.

Wrigley, Neil. "'Food Deserts' in British Cities: Policy Context and Research Priorities." *Urban Studies* 39, no. 11 (2002): 2029–40.

Yesin, Pınar. "Foreign Currency Loans and Systemic Risk in Europe." Federal Reserve Bank of St. Louis Review. May/June (2013): 219–36.

Zaloom, Caitlin. *Out of the Pits: Traders and Technology from Chicago to London.*
Chicago: University of Chicago Press, 2006.

Zerilli, Filippo M. "Sentiments and/as Property Rights: Restitution and Conflict
in Postsocialist Romania." In *Postsocialism: Politics and Emotions in Central and
Eastern Europe*, edited by Maruška Svašek, 74–94. London: Berghahn Books,
2008.

Ziuaveche.ro. "David: În Afara Granițelor Trăiesc între Șase și Opt Milioane de
Români." December 13, 2013. http://www.ziuaveche.ro/actualitate-interna/social
/david-in-afara-granițelor-traiesc-intre-șase-și-opt-milioane-de-romani-201479
.html/.

INDEX

acceleration, life defined by, 210n1

active retirement model, Romanian proposals for, 78, 207n11

addicts (*aurolaci*), as homeless classification, 14, 43

Adjective (film), 34

advertising, postcommunist rise of, 30–35

affect, boredom as, 17, 189n6

Agamben, Giorgio, 215n28

aging population: homelessness among, 72–95; part-time workers, lack of pensions for, 87–95; pre-retirement age workers in, 103–9; social services for, 94–95, 211n7. *See also* pension system

agricultural policies, postcommunist redistribution and, 29–35, 190n14

Ahmed, Sarah, 189, 194n53, 194n55

Anderson, Nels, 141, 218n16

Antena 1 television station, 34

anthropological research methods, xii–xiii, 185n1

"Anti-boredom Campaign" (Campanie Antiplictiseală), 34

anti-Ceaușescu uprising, 7–8

Augé, Marc, 202n1

austerity programs: in communist Romania, 19–20; global recession and expansion of, 40–43; introduction of, 9–10

bachelor parties, Bucharest as destination for, 177–78

Backwoods Shelter (pseudonym), xiii, 34–39, 42–43; aging residents of, 73–95; boredom in, 44–46; establishment of, 48–51; living conditions at, 51–57; selection process for housing in, 58–61

Bakhtin, Mikhail, 163, 224n10

Bardot, Brigitte, 47–48

bare life concept, slow death and, 215n28

Băsescu, Traian, 47–48, 203n5

Baudelaire, Charles, 213n17

Baudrillard, Jean, 144–46

Belzberg, Edet, 11

Benjamin, Walter, 108–10, 213n17

Benson, Peter, 225n15

Berdahl, Daphne, 187n13

Berlant, Lauren, 98, 210n2, 214n23, 223n6

Bhabha, Homi, 42

European Federation of National Organizations Working with the Homeless (FEANTSA), 11–12

European Union: debt crisis of, xi–xii; Romanian accession to, 33–35; pension reform and loans from, 75

false loans, in postcommunist real estate market, 77

family structure: aging pensioners and erosion of, 74–76, 211n7; communism's influence on, 223n7; migration from Romania and breakup of, 84–87; social death of homelessness and destruction of, 109–10; wives of homeless men in, 135–46; work and care conflicts and, 88–95. *See also* divorce; relationships

fiscal policies in communist-era Romania, 6–7

flâneur, homelessness and figure of, 108–9, 213n17

food supply: institutional solutions for shortages in, 192n39; low-income food deserts, 224n13; postcommunist privatization of, 29–35; scavenging by homeless for, 155–58, 161–62; shortages in communist Romania, 19–20, 24–25; social cohesion during shortages in, 25–28

foreign debt, burden in Romania of, 6–10, 40–43, 191n27

Foucault, Michel, 5, 51; on alienated labor, 68–69, 204n10; on biopolitics, 98–99, 211n5; on ethics, 184, 221n29, 228n21; on sexuality, 141–42, 218n18

Frederiksen, Martin Demant, 210n1

friendships: among homeless, 127–30; homelessness and destruction of, 100–103, 109–10

The Fundamental Concepts of Metaphysics (Heidegger), 190n10

Garcia, Angela, 211n7

gender, homelessness and, 136–46, 217n9

Genet, Jean, 221n26

Germany, citizenship and mass consumption in postunification era, 187n13

global economic crisis of 2008: impact of, 9–10; pension system and, 75–76

globalization: boredom linked to, 181–84; Eastern European postcommunist embrace of, 28–35; impact on Romanian pension system of, 74–95; infrastructure of displacement and, 69–70; labor mobility of, 142–44; postcommunist lost generation and, 103–9; socioeconomic instability and, 2–4, 188n2; technology and, 182–84, 226n12, 227n14; tourism and, 226n9

government policies: for aging pensioners, 74–76; homelessness and, 47–51; pension reform and, 74–76

government-subsidized housing, scarcity of, 58–61

Guattari, Félix, 221n25

Guess Who (hip-hop star), 34

Harvey, David, 181, 226n13

health services, 192n39; prostitution among homeless and, 145–46; for shelters, 56–57

Heidegger, Martin, 15, 190n10, 194n52, 217n17

The History of Sexuality (Foucault), 141–42

homelessness: absence of, during communism, 4; bureaucratic definitions of, 11–12, 185n5, 193n40; carnivalesque approach to, 162–71; categories of, 12–15; causes of, xiv–xvi; consumption practices and, 151–54; early research on, 192n38; estimates of, 12; interventions proposed for, xiv–xvi; passing aesthetic among, 158–71; of pensioners, 72–95; physical appearance as sign of, 12–15, 159–62; postcommunist rise of, 10–15, 34–35; Romanian terminology for, 12; as social death, 98–99, 210n1; stigmatization of, 33–35, 65–69

homeless service centers, piecemeal coverage offered by, 89–90

homophobia, 126, 139–46, 217n12, 219n21

homosexuality: informal sex economy and, 138–46, 218n18, 218nn15–16; masculine identity and, 141–42, 219nn19–21, 221n26

House of the People (Casa Poporului), 7

housing: for aging pensioners, 94–95, 210n27; communist program for, 4, 10; equality of access to, 53–57; postcommunist privatization of, 29–35, 205n15; real estate corruption and, 77–78, 88–90

Hungary, consumerism in postcommunist era, 187n13

"hunger circus" (*circul foamei*), 31

hyperconsumption: marginalization of homeless and, 157–58, 166–71; superfluity aesthetics and, 225n14, 225n16

idleness: boredom *vs.*, 22; in communist Romania, 19–20

IKEA, 156–58

illicit goods, black market for, 81–82, 110–15

import restrictions, postcommunist easing of, 30–35

industrial power: postcommunist collapse of, 103–9; postcommunist privatization of, 29–35; Romanian communist nationalization of, 22–24

informal sex economy, homeless participation in, 122–46

infrastructure of displacement, globalization and, 69–70

institutions: food supply programs of,

192n39; homeless people's use of, 110–18; inadequacy of, 44–46

International Monetary Fund (IMF), 9–10, 23; postcommunist market ideology and, 29; pension reform and austerity measures of, 75, 214n24

Isherwood, Baron, 223n9

isolation of homelessness, 44–46, 51–57; alternative relationships as response to, 115–18; consumption as antidote to, 172–74; growth of, 4–5; remoteness of shelters and, 48–51; risk of death and, 99–103; social death and, 109–10; for street homeless, 61–65

Kirsch, Stuart, 225n15

Krugman, Paul, xii, 186n8

labor market: communist control of, 23–26; global recession and collapse of, 35–43; participation of elderly in, 207n11, 208n19; part-time workers, lack of pensions for, 87–95; postcommunist changes to, 29–35, 82–87; redundancy in postcommunist era of, 103–9, 212n12; retirement from, 29–35, 82–87; work and care conflicts in, 88–95. *See also* black labor market

lads' weekends, Bucharest as destination for, 177–78

land reform, postcommunist redistribution and, 29–35, 190n14

Law 119, nationalization of private industry under, 22–24

Lefebvre, Henri, 222n2

leisure activities: of homeless, 54–57, 122–26, 205n22; market development and, 144–46; nightlife for homeless, 138–40

letting die, state of, 5, 97–99; asocial experience of, 109–10; labor redundancy and, 107–9

Li, Tania, 212n14

Malkki, Liisa, 227n19

malls and retail shopping space: cultural capital for employment at, 105; exclusion of homeless from, 64, 71, 145; homeless negotiation of, xiv, 149, 155, 158–71, 223n7; hyperconsumption promoted at, 154–56, 166–71; middle class support of, 3, 159–62; postcommunist emergence of, 8, 16, 31–32; privatization of public space and, 222nn3–4; semipublic resources of, 13

marginality of homelessness: class politics and, 158–62; shelters and, 60–61, 69–70; space-time expansion and, 210n1

market ideology: deprivation under, 22; Eastern European postcommunist embrace of, 28–35; inequality of access in, 52–57; pensioners and, 76–77, 94–95; socioeconomic instability and, 1–4

Marx, Karl, 25

masculinity: male intimacy and, 140–44; prostitution among homeless and, 136–46, 219nn19–20

Maynard, Steven, 218n15

Mbembe, Achille, 225n14, 225n16

McDonald's, homeless visits to, 155–56

media: coverage of communist-era shortages by, 24–25; foreign debt coverage by, 40–43; images of homelessness in, 11, 48–51; postcommunist expansion of, 30–35; poverty coverage by, 46–47; wages discussed in, 40

middle class: carnivalesque approach of homeless to, 163–71; homosexuality among, 138–40, 143–46; stigmatization of homelessness by, 65–70

migration: impact on families, 84–87; loss of pensioners due to, 75–76; unemployment and rise of, 31, 33–35, 40–43

mobility: economic deprivation and loss of, 36–43, 89–95; globalization and,

142–44; prostitution and, 128, 148, 216n7; of street homeless, 61–65

morality, economic theory and, 183–84

narratives of boredom: black labor market and, 110–15; social death in, 109–10

Nescafé Corporation, anti-boredom campaign, 34, 147–49, 171

Nietzsche, Friedrich, 15

nightlife: in Bucharest old-town district, 175–84; creation by homeless of, 138–40

nongovernmental organizations, homeless shelters run by, ix–xiiv

nonplaces, Augé's concept of, 202n1

North Atlantic Treaty Organization (NATO), 8

om fără casă (man without a house), 12–14

Oosterhuis, Harry, 220n22

optimism, cruelty of, 194n51, 194n58

orphanage scandal in Romania, 128–29, 216nn4–5

Padilla, Mark, 219n20

part-time workers: lack of pensions for, 87–95; postcommunist labor redundancy and, 103–9

paternalism of Romanian state: postcommunist demise of, 29–35; social cohesion under, 25–26

pathologization of homelessness, in communist Romania, 10–11

Patico, Jennifer, 187n13

pension system: aging homeless and, 73–95; contributions as basis for, 206n2; part-time workers, lack of pensions for, 87–95; postcommunist stresses on, 74–76; rates for benefits, 208n18; reform proposals, 94–95, 207nn9–10

places of consumption, homeless negotiation of, 154–71

Police (film), 34
politics: of leisure, 205n22; postcommunist trends in, 32–35, 191n25
poverty, 46–47: aging and, 72–95; boredom and, 15–17; postcommunist stigmatization of, 33–35
privatization: postcommunist embrace of, 29–35; in pension system, 207nn9–10
privilege, boredom linked to, 15–17
production: boredom and, 17; postcommunist alteration of, 105–9
property laws, postcommunist privatization and, 77
prostitution: in Bucharest Lipscani nightlife district, 175–76; informal sex economy of homelessness, 122–46, 216n7, 218n15; women prostitutes, 135–46, 218n16
pruning, government policy of, 98–99

queuing, daily routine of, in communist Romania, 19–20, 24–25

real estate market, postcommunist corruption in, 77–78, 88–95, 208n16
Realitatea Tv, 24–25
redundancy, homelessness and, 103–9
relationships: black labor market and importance of, 115–18; impact of homelessness on, xii–xv, 22, 101–3, 109–15, 211n10; male intimacy and, 140–44; postcommunist erosion of, 28–35; sexual relationships among homeless, 135–46, 221n28; social cohesion during communist-era shortages and, 22–28
remittances, 85–87, 209n24
resignation, boredom and politics of, 171–74, 225n15
Roma: barriers in labor market for, 35, 38–39; racism toward, 77–78, 88–89, 209n20; stereotypes of, 12, 39
Romanian Communist Party, 6–7; centralization of economy under,

22–24; cult-of-labor policy, 25–26; universal housing program, 4, 10
Romanian National Tourist Office, 177
Rosa, Hartmut, 210n2
rural population, economic decline of, 5–10
Russia: consumerism in post-Soviet era, 187n13; homelessness in, 212n13

Sachs, Jeffrey, 28–29
Schonberg, Jeffrey, 219n20
Scott, James C., 224n11
Second Chances night shelter, 48, 59–61; aging pensioners at, 74
Securitate, 26, 78, 208n16
security guards: bribery of, 134; harassment of prostitutes by, 134–46; monitoring of homeless by, 96, 114–15, 134; part-time employment for homeless as, 54, 82; at places of consumption, 155, 158–62, 167–71
self-destructive behavior, homelessness and risk of, 99–103, 118–21, 211n3
sexuality, homelessness and, 122–46
shelters: absence of programming in, 54–57; boredom in, 51–57; development of, 46–51; homeless population in, 12–13; inadequacy of, 44–46; infrastructure of displacement and, 69–70; remoteness of, 48–57; residency limits introduced for, 99, 204n14; pensioners in, 72–95; rules enforced at, 164–66, 224n12; selection process for, 57–61, 113–15; in United States, 60–61, 204n13
shortage economy in communist Romania, 19–20, 24–28
sleep, as escape from boredom, 151
slow death, Berlant's concept of, 98, 210n2, 215n28
social death: homelessness as, 98–99; social world of, 109–10; underconsumption and, 123–24
socialist-era urban planning, equalization in, 52–57

Social Security Act of 1935, 206n4

social services: for pensioners, 94–95, 210n27; postcommunist decline of, 81, 211n7; prioritization of housing by, 59–61; homelessness and, 11, 55–57; "third-sector approach" to, 205n16

Soviet Union, homelessness in, 193n40

space-time expansion: for aging pensioners, 88–95; class politics and, 140; consumption practices and, 152–54; globalization and, 181–84; during global recession, 35–43; marginality of homelessness and, 108–10, 210n1, 213n17; in postcommunist Romania, 15–17; privatization of public space and, 222n3; shortage economy in communist Romania and, 19–20, 24–25

squatter camps: in Bucharest old-town district, 176–77; construction of, 61–65; homeowner's use of, to conserve money, 138–40, 163

standard of living: cultural deprivation of poverty and, 62–65; global recession and decline of, 35–43; homeless persons' visions of, 62–65, 93–95, 205n19, 214n23; postcommunist expectations concerning, 30–35, 187n13, 194n51, 194n58

Stephenson, Svetlana, 212n13

Stewart, Kathleen, 189n6

stigmatization of homelessness, 33–35, 65–70

street homeless: deprivation of, 151–54; infrastructure of boredom, 61–65; labor redundancy and displacement of, 107–9; population of, 13; sexual relationships among, 135–46; social practices of, 60–61

suffering, boredom as, 101–3, 215n25

suicide, homelessness and risk of, 118–21, 211n3

surveillance, in communist Romania, 26–28

survival sex, performance by homeless of, 129–30, 142–43, 216n6

Tarde, Gabriel, 144–46, 221n25

Taussig, Michael T., 214n22, 221n26

temporary work visas, Romanian liberalization of, 31

The Thief's Journal (Genet), 221n26

țigani, 12, 39, 43

time expansion: for aging pensioners, 88–95; under communism, 19–20

tourism in Bucharest, development of, 176–84, 226n9

tourist visas, qualifications for, 93–94, 210n26

unemployment: absence of, in communist Romania, 6–10, 23–26, 64–65; black labor market and, 20–22; economic crisis and rise in, xi–xii, 186n8; loss of pensioners due to, 75–76, 207n6; permanent unemployment, 96–98, 212n12, 212n14

unintended consequences, Foucault's concept of, 51, 204n10

United States, retirement centers in, 206n4

universal housing: communist program for, 4, 10; equality of access with, 53–57; postcommunist privatization of, 29–35, 205n15

urbanization: Bucharest Lipscani nightlife district development and, 176–84; in communist Romania, 6–10, 22–23; early theories concerning, 189n7; exclusion of poverty and gentrification with, 48–51, 202n4; flâneur figure and, 108–10, 213n17; housing construction and, 10; inequality of access and, 52–57, 203n8

value added tax (VAT), 9

Veblen, Thorstein, 186n12, 223n8